The Word That Redescribes the World

The Word That Redescribes the World

The Bible and Discipleship

Walter Brueggemann

Edited by Patrick D. Miller

Fortress Press
Minneapolis

THE WORD THAT REDESCRIBES THE WORLD
The Bible and Discipleship

Cover design: Kevin van der Leek Design Inc.
Cover photo: © Trinette Reed/Photodisc/Getty Images. Used by permission.
Interior design: Beth Wright, Trio Bookworks

Library of Congress Cataloging-in-Publication Data
Brueggemann, Walter.
    The Word that redescribes the world : the Bible and discipleship /
Walter Brueggemann ; edited by Patrick D. Miller.
        p. cm.
    Includes bibliographical references (p.   ) and indexes.
    ISBN 0-8006-3814-X (alk. paper)
    1. Theology. 2. Christianity and culture. I. Miller, Patrick D.
II. Title.
BT22.B78 2006
230'.041—dc22
                                        2005035387

The paper used in this publication meets the minimum requirements of American
National Standard for Information Sciences—Permanence of Paper for Printed
Library Materials, ANSI Z329.48-1984.

Manufactured in the U.S.A.
10   09   08   07   2   3   4   5   6   7   8   9   10

For
Lee Carroll
and
Erskine Clarke

Contents

Editor's Foreword

The beginning point for this new collection of Walter Brueggemann's essays is not new at all. It is where he always begins—with the text of Scripture. Few persons in our time have been more committed in theory and practice to the significance of the words of Scripture for faith and life, for our time and for all times. Few also have been more self-consciously attentive to the problematic of the biblical text as much as to its possibility. There is a candor—a favorite word of Brueggemann's—to his interpretive work that does not hide or flinch from the alien character of the Bible and its humanity. Surely no contemporary interpreter better exemplifies Luther's image of the Bible as the Word of God in a very human, crude manger. Both the danger and the power of the word of Scripture are lifted up in his writing. So also he has insisted, and not without some strong opposition on the part of other capable interpreters, that we have no access to the reality of God except through Scripture. Its interpretation is thus difficult, dangerous, and absolutely necessary.

In what follows, my comments are not aimed at a summary of the essays. Rather I would point the reader to some of the themes and notes that are sounded throughout all of them. Each one is discrete in its focus and emphasis, but they also overlap in significant ways. So here are some of the things to watch for:

1. In the opening essays of this book and throughout, one encounters a mode of looking that is confrontational, not so much between author and reader as between text and the world in which we live. It is the text that confronts us and makes us uneasy or calls us to a new attention and consideration. At one point ("Proclamatory Confrontations"), Brueggemann speaks of preaching as "truth speaking to power." He is not unaware of the ambiguity of both truth and power. Indeed, he underscores the problematic. Yet there is a sense in which all of the essays here embody that definition of preaching as they place the text of Scripture, with its judgment and its hope, against the realities of the world in which we live.

2. That judgment and hope are always before the reader. One will note how often Israel's experience of exile is the focus of attention. It is precisely there that the community comes to know both judgment and hope. Brueggemann thinks that exile is not simply a moment in the history of ancient Israel. It is a metaphor for the church's contemporary existence. From careful attention to Israel's story of exile, the church may—and he would underscore the "may" because he is not primarily an optimist—discover where it is and why, what its future holds, and what is required for faithfulness in our time. A lot of attention is given these days to the significance of the exile and its aftermath as the time of composition of much of the Old Testament. Brueggemann is less interested in that literary history and more interested in whether the experience erupting in the text of Scripture can break through our academic arguments to mirror the present even as it tells the story of the past. After all, why do we bother to hold on to these texts?

3. Israel's way of holding on to the story that carried them through the present and into the future was by way of memory. Remembering forward and hoping backward is a construct that Dietrich Ritschl has used in his Christology (*Memory and Hope: An Inquiry Concerning the Presence of Christ*). It is also a way of thinking and living that is lifted up in Brueggemann's continuing recall of the biblical story, of the credo, of the redemptive acts of God, and his insistence that such memory is what feeds hope and creates identity.

4. Indeed, a concern for identity, which he finds so heavily in Scripture, is one of the communal requirements Brueggemann lays upon the contemporary church. Whatever marks go into that identity seem to come from an ethos that is heavily counter to the present way of living in this world. So again and again, Brueggemann hears the text of Scripture pressuring against the way things are and proposing an alternative or counter way—a counter culture, a counter lifestyle, a counter world, a counter economics. Brueggemann is deeply convinced that we have succumbed to a consumerist culture reflected in business—whose capitalist underpinnings are presumed as inherent and exclusive of other modes—sports, entertainment, and not least politics. At one point he asks: "How shall we practice a distinctive ethic of humanness in a society massively driven by the forces of the market economy toward an ethic of individualism that issues in social indifference and anti-neighborliness?" (151). The only way out of such a living death is via an ethic of resistance. Possible answers to his question, however, are

not confined to its immediate context. They are present throughout this collection of essays.

5. Among the necessities emphasized by Brueggemann are modes of *practice* and the possibility of *imagining* a different way and a different world. As it was with Israel, so it should be with those for whom Israel's story is definitive. Especially in the Torah but also in the story, Israel defined itself by various practices that both reflected its fidelity to the Lord and marked the community off from others without turning its back on "the other." As Brueggemann notes in these essays, like the people of God from the beginning, the church has to live between peculiarity and pluralism, between shaping ourselves as a different people—different not in our humanness but in our obedience—and living in relation to the other who is our immediate neighbor and also to the nation far off. For Brueggemann as he reads the prophets and the story, this is only possible by a constant use of imagination to evoke a new and different world. The prophetic imagination gives us the equipment to exercise our own imaginations against the culture and against the economic and political modes that seem to define our lives and continuously undercut our obedience to the one God who has redeemed and called us. If you are not sure how to use that equipment, Brueggemann is a helpful guide.

6. In the academy these days, Christian scholars are keenly aware of the fact that the Old Testament is a scripture shared by Jews. That is obviously reflected in the virtual abandonment of the term "Old Testament" in favor of the "Hebrew Scriptures." Pros and cons for such a move do not need to be debated in this context. What should be noted here is that Brueggemann, for whom "Old Testament" is a legitimate title, is deeply aware that the text he studies and lives by is a Jewish text as well as a Christian one. Indeed, it is a Jewish text before it is a Christian one. So he attends to its Jewishness and its reflections and resonances in Judaism, unabashed by criticisms of his daring to define its Jewishness.

7. If Brueggemann's attention to the rootedness of the Scriptures he studies and loves in the Jewish experience is something he risks attending to despite his Christian context, he is just as venturesome—and generally distinct from his colleagues in the same field—in yet another way: his attention to the whole of Scripture. While he is an Old Testament scholar, he is self-defined more deeply as a student of Scripture and so moves easily and unabashedly back and forth between Old Testament and New, probably more so than any other contemporary Scripture scholar. Thus

he reminds us that what we read and study and where the word of God addresses us is the *Bible*, not an Old Testament or a New Testament, but the whole, which is always more than a sequence or a sum of the two. It is, as such, a particular and peculiar reality of its own, a whole new thing. In this daring way, Brueggemann breaks through our academic compartmentalization, compelled once more by the very nature of the subject matter he studies. Would that more of us ventured to wander so freely through all of Scripture.

8. Finally, one must modify some of what has been said lest the reader of these essays miss one of the most characteristic features of Brueggemann's writings, here and elsewhere. I have spoken of the Scriptures as his subject matter from beginning to end. While that is true, it risks obscuring what is patent in the pages that follow. The subject matter may be the Scriptures, but only as they point to the true subject, the Lord of Israel. The reality of God, the mystery, the presence, the claims, the power of God, all of that and what it means for human existence and covenantal fidelity is what originally and finally Brueggemann seeks to illumine. To use one's imagination a bit, it is as if he is John the Baptist in Matthias Grünewald's Isenheim altarpiece, pointing that larger-than-life index finger to the crucified one with the words written behind his arm: *Illum oportet crescere me autem minui* ("He must increase, but I must decrease"). His scholarship is immensely helpful to all of us. It is also an act of devotion.

—Patrick D. Miller

Preface

To speak of "the Word that redescribes the world," using language appropriated from Paul Ricoeur, is to call attention to the fact that the biblical text functions among us as a "second thought," coming after the initial description of our life in the world according to the dominant metanarrative of our society. One function of redescription is to protest against that initial description and to insist that the initial presentation of reality is not an adequate or trustworthy account. The initial description of our current context may be a *secular account* of reality, preoccupied with power and the self-indulgent use of power in a way of entitlement or, alternatively, it may be a *supernaturalist fideistic presentation* of reality that misconstrues the claims of faith. Either way, such a description of reality will not do, for it distorts the truth of God's hidden reality amid the ordered workings of the world.

This collection of essays brings together papers that I have written and published in a variety of contexts, in response to a number of different questions and invitations. Consequently, there is a somewhat random quality to the collection and, inescapably, some repetition. Nonetheless there is a coherence to these chapters and a rough unity that is evident in the threefold arrangement of the sections, an arrangement shrewdly suggested by Patrick Miller and Neil Elliott.

The first section of the collection is preoccupied with the *biblical text*, with its dynamism and its relentless insistence upon being taken with contemporary seriousness. These four essays consider a way in which the biblical redescription may be practiced with authority in a cultural context where old patterns of authority will no longer serve. The sum of this section is the claim that the text itself is indeed a lively word that will have its dangerous, subversive say among us without excessive accommodation to either cultural or religious pressures.

The second section of the collection moves closer to the substantive claims of the biblical text, namely, that the Bible testifies to the claim that

God makes possible what the world takes to be impossible. I have learned from Karl Barth that we must begin, as much as we are able, not with what we think is *possible*, but with the *real* that staggers and shatters our unbelieving notions of the possible. Thus, for example, the biblical testimony testifies to the emancipation of the slaves from Egypt and to the resurrection of Jesus from the dead. These astonishing turns occur in the lived reality of the world but are beyond human explanation. They claim the continuing attention of Jews and Christians and leave us open for "abiding astonishment" (Martin Buber), a dazzled sense that the world is something other than we had understood it to be. The doxologies of ancient Israel, the lyrical soaring of Paul's Epistles, and the regular amazement evoked by the deeds and teaching of Jesus all converge in the stunning affirmation that the world is other than we had taken it to be, because the world is the venue for God's reign.

This of course is the stuff of biblical faith. But we have not of late reflected much on a point so well understood by Karl Barth, that this claim shatters all our conventional certitudes. As a result, moreover, if we consider the crisis points before the church in our society—the status of gays and lesbians, the mystery of creation and the workings of evolution, the intractable problem of our economy and the derivative issue of poverty, the cultural wars, and the engagement with other faith claims—it is clear that our old patterns of certitude yield no possibility for the future. All of these issues await a new possibility that would be a gift of God. And even while we gladly recite the old inventory of God's miracles, such new possibility about these issues seems implausible at best. That there should be a "third way" beyond "red" and "blue" on any of these issues is completely unlikely. Of course it is "unlikely" for "flesh and blood"; that, however, is the wondrous, subversive option kept open in the testimony of the biblical text. Our engagement with that text is to gather around the testimony and thereby to receive eyes to discern and lives to receive a third way of God that is characteristically "a way out of no way."

The third section of this collection considers the ways in which the impossibility of the text is not only to be understood but is to be lived out in glad obedience. It is my intention to move as far as a biblical exegete might reasonably move toward practical theology and the daily, bodily act of obedience to God-given possibility. What counts in the end is not a better understanding or a new idea; what counts is a community of concrete engagement that takes up the gift of transformation and acts it out in the world. The essays in this section reflect on fresh modes of holy obedience in a world of anxiety and a critical rereading of world power wherein even the capacity of the last standing superpower is made unarguably penultimate. The concreteness of praxis, of course, invites us beyond all extant certitudes and all long-held assumptions. The old cluster of memories of Exodus concerns a departure from old loyalties toward new commitments; the Easter memory concerns a gift of new life wrought out of death. This memory of *departure* and *new life* resurfaces for people gathered around the gospel. We are indeed summoned to a new obedience that is articulated through new freedom and new life.

The sequence of text as *redescription, possibility,* and *practice of discipleship* converges in what is now commonly termed a "postliberal" presentation. Of course I did not set out to be postliberal, even though I am much informed by the leading figures in what is now commonly named under that label. Rather, I set out to read the text vigilantly and in relationship to our particular social venue where we are to practice our faith. It is clear that the text—read according to the dominant description of our world, that is, according to the usual modes of belated capitalism—yields no energy for mission. When one pays attention to the text, it is clear that we are, in reading as in acting, summoned beyond the fixed world of Pharaoh or Caesar. While dominant descriptions want to terminate our reading, the inventory of miracles—exodus, resurrection—keeps the world open and insists on a better, more faithful, more dangerous reading. These essays constitute a part of our common effort in that more dangerous reading.

—Walter Brueggemann

Acknowledgments

I am indebted in this collection to many editors who have accepted my submission of articles and to many who invited me to speaking venues that evoked my many words. More specifically I am indebted to Tempie Alexander and now currently to Tia Foley, who shaped my probes into a manuscript. I am grateful to the several folk at Fortress Press, particularly Michael West, who continue to be receptive and attentive to my work, and to Chris Hooker who prepared the indices. Above all I am grateful to Patrick Miller who has again patiently moved these materials toward a coherent book form. In order to do that, he has done much more than put things together. He has paid enough attention to the argument to see the progression from *text* to *possibility* to *discipleship*. In this shaping he has seen the coherent intentionality of my work and I am grateful for his discernment. On all counts I am blessed to be in a community of support and challenge where my work is drawn to the issues that concern us all. Most particularly I am glad to dedicate this collection to Lee Carroll and Erskine Clarke, who are among my most generous colleagues and my most steadfast friends.

Credits

Chapter 1: "A Text that Redescribes," *Theology Today* 58:4 (2002): 526–40.

Chapter 2 first appeared as "Four Proclamatory Confrontations in Scribal Refraction" in *The Scottish Journal of Theology* 56:4 (2003): 404–26.

Chapter 3 first appeared as "Rescripting for a Fresh Performance Midst a Failed Script," *Reformed Review* 55:1 (2001): 5–17.

Chapter 4: "Faith at the Nullpunkt," pages 143–54 in *The End of the World and the Ends of God*, ed. John Polkinghorne and Michael Welker (Harrisburg, Pa.: Trinity Press International, 2000).

Chapter 5: "The City in Biblical Perspective: Failed and Possible," *Word & World* 19:3 (1999): 236–50.

Chapter 6: "Evangelism and Discipleship: The God Who *Calls*, The God Who *Sends*," *Word & World* 24:2 (2004): 121–35.

Chapter 7: "Options for Creatureliness: Consumer or Citizen," *Horizons in Biblical Theology* 23:1 (2001): 25–50.

Chapter 8: "Ecumenism as the Shared Practice of a Peculiar Identity," *Word & World* 18:2 (1998): 122–35.

Chapter 9: "Vision for a New Church and a New Century: Part I: Homework against Scarcity," *Union Seminary Quarterly Review* 54:1–2 (2000): 21–39.

Chapter 10: "Vision for a New Church and a New Century: Part II: Holiness Becomes Generosity," *Union Seminary Quarterly Review* 54:1–2 (2000): 45–64.

Chapter 11: "Patriotism for Citizens of the Penultimate Superpower," *Dialogue* 42:4 (2003): 336–43.

I.
The Word
Redescribing the World

CHAPTER ONE

A Text That Redescribes

It is more or less a given, by convention if not by conviction, that one must have a biblical text for a sermon. Sometimes the text is more than that, utterly absolutized. Often it is a lot less than that, a text read but not taken seriously. The text is a given, nonetheless, in the churches of the Reformation. It is a given that requires, in our time, a fresh consideration.

The Dominant Script

A fresh reconsideration is a requirement (1) because of our awareness, fresh awareness, of the problematic of the text with reference to historical questions; (2) because the text is seen to be laden with deep ideological force that is dangerous; and (3) because our church situation is now so greatly pluralized that the claim for this particular text—even in the church—is not obviously normative, as the slippage between text and gospel seems wide and gaping.

The text is problematic enough—historically and ideologically—that we might do better to leave off the text and go with "experience," what George Lindbeck terms "experiential-expressive" modes of discourse.[1] Except that it readily becomes obvious that when the church works from its experience—or, worse, from the experience of the preacher—things very quickly become thin, boring, predictable, and perhaps too congenial or, alternatively, too angry and coercive, depending on the preacher's "experience." Any large vision of saving transcendence, moreover, devolves into the family or tribe, either in blasé comfort or in militant crusading, either way with a very low ceiling. The failure of such thinness makes clear that we need a text that addresses us inscrutably, from beyond us, beyond the low ceiling of the congregation and the short horizon of the preacher.

If we cannot get along without a text, should we not be candid enough to say that we already have a text? We already have a text that we bring to

church and carry home with us. We may characterize that hidden, powerful, authoritative text in various ways, here all critical if not polemical. It
is the text of the Enlightenment, of modernity, which received its decisive
articulation within decades of the final edition of Calvin's *Institutes.* The
turn from the sixteenth to the seventeenth century—in Hobbes, Descartes,
Galileo, and Locke—worked an incredible gain of emancipation in Western culture—a knowing revolt against superstitious traditionalism in the
church, a rejection of the kind of absolutism that still operates in the "religious wars" of our own time— and produced the Thirty Years War, rendering Europe bloody. This new, emerging text, culminating in the immense
rational powers of Immanuel Kant, was perhaps a gift from God and was
received as such by its formulators.

That text has become an unquestioned, normative narrative that has
permeated Western consciousness, for believer and nonbeliever alike, with
reasonableness and autonomous freedom. It is, however, a huge leap from
the reasoned intentionality of the formulators of that text to the present-
tense derivations and extrapolations now so forceful among us: Its undis-
ciplined extrapolation shows up

- in the assumption that there is a reasonable, technical solution to
  every problem, so that "research and development" are the order of
  the day.
- in the self-worship of media idols in which human quality is reduced
  to sexual emanations.
- in professional sports, where physical strength is traded for bigger
  salaries, and macho images show powerful people who are unbridled by normal social restraints and expectations.
- in the piped-in, televised liturgies of consumerism that offer always
  one more "Elemental Helper"—offers that are interrupted only by
  occasional episodes of numbing entertainment.
- in systematic violence within the U.S. that is fostered by the gun
  lobby, which relies upon a constitutional amendment, itself an
  Enlightenment statement of autonomy.
- in endlessly developing military capacity of technique given over
  to violence, whether of Auschwitz or, currently, the U.S. imperial
  machine of war.

Do I go on too long with this? Do I overstate? I take so much time, because I believe this text that we already have—which is dangerous to criticize in public—is deeply embedded in the church and in our listening apparatus. The power of this text shows up in an excessive theological conservatism that has transposed fidelity into certitude and believes that if we go deep enough we will find certitudes that are absolutes about morality as about theology, as though somewhere there are rational formulations that will powerfully veto the human ambiguities so palpable among us. The power of this text also shows up in overstated theological liberalism in which every woman and every man is one's own pope, in which autonomous freedom becomes a fetish and all notions of communal accountability evaporate into a polite but innocuous mantra of "each to her or his own."

The Text Lost

In the presence of that powerful, extrapolated text of Enlightenment autonomy, we become aware of how feeble the biblical text has become among us. Likely, we should say that in the Bible we *had* a text for preaching; but it was largely, unwittingly lost among us and has stayed largely lost. In the interest of the recovery of that text, we may reflect on how we lost it.

We have lost the text, in a measure, because we have wanted to press the text to yield dogmatic certitudes that it does not offer. The playfulness of the text has left things too open—or, as we might say, "polyvalent"—for our comfort. Its playfulness, openness, and ambiguity were consequently made to yield to a scholastic pattern of conclusions that make the text almost too predictable and familiar to bother with.

We have lost the text, in a measure, because, like Uzzah in 2 Samuel 6:6, we touch the ark; we get too close to its inscrutability. Or, like the janitor in 1 Kings 8:9, we have looked into the ark and discovered it was empty, except for the tablets of Torah. We have become critically knowing and busy with explanation. Our loss has come with historical criticism, to which we all, in one way or another, are committed. The project of historical criticism began with an attempt to place and locate texts in context, in the belief that context illuminates text. But the project went on to make the text congenial to modern rationality, with the dismissal of inconvenience through glosses, the slicing into sources where the tension offends, all of which culminates, for example, in the Jesus Seminar. The outcome, of course, is a respectable text, one emptied of its unfamiliarity.

We have lost the text, in a measure, because we have become knowing and technologically competent, and one cannot build public greatness on the foundation of an irascible Holiness who subverts. Our controlling power and self-confidence have come to require a text not so disruptive, either this one smoothed to management or another one in its place.

We have lost the text, in a measure, because we have become self-sufficient and affluent, and we no longer need to be reminded of the more dangerous powers that still float around in our bodies and in the body politic. Self-sufficiency makes the primal categories of this text not only an unwelcome disruption, with its talk about gifts, wonders, and obedience, but also so remote that it sounds like a language we do not know and do not intend to learn. We are long aware of tales from the "mission fields" in Africa where it was so difficult to do mission because the peoples have no vocabulary for "grace" or "atonement" or whatever. *Mutatis mutandis,* we, in our technological affluence, have no vocabulary for "presence" or "holiness" or "discipleship." And the preacher chatters on in a foreign tongue.

We have lost the text, in a measure, because in our moral earnestness we have willed that the text should be relevant; by twists and turns of a thousand kinds, we have helped the text speak directly to us concerning our passionate convictions about sexuality, money, capital punishment, abortion, the Panama Canal, and whatever—a text now speaking to us in cadences that sound strangely like our own. Because the text is not so immediately interested in our burning contemporary crises, I think sometimes the text finds us not very interesting at all.

We have lost the text, in a measure. I have, by inference, been characterizing the text itself as the antithesis of each of these dimensions of loss. That is, the strangeness of the text itself illuminates the reasons we have scuttled it. With the inchoate recognition of loss, moreover, we hold many conferences on the recovery of the text. We may consider what would happen if we set about the recovery of the text in ways that

- moved past fascination with our own *experience,*
- moved past packaged *certitudes* familiar to us, and
- risked *unlearning* much that we have known too long.

Recovering the Text

I suggest that recovery entails and produces

1. a deep and inescapable awareness of how this text, and the life it fosters, lives in deep tension with the dominant text of the global market, a tension to be entrusted to those who speak and listen to this text.

2. an openness to a text that resists reduction and explanation, that traffics in metaphor, image, tease, and possibility, but that is short on conclusions and directives.

3. a hosting of the seething, unrelieved ambiguities hidden deep within human life that operate with enormous leverage among us. The seething ambiguities have now been channeled into counseling, an important legacy of Freud, who did not flinch from that which was denied. Counseling as a pastoral opportunity is surely important; as we practice it, however, it remains mostly unconnected to the public realities. We have arrived where we can scarcely acknowledge the unresolved ambiguities that characterize our life, public and personal.

4. a quality of danger and risk; danger when people sense the tension with another text, danger to the one who speaks, expressed not uncommonly as anger. Beyond that, this danger of openness stops short of resolution; it is the danger of acknowledging and living with ambiguous claims.

5. a readiness to be less relevant to the presenting problems of the day, for in truth this text gives little directly to such questions but cuts underneath to where the hidden issues of density hover, to the places where we redecide about trusting, doubting, giving, and resisting.

6. the loss of the "moneys of certitude"—the ones we gladly pay to be reassured that the troubles are all in fact contained—because such moneys do not respond easily to textual proclamation that is polyvalent, open, and subversive. A wager can be made that those relieved to have their lives opened by such a recovered text will, in immense generosity, outgive the loss of the moneys of certitude, but one never knows. That is, the recovery of the text likely brings with it a deprivileging and the need to find a new set of friends, as did Jesus with his circle of "publicans and sinners."

The Plot of the Text

It will be helpful to consider the large plot of this text to be recovered among us, a text that questions the dominant text of our culture, a plot that tells radically against the plot of modern consumerism. I understand and acknowledge the risks in such a large plot because the text is enormously variegated in its detail and nuance. To suggest such a large plot is for me to think too much like a theologian, or perhaps to echo too much the so-called Biblical Theology Movement. Nonetheless, such a suggestion seems inescapable.

I take recourse to Martin Buber and Franz Rosenzweig to speak of *creation-covenant-consummation* as an ordered account of faith, of the large way in which faith sees the life of the world. Of course, that plot line is too simple, too clear, and too coherent for the vagaries of daily life, the vagaries of the text, or the detailed nuance of careful reading. But, provisionally, the task of the preacher is to lead the church in situating its daily life—with all the ambiguities present and not to be denied—in this sweep. The plot of creation-covenant-consummation that the preacher works day by day, week by week, and text by text situates lived human crises in relation to large evangelical claims—the linkage between the immediate and the deep. It also links the detail of our life to the presiding God, intimately connected to but not domesticated by the truth of our daily existence.

- Creation is the claim of the text that the life of the world is bounded by the self-giving generosity of God. As deep and as far back as we can go, we will find that generosity. We cannot push beyond, will, or imagine our life outside the arena of Holy Generosity.
- Consummation is the claim of the text that the life of the world is bounded by God's utterly reliable fidelity. As deep and as far forward as we can go, we will find that fidelity. We cannot push beyond, will, or imagine our life outside the theater of Holy Fidelity, all the way home.
- Covenant is the claim of the text that the current life of the world is intimately and determinedly held in relation to God's governance. This governance, moreover, is marked by summons, expectation, and demand toward the neighbor, and we cannot outdistance that demand. We cannot push beyond, will, or imagine our life outside the demand of that Holy Neighbor who marks all our other neighbors by holiness.

What a mouthful of daring assertion! A mouthful uttered over and over in the text. To be sure, Israel always knows that its most profound claims are at the same time inescapably and deeply problematic.

- Creation bespeaks abundance, but the creation texts live close to issues of *idolatry*, whether the world in some way and to some extent is governed by powers that are not generous.
- Consummation bespeaks fidelity, but the text is haunted by a defining sense of *absence* in which the allegedly faithful one can only be addressed on occasion in demanding accusation and disputatious summons.
- Covenant bespeaks neighborly command, but the text is endlessly aware that the ones given as neighbors turn out, with some regularity, to be *enemies*.

Creation-covenant-consummation yields a sweeping metanarrative to which the preacher bears witness. But Israel will not lie. It knows about this other triad of *idolatry-absence-enemies;* it knows about this other triad even as do we and as do the ones who attend to our preaching. Thus it is the case that preaching is not only a championing of this metanarrative that makes sense and gives coherence to daily vagaries, but preaching is also wrestling with the problematic in candor. The outcome, moreover, is not always clean, unscarred, and without ambiguity. The recovery of the text is in the interest of both the large coherence of metanarrative and the candid engagement of the problem left by that metanarrative and by our life in the world. In what follows, I consider three aspects of the large claim as it functions as countertext, as text counter to the dominant text.

Memory against Dominant Amnesia

The recovery of the text is in order to *mediate a memory of generosity* in the face of a *dominant text of amnesia.*

The dominant text of our culture is one that is programmatically committed to amnesia because what is past is over and done. This commitment to technical reason means that the lively retention of lore as a way of embedding the present in the past and importing the past into the present is a devalued and delegitimated project. Henry Ford, a great practitioner of modernity, famously opined, "History is bunk!" Ronald Reagan, after him, led a parade of deniers whose defense of their shabby present was a dismissive "I cannot remember," that is, I am unable to remember, I do not want to remember, I refuse to remember. Such a posture leaves the present unembedded and necessarily thin. Amnesia renders the human community lean and without resources, unprotected from the past, and left with the need to invent and reinvent endlessly. A nonremembering user of present-tense data never has the finger far away from the delete button; what was vanishes completely.

The recovery of this text, with its rootage in the generosity of the Creator, gives the preacher the task of mediating the past as both resource and as problem for the present. While the past given by the text is variegated, here I consider only one dimension of that past, namely, the memory of Israel that is saturated with miracle, wonder, wondrous deeds, mighty acts. The past that Israel celebrates is a collage of remembered transformations that attest that the world is open to generous, inexplicable transformation.

Israel concedes nothing to such technical reason. It proceeds in lyrical, poetic, narrative, imaginative modes of discourse to give testimony that refuses the monitoring of modernity. Thus preacher and congregation, from the outset, proceed in a very different and odd rhetoric; the task of communication consists in willingness to use rhetoric that modernity (in the form of historical criticism) can hardly tolerate. One may suggest that in entering into liturgy and preaching one agrees to engage a world of alternative discourse that bespeaks an alternative to the world of technical, self-sufficient management that remembers nothing.

The recital of miracle that constitutes Israel's past has, of course, focused on Gerhard von Rad's credo hypothesis.[2] While that hypothesis is subject to all kinds of critique with reference to dating and the rhetoric involved, it cannot be denied that von Rad saw clearly that Israel's worship life was regularly an engagement with the past, a past constituted by YHWH's wonders to which Israel endlessly attests.

The so-called early credos of Deuteronomy 6:20-24 and 26:5-9 and Joshua 24:1-13 provide a shaping inventory of that wondrous past: exodus-wilderness-land. The liturgical recital holds to the story line that smacks of *particularity* and, at the same time, readily becomes a *typology* of departure and arrival, of relinquishment and reception that can be reread in many different contexts. That story line yields three accents for attention. First, the action of transformation features YHWH, the subject of the verbs, as the characteristic and decisive agent. Israel has no past except a past centered on YHWH. Second, the actions recited are all acts of gift in which YHWH wills and enacts a better life for Israel: emancipation from bondage, sustenance in the wilderness, settlement in a land of abundance. None of these acts could be expected or explained. Each is a wonder that lies beyond human achievement and can only be understood as gift. The past is a collage of gifts. Third, the gifts are jarring and dynamic, marked by a disruption and discontinuity that radically resituate Israel. The memories are not of ongoing conditions but of emerging new conditions willed by the Initiator against the circumstances over which Israel has no control.

The primal substance of the credo, as von Rad saw, is exposited in the great doxological recitals of Psalms 78, 105, 106, 135, and 136, each with a similar story line but with important distinctive developments. Here I comment only on Psalm 136 as an extreme expression of Israel's doxological memory. Von Rad has seen that these expansive Psalms are connected to the leaner credos but go well beyond them. In Psalm 136, in addition to the accents on the exodus (vv. 10-15), the wilderness (v. 16), and the land (vv. 17-22), there is an opening element on creation (vv. 4-9). Thus, the particularities of Israel's memory are embedded in a larger, deeper recall of creation. But, of course, what counts most in the Psalm is the regular refrain of each verse, "for his *ḥesed* ("steadfast love") endures forever"; that is, this second line shows Israel making a characteristic interpretive move that finds in the particular memory a generic affirmation of YHWH's fidelity. The entire sketch of the past is read as a mass of evidence that the lived world of Israel and the life of all creation is a transaction of elemental fidelity that is an enactment of YHWH's character. Memory is an engagement with fidelity from a God who takes endless initiatives in life-transforming, life-guaranteeing actions of generosity.

This public recital of the past as life-guaranteeing fidelity is matched in songs of thanksgiving that remember intimate, personal, albeit stylized, rescues. Psalm 107, for example, cites four typical rescues: from desert thirst (vv. 4-9), from prison (vv. 10-16), from sickness (vv. 17-22), and from storm (vv. 23-32). What is interesting yet again is Israel's capacity to move from the transformation to an act of gratitude focused on YHWH's *ḥesed*:

> Let them thank YHWH for his steadfast love,
>> For his wonderful works to humankind.

Again, memory is shaped like life-saving fidelity. Thus, in credo, hymn, and song of thanksgiving, Israel counters amnesia with concrete memory and affirms active *ḥesed* against a neutral or hostile environment for life.

Characteristically, the past is given in doxology, not in positivistic reportage. Remembering is a lyrical, imaginative, hyperbolic construal that empowers Israel to move beyond every fearful calculation to a glad ceding of self, a bodily, emancipated gesture of the transference of energy, attention, and passion beyond self to YHWH who is the object of worship and the true subject of life. Israel enacts poetic *ceding* against a prosaic, technical *retention* of self. In this act, Israel does not insist on its own autonomous past but gladly submits its past to the larger story of YHWH's own life in the world. As the dominant text of Western culture is a *turn to* the private subject, so doxological remembering is a *turn away* from a private subject to the grandeur of the faithful Holy One who dominates the true story of the world.

This collage of doxologies about YHWH's wonderful works prepared the way for the church's earliest attestation of Jesus, namely the collage of narratives about his amazing acts of transformation wrought concretely in the life of the world. From the outset, the church has cherished many specific accounts of the raising of the daughter of Jairus, the giving of sight to Bartimaeus, and the cleansing of the lepers. The church has never explained but has treasured a remembered narrative that constitutes the world as a place of bottomless transformative generosity. The specific narratives remembered about Jesus can be given in summary form: "Go and tell John . . . the blind receive their sight, the lame walk, the lepers are cleansed, the deaf hear, the dead are raised, the poor have good news brought to them" (Luke 7:22). Go tell John and let Herod notice. Go tell the church and let the world wonder. Go tell that we have these testimonies of the way in which the generous, life-giving power of God has come bodied to make things new. Nothing explained, nothing doubted: The memories of Jesus, like the memories of YHWH, tell the world differently. Those who live in this told world have our amnesia overcome, have the pressured requirement of self-sufficiency vetoed by the panoply of gifts, and have pervasive prosaic calculation flooded with doxology that leaves us amazed and grateful. Such is the first gift of the text.

Hope against Dominant Despair

The recovery of the text is to mediate *hope of utter fidelity into all futures* in the face of a *dominant text of despair.*

I need use little energy arguing that the dominant text of our culture is a practice of despair. A closed, settled world of reasonableness requires that there are no new gifts to be given, and there is no Giver who might give gifts. There is nothing more than management and distribution of what is already there, distribution and redistribution, wars about distribution of land and oil and water, no more gifts. Everything is limited and scarce, to be guarded and kept, to be confiscated and seized. It is so in the public domain of economics, not less so in the intimate world of human transactions and emotional need—not enough of love, a shortage of forgiveness, and finally a deprivation of grace in this age and in the age to come. It was perhaps Marlene Dietrich who eloquently concluded, "When you're dead, you're dead." Since death is so final, so daily, so immediate, and so palpable, it leaves adherents to this dominant text in despair, either the despair of glad complacency or the despair of wretchedness—but, in either complacency or wretchedness, without a chance for new gifts.

The recovery of the biblical text includes the daring, pervasive conviction that God's fidelity outlasts every circumstance. In the face of every circumstance, it is assured in the faithfulness of YHWH that, in the words of Julian of Norwich, in the end "all shall be well, and all manner of things shall be well."[3] What an incredible mouthful! All will be well, because YHWH is no quitter, is not defeated by death, but will prevail against every negation with a primordial "Yes" (2 Cor. 1:19) from which we can never be separated by death or by life or by angels or by rulers or by things present or by heights or powers or things to come, not separated because that fidelity reaches all the way toward us.

Such talk of assured fidelity over the future is not easy. It is the privilege of every preacher to do Romans 8 at funerals. Too bad we do this text primarily at funerals, for the seething power of despair is more dangerous and insidious in many other contexts of wretchedness, anxiety, and greed. Perhaps funerals are an easier place, for there is a readiness for going beyond. To counter despair in an economy of scarcity or in communities of rage, however, is more difficult.

The promise-generating reality of YHWH is as old as the first utterance to Abraham: "Go . . . I will make of you a great nation, and I will bless you, and make your name great, so that you will be a blessing" (Gen. 12:1-2). Abraham, Sarah, and all members of this text are summoned into a future they do not see or have in hand. It is a future beyond our poor powers of imagination. It will be a good land, a land of milk, honey, houses, vineyards, olive trees, and water; and it will be given. Faith—"reconed as faith"—is to trust present-tense life to future gifts not yet in hand.

The promise to the ancestors is a shadowy promise in the community of Moses, not much voiced—until exile! In exile—the defining moment of despair for Israel when YHWH was silent, remote, and uncaring, in a context where the "No" of reality might have had the last word—the promises from the ancestors surge; it is amid the wretchedness of exile and all its marks of abandonment that the poets arise to voice God's new gifts of homecoming.

The lyrical poetry of Jeremiah can imagine a renewal of the covenant that is rooted in forgiveness. Ezekiel can anticipate a new temple with abiding glory and assured presence and, beyond that, a trace of resurrection with the vision of the valley of dry bones. Second Isaiah can imagine most vividly the defeat of the powers of the gods of negation. In that ancient world, the defeat concerned Babylon; perhaps in our time it is transnational corporate wealth and its totalizing ideology—entrenched, with our collusion, in exploitative ruthlessness. The poet looks beyond such negation, precisely because YHWH's fidelity toward YHWH's world is not curbed by empire, not defeated by exile, not limited by any closed circumstance. Newness springs forth laden with well-being.

The beginning of promise—quite concrete, text-specific oaths on the part of YHWH—pushes even beyond Israel's loss. On one hand, the hope is cosmic, new heaven and new earth. That newness will be urban, a new Jerusalem. On the other hand, at the edge of Israel's text, the poetry imagines the defeat of the last force of despair:

> he will swallow up death forever.
> Then the Lord God will wipe away the tears from all faces,
>   and the disgrace of his people he will take away from all the earth.
>   (Isa. 25:7-8)

Israel's buoyancy is in the conviction, not that we shall never die, not that we shall meet our loved ones, but that God's governance will not be disrupted or diminished.

The gathering of all these hopes—to the ancestors, to the exiles, to the cosmos, against death—is in the Christian Bible at the pivot point of the Old Testament, as we make the close, huge leap from Malachi to Matthew. For just at the last moment, this is the last utterance of hope of the Old Testament: "Lo, I will send you the prophet Elijah before the great and terrible day of the LORD comes. He will turn the hearts of parents to their children and the hearts of children to their parents, so that I will not come and strike the land with a curse" (Mal. 4:5-6). This assurance is picked up directly in Luke's anticipation concerning John, who will precede Jesus: "With the spirit and power of Elijah he will go before him, to turn the hearts of parents to their children, and the disobedient to the wisdom of the righteous, to make ready a people prepared for the Lord" (Luke 1:17). Israel hopes relentlessly because the world will be made new in God's good time. The church is one of those who takes this hope seriously, along with synagogue and mosque.

This hope is a claim beyond data, beyond circumstance, and clearly beyond the myth of a closed world. The New Testament does not know how to say it well, but does not believe that the end of the life of Jesus is the end. There is more. And so it says:

> Truly I tell you, there is no one who has left house or brothers or sisters or mother or father or children or fields, for my sake and for the sake of the good news, who will not receive a hundredfold now in this age—houses, brothers and sisters, mothers and children, and fields with persecutions—and in the age to come eternal life." (Mark 10:29-30)

And so the text ends:

> The one who testifies to these things says, "Surely I am coming soon."
> Amen. Come, Lord Jesus!
> The grace of the Lord Jesus be with all the saints. Amen.
> (Rev. 22:20-21)

And so we say regularly at the table:

> For as often as you eat this bread and drink the cup, you proclaim the Lord's death until he comes. (1 Cor. 11:26)

Until he comes!

This capacity to counter despair is seductive, for it can make us simply the happy optimist in town. I want only to insist that this hope is text-specific. It is not a generic generalization. It is a collection of texts that are precise, holy utterances in which God has taken an oath, vowed a vow, made a promise. It is this set of utterances, inscribed in text, that had been spoken over the world. The preacher and the church cling not to a generic sense of things but to specific promises over which God keeps watch. The hope that overcomes despair in its assertion of fidelity is as text-specific as is memory over amnesia that asserts generosity. The preacher and the church are always relearning that the despair sponsored by the dominant text is false. The scarcity it breeds, moreover, is a phony construct designed for power and greed, an excuse for violence. For, in the end, the antithesis of hope is indeed violence.

Neighborliness against Dominant Selfishness

The recovery of the text is to mediate a *present tense of covenantal neigh-borliness* in the face of the dominant text of *anxious selfishness and alien-ated greed.* The present, any present tense, is given its tone, character, and potential by the way in which it is related to past and future.

In the dominant text, I have traced a nonexistent past of *amnesia* in which there is no fund of miracles and no memory of gifts but only the hard, endless work of self-invention. I have traced, in like fashion, a future of *despair* in which there are no more gifts to be given, but only a no-win struggle against scarcity. If that dominant text, as I suggest, is marked by an amnesia requiring self-invention and a despair requiring self-sufficiency, it is not surprising that the present becomes a jungle of frightened meanness. The theologian of such a thin present tense, Gordon Gekko, a character in the movie *Wall Street*, made it a credo to say, "Greed is good." That credo is not only shameless. It is inescapable if one's past tense is burdened by self-invention and one's future tense is limited to self-sufficiency. It takes no imagination to see that technological consumerism, unable to host past miracles or future promises, has given us a present tense of greed powered by anxiety and issuing in shameless brutality against the neighbor. The world, in such limited horizon, really has no option.

I suggest that the recovery of the biblical text is urgent, the most urgent "social action" that can be undertaken. For it is only when the past is brimming with miracle and the future is inundated with fidelity that the present can be recharacterized as a place of neighborliness in which

- scarcity can be displaced by generosity;
- anxiety can be displaced by confidence;
- greed can be displaced by sharing;
- brutality can be displaced by compassion and forgiveness.

In the great covenantal traditions of Moses, Deuteronomy, and the prophets, there is a sustained vision of covenantal neighborliness. Whether the texts are dated early or late, Norman Gottwald is surely correct to say that Israel—and consequently the synagogue, the church, and the mosque—is a "social experiment" in the world, a revolutionary alternative to see whether the daily social relationships, policies, and institutions in the world can be ordered differently.[4] The Torah of Israel is a mandate from heaven, precisely located between deep generosity and long fidelity, that Israel take the world as a neighborhood. The most radical summons on behalf of the neighborhood is what Patrick Miller terms "the sabbatic principle," enacted as a year of release and jubilee, whereby the strong give back to the weak their proper entitlement, precisely because the strong and the weak are bound in a common destiny.[5] It is impossible to overstate the radicality or the centrality of this mandate, whereby Israel, in God's *timefulness*, repeatedly breaks the vicious cycles of anxiety, greed, and brutality.

The particular subject of this recognition and entitlement, at the core of covenantal ethic, is regularly widow, orphan, alien. Indeed, that triad in Deuteronomy and the prophets is like a mantra, a mantra of neighborliness that characterizes the vulnerable, marginalized, and most at-risk people as the proper subjects of communal investment. The prophetic tradition is not so much about scolding and threat as it is a massive act of imagination that asserts that the world could be different, if the present is informed by a freighted past and an assured future.

The mantra of widow, orphan, alien rings in the ears of Jesus as it rang in the ears of Israel. He had, presumably, been nurtured as a small child while his mother sang about "filling the hungry with good things" (Luke 1:53). The cadences of widow, orphan, illegal alien are transposed in his text into tax collectors and sinners (Luke 5:30, 7:34). But it is all the same. It is action that is transformative of social relationships, action disapproved in a less generous horizon by a world schooled in infidelity that cannot share because there is not enough.

The church of late has mostly forgotten how remarkable and upsetting is the self-giving of Jesus. The church has gotten into the fear, scarcity, and survival business, precisely a denial of its Lord and its text, busy supervising a morality of scarcity, trying to keep the old world of anxiety in place. The text, of course, is otherwise. The giving of God that populates our past and the reliability of God that marks our future make life in the present different. It is our capacity to be amazed that equips us to enact the present tense outside normal boundaries and procedures. It is the chance of the preacher, out of this text, to amaze.

The Chance of the Preacher

At this juncture in our common life, the chance of the preacher is crucial—as it has not been in a long time—precisely because the dominant texts are failing. It is sad for a trusted text to fail, sad to watch while people continue to act it out in its failure:

- We have seen the old text of racial superiority fail in South Africa, while apartheid continued.
- We have seen the old text of communism fail in China, while oppressive control goes on.
- We are watching while the old text of hate in Northern Ireland collapses in a yearning for otherwise.
- We are watching while the old text of self-destruction in the Balkans runs out in exhaustion.
- We are watching while some seek to keep the U.S. "pure" by excluding immigrants, even though our nation has a history of welcome.
- We are watching churches exclude people duly called by God to ministry because of some genital practice that frightens us.
- We are watching our young people being devoured by consumerism in the mad pursuit of commodity.

It would be a shame and a pity if we mark the failure of all these old texts and did not notice that the text of self-invention and self-sufficiency that engenders fearful selfishness is also failing among us. The beneficiaries of that old text have huge muscle among us and include most of us; but it has failed.

It is a task of the church—with synagogue and mosque—to offer this countertext of generosity, fidelity, and neighborliness. It is the chance of the preacher to permit people to give up old, failed textual construals and to reimagine and redescribe using this countertext. It is our human work to switch texts, and we do not do that easily. We do not do it unless the alternative text is visible, credible, and available.

Moses said:

> ONLY DISCIPLES WHO ARE
> LIVING OUT THEIR HOPE IN
> JESUS MAKE DISCIPLES WHO
> BELIEVE IN THE POWER OF
> HIS LIFE .

> I have set before you today life and prosperity, death and adversity. . . . Choose life. . . . (Deut. 30:15, 19)

Jesus said:

> Enter through the narrow gate . . . for the gate is narrow and the road is hard that leads to life, and there are few who find it. . . .
> Everyone then who hears these words of mine and acts on them will be like a wise man who built his house on rock. (Matt. 7:13-14, 24)

And Matthew added:

> Now when Jesus had finished saying these things, the crowds were astounded at his teaching, for he taught them as one having authority and not as their scribes. (Matt. 7:28-29)

What an authority given us in doxological memory, oracles of promise, and summons to alternative! It is an oddness entrusted to us. The techno-speak of a computer lacks the thickness we require to be human. That thickness must come from preachers who love and live in this odd text.

Proclamatory Confrontations

In the discussion that follows, consideration will be given to the contested environment of preaching in the United States church where traditional patterns of homiletical authority no longer pertain, thus requiring an alternative perspective that is undertaken intuitively by knowing preachers. This changed environment invites attention to an important new awareness in Old Testament studies, namely, that the texts of confrontation between truth and power (prophet and king) in the Old Testament have now been belatedly refracted through scribal interpretive intentionality. Consequently, what the preacher and the church now have in the Bible is not a report on an encounter (an easy assumption of historical criticism), but a text behind which we cannot go. The implication is that the preacher has the role of a scribe who champions text and not the role of a prophet who participates in the confrontation. Such a perspective invites immense reliance on the text and removes the preacher as the point of impact in the confrontation between truth and power.

We may readily characterize preaching as *truth speaking to power*. Preaching is the difficult, daring act of enunciating a truth from outside conventionally assumed reality that accommodates none of the presuppositions of a conventional listening community. It aims to assure by an alternative, to jar by exposé, and to impel action in a new direction. It is no wonder that preaching is demanding and often dangerous work.

I

This chapter will consider, as a basis for the study of *truth speaking to power*, four scriptural confrontations that are familiar to us because they are classic cases. In each case the "hero," the one with whom we are intended to side in the narrative, is the one who has been authorized to utter truth that exists outside the horizon of the ones addressed.

1. The primal case of truth to power in the Old Testament is *Moses speaking truth to Pharaoh*. Moses as a truth-teller had long preparation for his call:

- He was birthed in danger because Pharaoh, the quintessence of power, had already generically decreed his death as a baby (Exod. 2:1-10; cf. 1:8-22).
- He was schooled as a freedom fighter (read "terrorist") who, along with his people, resented the Egyptian administrators. He so resented them that he killed an Egyptian (Exod. 2:11-12). For his moment of rage he had to flee as a fugitive, a *persona non grata* in the empire (Exod. 2:13-15).
- In his status as a fugitive, he is addressed by this Voice from the burning bush who summons, authorizes, and dispatches him to Pharaoh (Exod. 3:1-10).
- In response, Moses can think of at least five reasons not to undertake such a risky venture as truth to power:

  1. He is inadequate (3:11): Who am I?
  2. His people want to know who the God is who sends (3:13).
  3. Israel will not believe (4:1).
  4. He is inadequate in speech (4:10).
  5. Moses proposes the dispatch of an alternative messenger (4:13).

Moses seems to know that the mission upon which he is sent by YHWH will not succeed, or in any case is much too risky.

The protests of Moses to YHWH, however, are ineffective. The One who calls and voices truth will not be put off. Truth must be uttered. Finally, in chapter 5, truth is uttered to power:

> "Thus says the Lord, the God of Israel: 'Let my people go, so that they may celebrate a festival to me in the wilderness.'" (5:1)

That is all! That is the truth from YHWH! Moses utters the truth of YHWH. The familiar "Let my people go" is in fact an imperative: "Send my people!" Through Moses, YHWH issues a directive to Pharaoh; the king of Egypt was not accustomed to hearing imperatives spoken to him, for the truth of the imperative is that Pharaoh is penultimate and accountable to YHWH.

The truth, moreover, is that the authorization of a festival to YHWH is a highly political act, for the festival is an acknowledgment of sovereignty; a response in festival is visible obedience to YHWH as an alternative to Pharaonic obedience. The truth to be told and visibly enacted is that Pharaoh is exposed as a fraudulent authority.

Over the course of the Exodus narrative, Moses has many occasions for truth-telling, truth that is finally put in this way in Exodus 11:4-7:

> Moses said, "Thus says the LORD: About midnight I will go out through Egypt. Every firstborn in the land of Egypt shall die, from the firstborn of Pharaoh who sits on his throne to the firstborn of the female slave who is behind the handmill, and all the firstborn of the livestock. Then there will be a loud cry throughout the whole land of Egypt, such as has never been or will ever be again. But not a dog shall growl at any of the Israelites—not at people, not at animals—so that you may know that the LORD makes a distinction between Egypt and Israel."

The narrator, in what follows, confirms the truth of Moses' utterance:

> Then [Pharaoh] summoned Moses and Aaron in the night, and said, "Rise up, go away from my people, both you and the Israelites! Go, worship the LORD, as you said. Take your flocks and your herds, as you said, and be gone. And bring a blessing on me too!" (Exod. 12:31-32)

That is the truth! The truth is that YHWH, not Pharaoh, is sovereign. YHWH is glorified and the power of Pharaoh is dissolved. As a consequence and by-product, Israel is emancipated. That is the truth. It is the truth of YHWH; it is, moreover, the disastrous truth of Pharaoh. Moses, frightened, mumbling Moses, is engaged in proclamation that changed history and founded the missional people of God in the world.

2. A second familiar case study of truth to power, a proclamation that jars and invites, is the encounter of Nathan with David in 2 Samuel 12. The narrative of David's success is well known. From his youth, David was a privileged child who quickly passed over his seven older siblings in favor (1 Sam. 16:1-13). Even as a little boy, a giant-killing little boy, he was an anointed king and Messiah. The story of his rise to power given us in the Books of Samuel is an amazing saga. The women adored him (1 Sam. 18:7); the men trusted and admired him—a man's man, a soldier, a chief,

an intimidator (2 Sam. 23:13-17). Everything happens for his benefit and advancement. Very few people ever are able to say "no" to him, and one who does say "no" promptly dies (sec 1 Sam. 25:37-38). Indeed, David is the beneficiary of many convenient deaths, so many that he is endlessly under suspicion for murder (2 Sam. 1:15-16; 3:28-37; 4:11). He himself asserts his innocence in his eager self-announcement to Abigail:

> David said to Abigail, "Blessed be the LORD, the God of Israel, who sent you to meet me today! Blessed be your good sense, and blessed be you, who have kept me today from bloodguilt and from avenging myself by my own hand!" (1 Sam. 25:32-33)

That assertion of innocence did not persuade everyone, however, as Shimei calls him by another name:

> Shimei shouted while he cursed, "Out! Out! Murderer! Scoundrel! The LORD has avenged on all of you the blood of the house of Saul, in whose place you have reigned; and the LORD has given the kingdom into the hand of your son Absalom. See, disaster has overtaken you; for you are a man of blood." (2 Sam. 16:7-8)

In any case, David arrived in power with a long winning streak, successful and innocent (2 Sam. 2:4; 5:1-5). He was seven years king in Hebron, then promoted to Jerusalem, and in Jerusalem, settled—safe, prosperous, and then bored. He was so bored that he needed diversion. He spotted Bathsheba (2 Sam. 11:2-3). She, like everyone before her, did not resist him and the rest, as they say, is history. What follows is a narrative of cover-up. And then an act of murder. It is all in the interest of protecting this king who is above the Torah, who has no restraints, who will have what he wants, who bends the whole world to his whim. That's power!

Enter truth! Enter Nathan, the prophet on the payroll of the king who, back in chapter 7, had given an oracle of divine assurance to David. In that oracle the Creator of heaven and earth signs a blank check to this ruthless, self-indulgent king. That had been an easy truth to speak to power:

> But I will not take my steadfast love from him, as I took it from Saul, whom I put away from before you. Your house and your kingdom shall be made sure forever before me; your throne shall be established forever. (2 Sam. 7:15-16)

But now, in the wake of 2 Samuel 11 and Bathsheba and Uriah, this same truth-teller has a more demanding, dangerous assignment. He must still tell the truth, the truth from the same God to the same king. It turns out, however, that the God of the wondrous *royal oracle* of 2 Samuel 7 is also the God of the *sturdy Torah* who must communicate this uncompromising truth to this king who had accepted no restraints. It is the truth that there is an intransigent restraint in YHWH's Torah that cannot be violated.

This truth-telling assignment given to Nathan is daring and dangerous: The challenge is to announce restraint to an unrestrainable, unrestrained, spoiled, self-indulgent king! The prophet Nathan wisely resorts to a figure of speech, a parable. He employs an artistic euphemism to soften the truth, hoping that the king will not too readily notice or understand what is now to be said as truth.

The parable does its effective, dangerous work (2 Sam. 12:1-4). Ever since that moment, moreover, preachers who must speak truth to power have been employing euphemisms and figures of speech and other rhetorical strategies that we call "illustrations." Nathan's chosen artistic articulation concerns a rich man with many sheep and a poor man with one sheep. David gets the point immediately and expresses his indignation, unwittingly condemning his own royal action:

> Then David's anger was greatly kindled against the man. He said to Nathan, "As the LORD lives, the man who has done this deserves to die; he shall restore the lamb fourfold, because he did this thing, and because he had no pity." (2 Sam. 12:5-6)

The ploy of Nathan works. Nathan the truth-teller, however, is not finished. He still has to draw his point directly to the king. In English, Nathan has to say four dangerous words to David: "You are the man!" In Hebrew, Nathan can get by with only two. But two words or four words, these are dangerous words whereby the indignant king is quickly moved from recipient of a parable to the main character in the transaction, the one who is condemned out of his own mouth. Our interest, however, is not in King David, but in Nathan the truth-teller. What an act of courage and what a risk! At stake in this two-word interpretive act is Nathan's office, his prestige, his future, surely his well-connected wealth. He must speak that truth! Nathan must deconstruct royal self-regard in order to assert that before the intransigence of the Torah the king stands exposed and equal to every other Israelite, nothing special, no exception. It has been a very long time since anyone had risked telling David that he was nobody special!

It may well be that that is all that Nathan said, all that he needed to say, all that he dared to say. The critics have concluded that after the narrative, in its artistic coolness, there comes the moral intensity of the Deuteronomist to make things specific so that nobody will misunderstand the truth that has been uttered and the power that has consequently been deconstructed:

> "Why have you despised the word of the LORD, to do what is evil in his sight? You have struck down Uriah the Hittite with the sword, and have taken his wife to be your wife, and have killed him with the sword of the Ammonites. Now therefore the sword shall never depart from your house, for you have despised me, and have taken the wife of Uriah the Hittite to be your wife. Thus says the LORD: I will raise up trouble against you from within your own house; and I will take your wives before your eyes, and give them to your neighbor, and he shall lie with your wives in the sight of this very sun. For you did it secretly; but I will do this thing before all Israel, and before the sun." (2 Sam. 12:9-12)

In the hands of the Deuteronomists, the artistic parable of Nathan becomes a prosaic speech of judgment that places the king under severe and inescapable penalty. The royal house will be troubled and humiliated; this house of privilege will become the house of embarrassment, and that right soon.

It belongs to David's magnificence that in this dangerous moment he responds to Nathan's parable as an obedient son of the Torah. He utters six words of acknowledgment, "I have sinned against the Lord," only two in Hebrew (2 Sam. 12:13). The truth has prevailed and David in his power has repented. This is exactly the way such encounters are supposed to work. What a relief, because Nathan had no assurance that his confrontation with the king would work so well. Very often power does not yield to truth. This time, in any case, it did; Nathan had risked his life and future for the sake of Torah truth, and power had embraced that truth.

3. The third well-known case of truth to power is in 1 Kings 21, the tale of "Naboth's vineyard." It is interesting that we name the narrative so, for Naboth speaks only once, a minor truth-teller to the king:

> But Naboth said to Ahab, "The LORD forbid that I should give you my ancestral inheritance." (1 Kgs. 21:3)

That is all Naboth ever is permitted to speak. His utterance, however, is a remarkable act of resistance to the king, whereby the acquisitive will of the king is thwarted by old tribal notions of patrimony. Our interest, however, is in the king, Ahab. He is, after his father, the second king of the dynasty of Omri. The dynasty of Omri lasted forty years or so and amassed great wealth and power. It also attracted to itself narratives that seemed to deconstruct its claims to legitimate power. The dynasty of Omri receives attention in the Bible, however, only because it is the public arena for the stunning performances of the prophets Elijah, Elisha, and Micaiah. The occasion for these awesome truth-tellers is that the Omri dynasty, according to this version, is dead set against the tradition of Torah. These Omride kings are practitioners of Baalism, certainly a heterodox religion from the perspective of the Deuteronomist; to judge from their actions, a religion that bespeaks social policies of aggrandizement, acquisitiveness, and exploitation.

In biblical focus, everything turns on this Ahab, son of Omri. He attracts great narrative attention and is the focus of power to which all of this prophetic truth must be addressed. The narrative of 1 Kings 21 concerns a modest real estate deal. It is amazing how great enterprises of state often turn on small, inconspicuous transactions that of themselves amount to nothing, as in the cases of Watergate, Whitewater, and Enron. In this case, Ahab wants a tract of land owned by Naboth for his vegetable garden (1 Kgs. 21:2). The king offers to pay for the property because he assumes, in good Baalistic fashion, that everything and everyone is a purchasable commodity. The king is stunned when Naboth, a powerless Israelite, refuses the request of the king. Ahab is defeated by the resistance of Naboth; he went home and to bed; he would not eat and he sulked (1 Kgs. 21:4).

The story would end there except for his wife, the queen Jezebel. She is from Tyre, not native born, not Israelite, not child of Torah, not subject to old tribal restraints. She knows how to move in the world . . . and she moves. She scolds her husband and makes a promise to him:

> His wife Jezebel said to him, "Do you now govern Israel? Get up, eat some food, and be cheerful; I will give you the vineyard of Naboth the Jezreelite." (1 Kgs. 21:7)

Jezebel orchestrates a judicial scenario against the innocent Naboth, frames him, and gets him stoned by the indignant citizens as an enemy of God and state (1 Kgs. 21:8-14). The mastery of public opinion is indispensable for the practice of ruthless power. As the narrative goes, all's well that ends well for the powerful royal couple:

> As soon as Jezebel heard that Naboth had been stoned and was dead, Jezebel said to Ahab, "Go, take possession of the vineyard of Naboth the Jezreelite, which he refused to give you for money; for Naboth is not alive, but dead." As soon as Ahab heard that Naboth was dead, Ahab set out to go down to the vineyard of Naboth the Jezreelite, to take possession of it. (1 Kgs. 21:15-16)

End of story! No doubt, had Naboth had a clue about the rapacious quality of royal power, he would have sold his land promptly to the crown at the first offered price; but he was innocent, and before real power the innocent have short lives.

The story should have ended there. Land acquired, crown vindicated, case closed! Except that in the truth-telling horizon of the Old Testament, only now does the narrative really begin. Only now does the key character, Elijah, appear on the scene. Elijah gets only a few narratives in Israel, but when on stage he utterly dominates. He has been introduced in 1 Kings 17:1-7 as a dangerous character who ate no royal junk food but lived on the supplies flown in by bird and what he could drink from the brook. He lived completely outside the world of royal management and the flow of consumer goods. Even before our narrative concerning Naboth, Elijah had, with immense pastoral passion, enacted God's truth of life against the power of death when he raised the dead boy, son of the widow of Sidon, to new life (1 Kgs. 17:17-24).

In our particular narrative, Elijah does not exhibit much of what we might call "pastoral presence." He is dispatched by YHWH, the ultimate truth-teller, to meet the king:

> Go down to meet King Ahab of Israel, who rules in Samaria; he is now in the vineyard of Naboth, where he has gone to take possession. You shall say to him, "Thus says the Lord; Have you killed, and also taken possession?" You shall say to him, "Thus says the Lord: In the place where dogs licked up the blood of Naboth, dogs will also lick up your blood." (1 Kgs. 21:18-19)

The God of Israel had read the scholarly literature about "prophetic law-suits" and utters a perfect "prophetic lawsuit" with appropriate *indictment* and corresponding *sentence*. This utterance is voiced in the divine dispatch on the lips of YHWH. Elijah, obedient to truth, swoops down on the king who calls him an "enemy" (v. 20). Elijah is devoted to the urgency of truth-telling and so minces no words with the king. He delivers an incredibly harsh oracle of punishment against Ahab and against the entire dynasty.

Indictment:

> Ahab said to Elijah, "Have you found me, O my enemy?" He answered, "I have found you. Because you have sold yourself to do what is evil in the sight of the Lord." (1 Kgs. 21:20)

Threat against the dynasty:

> I will bring disaster on you; I will consume you, and will cut off from Ahab every male, bond or free, in Israel; and I will make your house like the house of Jeroboam son of Nebat, and like the house of Baasha son of Ahijah, because you have provoked me to anger and have caused Israel to sin. (1 Kgs. 21:21-22)

Threat against Jezebel the instigator:

> Also concerning Jezebel the Lord said, "The dogs shall eat Jezebel within the bounds of Jezreel." (1 Kgs. 21:23)

More threat against the house of Ahab:

> Anyone belonging to Ahab who dies in the city the dogs shall eat; and anyone of his who dies in the open country the birds of the air shall eat. (1 Kgs. 21:24)

The truth told here against royal power is breathtaking. It is so sweeping as to leave no exception to death:

- every male, bond or free
- anyone belonging to Ahab
- who dies in the city . . . dogs
- who dies in the country . . . birds.

The severity of this judgment seems disproportionate for seizing one vegetable garden and killing one small farmer. But of course Naboth is only an instant in a general policy of ruthless royal acquisitiveness, the kind of acquisitiveness that the God of Torah will not tolerate. Elijah is fearless and pulls no punches before the king. We should not, however, gloss over the risk of truth-telling. Elijah does not blink at killing; but the truth must be told.

So truth is told. Astonishingly, Ahab responds:

> When Ahab heard those words, he tore his clothes and put sackcloth over his bare flesh; he fasted, lay in the sackcloth, and went about dejectedly. (1 Kgs. 21:27)

Critics judge that this note of repentance on the part of Ahab is not authentic, but for the sake of coherent chronology: Ahab in the narrative could not die yet. It turns out in the full telling, as we discover belatedly, that Elijah's word is true. Ahab dies in chapter 22 (see vv. 34-40); it takes longer for Jezebel, who dies ignominiously in 2 Kings 9:33-37:

> He said, "Throw her down." So they threw her down; some of her blood spattered on the wall and on the horses, which trampled on her. Then he went in and ate and drank; he said, "See to that cursed woman and bury her; for she is a king's daughter." But when they went to bury her, they found no more of her than the skull and the feet and the palms of her hands. When they came back and told him, he said, "This is the word of the LORD, which he spoke by his servant Elijah the Tishbite, 'In the territory of Jezreel the dogs shall eat the flesh of Jezebel; the corpse of Jezebel shall be like dung on the field in the territory of Jezreel, so that no one can say, This is Jezebel.'" (2 Kgs. 9:33-37)

It is the truth. The truth given by Elijah. And that truth—rooted in YHWH, concretized in Naboth—will not be mocked by power.

4. The fourth case I cite is less well known among us. It concerns Nebuchadnezzar in Daniel 4. He is the king of Babylon, and, even more than Pharaoh before him, he is the quintessential cipher in the Old Testament for all intransigent, acquisitive power. Nebuchadnezzar, it is reported, had had a terrible nightmare, the kind one has when power sits uneasy in anxiety. He is king of everything, but, we are told, his entire research-and-development cadre now fails him. None can interpret the dream because

dreams are secret; they are nighttime messages from God that lie outside
the purview of technocrats.

In a last desperate maneuver to learn the truth of his nightmare about
power, Nebuchadnezzar summons Daniel who is known to be a peculiar
Jew endowed with incomparable hermeneutical capacities. Nebuchadnezzar renarrates his dream to Daniel, a remarkable practice for power in a
position of deference before truth. Nebuchadnezzar, so the story goes, has
confidence in this Jew with peculiar gifts of wisdom.

> You are able, however, for you are endowed with a spirit of the holy
> gods. (Dan. 4:18)

Daniel hears the dream and immediately knows its meaning. He is, however, "severely distressed" (v. 19). The news he must enunciate for Nebuchadnezzar is not good, and Daniel trembles at the risk that his interpretation will entail for him. The king reassures him but Daniel parries:

> The king said, "Belteshazzar [Daniel], do not let the dream or the inter-
> pretation terrify you." Belteshazzar answered, "My lord, may the dream
> be for those who hate you, and its interpretation for your enemies!"
> (Dan. 4:19)

In any case, Daniel finally tells king the meaning of his dream. The dream
anticipates that Nebuchadnezzar will be severely demoted from his glorious power, driven away from human society to dwell among wild animals.
This sorry, humiliating condition of the king will last, so says Daniel,

> until you have learned that the Most High has sovereignty over the
> kingdom of mortals and gives it to whom he will. (Dan. 4:25)

Indeed, is that not the lesson that truth must always speak to power? The
word of the dream beyond royal control is that power invested in human
agents is endlessly, intractably penultimate. Daniel goes so far as to suggest
to the king action that he might take, even though the king has not asked
him for advice:

> "Therefore, O king, may my counsel be acceptable to you: atone for
> your sins with righteousness, and your iniquities with mercy to the
> oppressed, so that your prosperity may be prolonged." (Dan. 4:27)

The advice of Daniel, so quintessentially Jewish in tone and substance, goes unanswered by Nebuchadnezzar and, as far as we know, unheeded.

The reader is not surprised to find that Daniel the truth-teller is vindicated. The dream comes to reality as Daniel had said; the power of Nebuchadnezzar is deconstructed as Daniel anticipated. Nebuchadnezzar becomes like an animal who eats grass, grows long hair, and has nails like claws. He is utterly ungroomed and his being ungroomed is a sign of his new status of powerlessness. He is, by the hidden sovereignty of God, uncreated, now less than the creature God had made him. All this Daniel had seen and announced to the waning king.

The astonishing feature of this narrative is that it does not end in radical deconstruction of power, as we might have expected. The narrative continues until it can report restoration of the king. Nebuchadnezzar, we are told, recovers his sanity. In his sanity, moreover, he does the most sane thing imaginable. He sings doxology to the Most High, a public, lyrical act of ceding ultimate authority out beyond himself to the creator God:

> When that period was over, I, Nebuchadnezzar, lifted my eyes to heaven, and my reason returned to me.
>> I blessed the Most High,
>>> and praised and honored the one who lives forever.
>> For his sovereignty is an everlasting sovereignty,
>>> and his kingdom endures from generation to generation.
>> All the inhabitants of the earth are accounted as nothing,
>>> and he does what he wills with the host of heaven
>>> and the inhabitants of the earth.
>> There is no one who can stay his hand
>>> or say to him, "What are you doing?" (Dan. 4:34-35)

With that defining concession, the narrative comes full circle. Nebuchadnezzar is reestablished, "and still more greatness was added to me" (v. 36):

> Now I, Nebuchadnezzar, praise and extol and honor the King of heaven,
>> for all his works are truth,
>>> and his ways are justice;
>> and he is able to bring low
>>> those who walk in pride. (Dan. 4:37)

Only now, having been addressed by truth, this man of power is remade so that his power is marked now by truth, justice, and lowliness. This practice of power for Nebuchadnezzar is one that was not possible before doxology. The doxology the king now sings was not possible until he had heard the truth. It was not possible as long as Nebuchadnezzar imagined his power to be ultimate. He now knows that his power is decisively pen-ultimate. The dream of the night was a truth that subverted the illusion of the day.

II

These four cases of truth to power are typical and representative. All of us could cite other cases in scripture and beyond scripture, notably Jesus before Pilate . . . or Pilate before Jesus. It would be enough for one to say to courageous preachers, "Go and do likewise." It would be enough to say that and stop.

Except that I have cited these four characteristic cases precisely because I have wanted to consider the challenge of truth to power and the deep problematic of such a formula posed for contemporary preaching. In the end, I would not want to detract from that long-standing crisp model of preaching; at the same time, however, I want to underscore the problem-atic. Truth to power is a simple (simplistic?) model that almost no credible contemporary preacher can readily embrace, unless one is tenured, or at the end of a career, or has a reliable patron. Those who preside over insti-tutions with programs, budgets, and members filled with anxiety are not likely to practice, with any simplicity, the notion of truth to power. Perhaps most contemporary preachers are too well kept and too cowardly. We are, in our present circumstance,

- short of being a fugitive like Moses,
- short of being a raven-fed figure like Elijah,
- short of being on the royal payroll like Nathan,
- short of being clairvoyant like Daniel.

No contemporary preacher is likely to speak truth to power like Moses, so clearly and so effectively that the utterance will dismantle an empire and free slaves. No contemporary preacher likely will crash the palace like Nathan to tell an indicting parable to the king. No contemporary preacher, surely, will like Elijah be the king's enemy and announce the death penalty. No contemporary preacher like Daniel likely will interpret royal dreams.

Beyond those brute realities, however, there are other reasons that truth to power is problematic—beyond our cowardice, our ineffectiveness, or our inclination to accommodate. I submit that the problematic we face in preaching is that any simplistic notion of truth and power is now situated in a postmodern world where such easy assumptions of authority are profoundly precarious.

I do not want to deny that there are occasional dramatic moments when truth can be spoken directly to power, and must be spoken directly to power. I believe, however, that this model, on the whole, is not possible in our society and is certainly not possible in local congregations where one is cast as preacher, but also as administrator charged with maintenance.

Consider *power*, clear enough in the four cases cited. Power, however, is less clear in a complex world of interlocking systems. The fact is that those who have power among us sense relative powerlessness about themselves. Before being addressed as power, moreover, the pastoral task is empowerment, that is, the readiness to accept and affirm what power there is or could be, had we courage. That task of empowerment in pastoral scope requires a different perspective from any flat critique of power. In fact, it is the case in a postmodern world that power is endlessly subtle, complex, and elusive. Those who sit in the midst of contemporary preaching characteristically are not carriers of immense power.

Conversely, consider *truth*. There was a time when the church was a primal authority and the authority of the preacher was immense. There was a time when the preacher was the best-educated *man* in town. There was a time when issues were less complex; but not now. Now it is the case that truth has become democratized and secularized, and held in many quarters. Every preacher knows to pay attention when drawing near to the specialized learnings that are present among others in the congregation.

- If by "truth" we mean simply the claim of the Lordship of God—Father, Son, and Spirit—that can be proclaimed readily, simply, and directly. But of course truth never stops there. If we focus on the big dramatic moments of confrontation and think about the great heroes through the history of the church who have confronted power, then we can speak simply enough; but such occasions do not come often to most of us.

- If we think truth is peculiarly allied with pain—as in our defining Friday of the Cross—not many of us have suffered inordinately and, in any case, we have no monopoly on such suffering.
- If we mean that the truth of the Gospel should have real influence on the specific needs and problems of the world, then our utterance requires exposition that fully recognizes the complexities whereby God's suffering love touches the world in transformative ways.

Thus, in a postmodern world, both *truth* and *power* are complex and elusive; contemporary preachers are not permitted an easy assumption of our own certitude or importance. There is an endless temptation, when reading Exodus 5, for preachers to cast themselves as Moses and address all the Pharaohs when we ourselves are implicated in the sins of acquisitive power. There is a readiness to know the sin of royal power and play the part of Nathan or of Elijah, and every contemporary preacher probably would like to be Daniel, urging "mercy to the oppressed" in the ear of the haughty Babylonian king who is fated to eat grass. Such a stance is impossible, however, except for the very young and the very innocent, or the tenured and the very foolish.

III

Thus my review of the four cases and my statement of their inescapable problematic for preachers bring me to my primary reflection. It does not follow, I suggest, that because these texts of confrontation, and many like them, are problematic for our rendering that they are useless or that we need to find more palatable texts. Rather, I want to insist that these confrontational scenarios are *texts* and need to be taken as such. This of course is obvious; but notice that our common assumptions for texts are propelled by historical criticism. We know best how to go *behind the text* to the *drama of real life* that we can then reenact. What we have in the Bible, however, is not real-life historical drama. And if not real-life historical drama, then not drama to be reenacted by us. If we go behind the text to the interaction, we sense ourselves both obligated and empowered to reenact confrontations reported in the text as contemporary confrontations. But we do not in fact have a report on such encounters. What we have, rather, is a *text* that stands some distance removed from whatever historical encounter might have happened, a text that has its own interpretive offer that is surely remote from actual encounter. That we have a *text* means:

- that it stands some distance from the reality of raw facticity;
- that it is a stylized, artistic act of imagination;
- that that act of imagination has transposed whatever may have been of history into artistry, an artistry that may be instructive but nonetheless art;
- that this artistic transposition from factual happening (to which we have no access) to text (that we have in our hands) is accomplished by the imaginative and intentional work of real, self-conscious agents who intentionally make text.

While we do not know some things about the formation of the text as given to us, we do know (or at least think we know) that the forming of artistic imagination into narrative text happened in the Persian and Hellenistic periods of ancient Judaism. This time of text-making was a time of no more kings in Israel and very few prophets. The agents that remained after the withdrawal of kings and prophets, and who became a driving force for Judaism, were scribes.[1] Thus, as in my title, what we have in the text are "remembered confrontations" (between power [kings] and truth [prophets]) given us through scribal refraction, that is, through an intentional, self-conscious, interpretative editorial process that came later and eventuated in canonical text. That process of scribal refraction, now front and center in scholarly work, was not at all on the horizon of our long-established historical-critical work that sought to get behind text to lived reality; the process of scribal refraction, against more established assumptions of historical criticism, is a recently recovered scholarly interest. I suggest that scribal refraction (called "canonization" by Brevard Childs, called "ideology" by Robert Carroll) is not only important in understanding the text, but is also an important clue for contemporary preaching if the simple model of truth to power can no longer be defining for us.

I want then to speak a good word for scribes as the ones who have mediated for us canonical text. Our stereotype, from New Testament polemics, is to group the scribes with "Pharisees and hypocrites" (Matt. 15:1-7, 23:13, 15, 25, 27, 29) in a negative stereotype. In fact, the scribes are the school men and the book men who gathered old traditions and memories and preserved them in text form. They are the scroll-makers who stand at the head of the canonizing process.² Among the best known of these is Baruch who created some form of the Book of Jeremiah and his brother, Seraiah, who also served Jeremiah by writing (Jer. 36:4; 51:59-64).³ After them, we may focus especially on Ezra the scribe, the primal figure in creating Judaism. It is Ezra who formed Judaism into a community of text practice, whereby the lively, generative work of interpretation became definitional for Judaism, the Judaism of which Jesus is surely an heir. In Nehemiah 8, in a dramatic meeting, it is reported that Ezra presided over an assemblage of "men and women and those who could understand" (vv. 1-2). There he read the Torah to the community. He

> helped the people to understand the [Torah], while the people remained in their places. So they read from the book, from the [Torah] of God, with interpretation. They gave the sense, so that the people understood the reading. (vv. 7-8)

This was a gathering of people of Jewish descent who had been tossed about by the vagaries of historical circumstance and who had largely forgotten their theological identity in the rootage of Moses. What Ezra did was to *retext* this community to turn the imagination and therefore the practice of the community back to its most elemental assurances and claims. From that dramatic effort, moreover, comes canon, the community of Judaism, and the ongoing rabbinic teaching through which Judaism marks and sustains its identity.

Mutatis mutandis, my bid is that contemporary preaching in the postmodern U.S. setting addresses folks of Christian descent who have been tossed about by the vagaries of historical circumstance and who have largely forgotten rootage in Moses and in Jesus and the ongoing teaching tradition. The task, in such a critical context, is to *retext* this community, to turn the imagination and the practice of the community of the baptized back to its most elemental assurances and claims. I suggest nothing less than *reimagining* and *recontextualizing* the primal congregational venue for preaching, worship, and teaching as an arena for *retexting* a community that has largely forfeited its text and so its identity.

The import of such an interpretive maneuver is to give up an attempt to replicate or reenact the work of thirteenth-century Moses or of tenth-century Nathan or of eighth-century Elijah or of fifth- (or second-) century Daniel; instead, the task is to take on the work of a belated scribe who does not conduct the direct encounter of truth and power, but who keeps alive, available, and credible—in belated practice—textual newness and imagination of earlier confrontations to which we have no direct access. The defining mark of the text, in all its parts, is not the boldness of the prophetic character. It is, rather, that the Key Character in every such narrative encounter is YHWH, the One who promises, delivers, and commands, the One who endlessly summons people away from life without promise, without deliverance, without commands, into a world that the text provides and proposes as normative. This Key Character is not enacted by the preacher; rather God's own self is known and available through the *reperformance* of the text by the scribe.

This task of retexting requires the scribal preacher to be a text-man or a text-woman, to engage in study, to trust the text and be led by the text, to have confidence that the text, in all its vagaries and complexities, in all its characteristic and confounding cadences, merits our primal attention as a word of life.[4] This perspective requires that we submit our modernist rationalistic assumptions to the text and, even when the text sounds in violence and all of its unbearable harshness or other objectionable cadences, still to assume that engagement with this text is a primal engagement out of which comes missional energy, imagination, and identity. To be sure, such engagement with the text does not consist in blind acceptance of the text. Such engagement evokes, as well as assent, desperation, and protest. Nonetheless, such engagement makes possible a new field of courage and freedom.

Beyond attentiveness to the text, however, this mode of preaching requires attentiveness to the listening congregation in a particular way. In part, the congregation already knows this text; but in part, the congregation *is textless,* having been influenced by what George Lindbeck calls "expressive, experiential" perspective, which believes that one can live out of one's autonomous experience without any text.[5] Or the congregation assembles, bringing with it the *weak, thin text* of technological, therapeutic, military consumerism that is an odd mix of moralism, market ideology, self-congratulations, and anxiety. That is, the scribe does not do text work in a vacuum, but (a) *in the face of resistance* that rejects any text, (b) *in the face of thin text* that claims excessive and disproportionate authority, or (c) in the presence of those who are inclined to this text but who have *little clue about the text* or how to hear the text so that it could function as identity-giving.

IV

Thus, I consider the scribal, textual refraction of the four proclamatory encounters I have mentioned. The matter of speaking truth to power is indeed present in each of these texts in a quite direct way. But when considered in scribal refraction, these offers of truth and power are playfully open and not so unambiguous as our usual confrontational reenactment might assume. Thus, I attend to a distinction that is characteristically made by belated scribes between what is *in the text* and what is *our engagement with the text*.

1. The first case concerns truth (Moses) speaking to power (Pharaoh) in Exodus 5. The task in scribal refraction is to let the text be a resource for retexting the imagination, energy, and identity of the community through the retexting enterprise. The transaction of the text is simple:

- YHWH commands,
- Moses confronts,
- Pharaoh resists,
- YHWH prevails.

The narrative process maps the world of faith, the world of social power, the world of economic tension between labor and capital, between haves and have-nots, between power and powerlessness. It may also map familiar power grids in families and churches and seminaries. It may invite us to play all roles and every role and many roles in the narrative drama. We may listen as the one addressed or as the one sent. We may imagine ourselves as resistant to address or we may assume a new role for Pharaoh, willing to be addressed and repent, capable of imagining the Exodus narrative with a different outcome. Note well, in any case, that scribal refraction is not excessively "hot" about relevance. While the text, in our scribal imagination, may send out lines of connection and allude to contemporaneity, for the most part the interpretation stays within the text and lets the listening congregation stay within the text without being scolded or shamed or threatened.

Inside the text, *those in textless autonomy* may imagine that they live in an unaddressed world not thick with tradition, and now this text is planted thickly in imagination for future reference. Those who come with the text of military consumerism may sense that there is a countertext so that choices are possible between texts. And those who have "the Jesus text" in a vacuum may notice that Jesus, in all his confrontations before Caesar and Pilate, exposes old, established powers. All those engaged in "text time"—(a) the *textless*, (b) the *already texted*, and (c) those with *alternative texts*—are drawn to see that the confrontation between truth and power has within it a Third Factor, holiness beyond our usual truth and beyond our usual power and, perhaps, endlessly unsettled. Indeed, it is in the nature of the Key Character in these texts to unsettle and to be unsettled.

2. The situation is very similar but somewhat different in our second case: Nathan and David. Nathan is the voice who speaks both the guilt before YHWH and the favor of YHWH that surely hovered over David. Unlike Pharaoh, David is a child of the Torah. He knows about the ten prohibitions from Sinai. Until the matter is uttered as a prophetic speech of judgment, however, David did not need to deal with the problem and perhaps could not. Thus, Nathan is the voicing of the relentless, unvoiced agony of a failed child of Torah. Nathan did not say something new to David. He said what was known and waiting to be voiced yet again. That is why David caught the parable so quickly; indeed, that is why David answered so quickly, "I have sinned against YHWH." Nathan is a harsh judge; in fact, however, Nathan's work is to relieve David, to unburden him, albeit in costly ways, in order that he may try again in his thin, failed life to become who he is. Nathan's speech of judgment makes available to David the givenness of Torah from which David had momentarily imagined himself immune. Thus the Deuteronomist has Nathan speak of "take his wife" and "killing," voicing a given that is not available to people in autonomous reason and that is not available in the text of consumer indulgence (1 Sam. 12:9). The congregation is invited to ponder the deep voicing of failure, the intransigent givenness of Torah, the costly way of forgiveness, and the wonder of a post-forgiveness life beginning again, "born from above" (see John 3:7).

3. The third case of Elijah and Ahab is severe and without pastoral nuance. We have seen that Pharaoh was an *outsider* to the Israelite tradition and did not know YHWH until very late. We have seen that David was an *insider* to the Israelite traditions and knew what is required. Ahab, in contrast to both Pharaoh and David, was an *ambiguous figure*. He should have known as an insider. Perhaps he did know and that is why he, himself, did not press the point of dispute with Naboth (1 Kgs. 21:4). He had,

however, lived a long time outside the tradition, connected with Jezebel. In contrast to Ahab, Jezebel had no compunction in her ruthlessness and did not understand Israelite convenantalism. Perhaps Ahab admired Jezebel's freedom and ruthlessness. Perhaps he yearned to be as free from ambiguity as was she. Perhaps he feared her and wished he had the courage to resist her. Perhaps Ahab was *double-minded* and that is why he pouted and turned his head to the wall and would not eat, unable and unwilling to decide between a Torah tradition that he was supposed to honor and an acquisitive alternative that suited him better (1 Kgs. 21:4). Ahab could not decide.

I imagine that in any group that considers this text, Ahab will not be the only one in the room who does not want to decide. The congregation is filled with people who could not decide, whose energy is sapped by ambivalence. Of course it is no better for those who have already decided, like Jezebel, for such decisions bring the power of death, not suddenly but inescapably. Ten chapters are required for Jezebel to die (2 Kgs. 9:30-37). Indeed, it takes a long time to die if we stand in resistance to the will of the true God, a long time but nonetheless sure. Ahab repents. He repents in the face of harshness:

> When Ahab heard those words, he tore his clothes and put sackcloth over his bare flesh; he fasted, lay in the sackcloth, and went about dejectedly. (1 Kgs. 21:27)

Ahab did the proper acts of repentance; he was, however, not a free man because he was still "dejected" (1 Kgs. 21:27). He was still depressed because the popular, self-indulgent alternative of Jezebel still attracted him.

We may read the narrative of Naboth's vineyard in relation to whatever it is that we desire but to which we are not entitled. The very phrase "Naboth's vineyard" invites a thought against self-indulgent acquisitiveness that coincides with Jezebel's relentless entitlement. Astonishingly, *Naboth's Vineyard* is the title of a study from the U.S. State Department written by the Associate Secretary of State Sumner Welles under the administration of Franklin Roosevelt.[6] Welles used the phrase to describe his review of U.S. policy in Central America, for the U.S. has been Ahab (or Jezebel) to Naboth's vineyard in Central America. We live in a world and a system of endless strategies for taking the vineyard of the little guy, not unlike the one lamb in Naboth's vineyard. Naboth, Nathan—our narrative imagination is peopled by phalanxes of old characters who keep turning up to expose our entitlements, which are, in fact, seizures, rapacious seizures that have the smell of death about them.

4. The fourth case, Daniel and Nebuchadnezzar, is something of a fantasy not so close to reality. The plot nonetheless engages us because it suggests that unlimited power, uncurbed entitlement, and the absolutizing of one's personal claims leads not only to loss but to insanity. Rapacious self-aggrandizement will produce craziness! The narrative poses the question about how the practice of power in the world may be a cause of craziness and a practice of madness, a germane point given the unilateral propensity of "the last superpower"! This narrative of craziness nonetheless holds out promise. Unlike the accounts of Pharaoh and Ahab, there is here a chance of rehabilitation and restoration to power. The move from self-destructive insanity to restoration and doxological sanity is marked by two moves.

First, Nebuchadnezzar is capable of doxology, capable of publicly ceding ultimate authority beyond himself to God. The very act of doxology, if properly understood, is the surrender of the self to the one praised.[7] But second, the trigger for this move of Nebuchadnezzar to sanity via doxology is the introduction of the primal Jewish notion of obedience into the narrative:

> "Therefore, O king, may my counsel be acceptable to you: atone for your sins with righteousness, and your iniquities with mercy to the oppressed, so that your prosperity may be prolonged." (Dan. 4:27)

This urging to power in Daniel's voice of truth is deeply Jewish. It appeals to the deepest claims of Torah and invites Nebuchadnezzar to imitate YHWH, the God of mercy and righteousness. This single imperative that destabilizes failed power is rooted in Moses. It finds resilient echo in Jesus, child of the Torah:

> "Woe to you, scribes and Pharisees, hypocrites! For you tithe mint, dill, and cummin, and have neglected the weightier matters of the law: *justice and mercy and faith*. It is these you ought to have practiced without neglecting the others." (Matt. 23:23)

Doxology is an outgrowth of justice. Mercy lives on the wings of doxology whereby all things are made new, when power concedes that the Most High has sovereignty over the kingdom of mortals and gives it to whom he will. (Dan. 4:32)

Scribes are modest people. They do not claim too much for themselves. They do not push people into corners, nor do they issue strong imperatives. They tell the truth and stage "text time" for engagement with that truth.

- They invite people who live *without texts* to try a text that has Holy Presence at its center, Presence that shapes the world toward life.
- They invite people with *thin texts* to a thickness that cannot be had apart from the God who governs.
- They invite people already *in this text* to ponder more closely, to notice nuance and cadence and the lines sent out to contemporary life.

The text is a voice of truth, albeit elusive. When text time is well managed this text reaches to those with power. There is truth to power in such interpretive transactions, but it is not the advocacy of the preacher.[8] The preacher is cast more in a role not unlike that of a pastoral therapist. The preacher-therapist seeks to let the power of illusion and repression be addressed by old, deep texts that swirl around us. The text is not the possession of the preacher but it lives in, with, and under the memory of the community. The preacher gets out of the center of the confrontation, *trusts the text* to have its own say—powered by the spirit and not dependent on us—*trusts the listening congregation* to make the connections it is able to make. While engaging in such trust toward text and toward congregation, the scribe finds himself/herself also drawn into the deep place of *truthful power* and *powerful truth,* a deep place that permits even text-championing scribes to reimagine and redescribe. Such an act of reimagining may issue in repentance, perhaps a turn that makes all things new.

V

I finish with two concluding comments:

1. Jesus taught his disciples about the kingdom by means of parables, that is, not by confrontation (Matt. 13:40-50). And then he said to them, "Have you understood all of this?" (v. 51). Jesus clearly is a teacher and he is asking for feedback. And the disciples answer, "Yes."

> And he said to them, "Therefore, every scribe who has been trained for
> the kingdom of heaven is like the master of a household who brings out
> of his treasure what is new and what is old." When Jesus had finished
> these parables, he left that place. (Matt. 13:52-53)

It cannot be unimportant that Jesus instructs his disciples by reference
to scribes. Perhaps he invites them to be scribes trained for the new age.
Perhaps he references himself as a scribe. Either way, the scribe here is
nothing like a Pharisee or hypocrite (in the usual stereotypical modes of
conventional Christian interpretation), but is an agent who is equipped
for God's coming new reign. What that agent is to do for the sake of
God's newness is to have a rich treasure—things old and things new. The
scribe is called to preoccupation with text—a treasure of texts, *old texts,
new interpretations,* all in order to open to God's newness. This teaching
of Jesus may be an invitation to reimagine the preaching role as the careful
custodial management of old things and new things for the sake of God's
rule. That, of course, is what the scribes did:

- The old text of Moses and Pharaoh continues to empower the *new
  community of emancipated obedience;*
- The old text of Nathan and David continues to invite *practices of
  compassionate power;*
- The old text of Elijah and Ahab continues to open *new modes of
  stewarding the resources of the community, and especially the land;*
- The old text of Daniel and Nebuchadnezzar continues to
  describe the *new world of Jews and Gentiles shaped by doxological
  penultimacy.*

Old and new, coming rule, and the scribes manage. . . .

2. William Cavanaugh, in his remarkable book *Torture and Eucharist,*
tells how, albeit belatedly, the Roman Catholic bishops in Chile came to
understand that the community-creating power of Eucharist was an effective antidote to the community-destroying torture of the dictator Augusto
Pinochet. They discovered that *Eucharist* was stronger than *torture.* At the
end of Cavanaugh's book, he writes about a fictional character in a novel
concerning this crisis. He refers to "Carlos" but, in fact, means the community-creating capacity of the Church.

> Carlos's gift is more than just the gift of seeing; his stories about people can actually alter reality. . . . Carlos's friends nevertheless remain skeptical, convinced that Carlos cannot confront tanks with stories, helicopters with mere imagination. . . . Carlos . . . rightly grasps that the contest is not between imagination and the real, but between two types of imagination, that of the generals and that of their opponents.[9]

Carlos, in the novel, comments:

> We have to believe in the power of imagination because it is all we have, and ours is stronger than theirs.[10]

And Cavanaugh himself adds,

> To participate in the Eucharist is to live inside God's imagination. It is to be caught up into what is really real, the body of Christ.[11]

Scribes for the kingdom—engaged in an imagination that is stronger than the imagination of military consumerism—ponder old texts and find them contemporary. This counterimagination is the treasure of the scribes of the kingdom. It happens by *texts* and bread and *texts* and wine and *texts* and *texts*. The oldest stories become the newest songs, stories from Moses and Nathan and Elijah and Daniel and a host of others' old stories that let the Church sing—free, dangerous, energized, filled with courage. Very much depends on scribes who are trained for the kingdom.

CHAPTER THREE

A Fresh Performance
amid a Failed Script

The present moment is a splendid opportunity for rethinking the task of education and socialization of our young in the church. The church has suffered for a long time from timidity and collusion with dominant values in our culture. And now is a time when the church can, with some boldness, dare to assert that the demands and gifts of the gospel matter in a society that is heavy on coercive demands and seductive in its offer of phony gifts. We will need to think carefully about how to communicate our alternative with integrity.

In order to see clearly the task of Christian formation in our present situation, we must keep four observations in mind:

1. The great fact for so-called mainline Protestantism in the United States is the *deprivileging* of the church as a result of pluralism and secularism. This deprivileging constitutes a threat to business as usual, but it also provides an opportunity for fresh articulation of the peculiar missional identity of the church.

2. I will line out my argument in terms of the *Old Testament*; it will, however, require very little imagination to transpose my argument into the categories of New Testament faith.

3. Church education in the United States takes place in the midst of the scripting of *technological, consumer militarism,* a script that is powerfully seductive but, I suggest, manifestly a failure in its capacity to deliver either happiness or security or both.

4. *Baptismal identity* as a genuine alternative to that failed scripting is the task of church education; it is an identity rooted in deep gospel claims and manifested and exhibited in an alternative life in the world.

I

Thesis: The Bible, the tradition, and the long history of church practice constitute a peculiar, distinctive, clear, but flexible, script according to which life in the world may be lived out differently. This scripting of life as a *counterscripting* is the primal task of education; that work does not guarantee, but makes possible, an *alternative performance* of human life in the world, a performance that requires precisely the kind of imagination, courage, energy, and freedom for which this script vouches in peculiar ways.

II

The first dimension for rescripting that may generate a fresh performance marked by imagination, courage, energy, and freedom is that there is a *normative narrative memory* upon which an alternative life is staked, a memory that must be learned, reiterated, inhaled, and embraced. This normative givenness is not negotiable and does not arise from contemporary experience, but it is a given that was there before us, awaits us, addresses us, and includes us in its peculiar rendering of reality. In the New Testament, in all its variations, this given normativeness behind which criticism cannot go is what C. H. Dodd termed "the kerygma" (1 Cor. 15:3-4).[1] In the Old Testament, that given narrative is at bottom the Torah, the five books of Moses, that are endlessly interpreted but not questioned as norm and basic truth that must be accepted as a true rendering of the past that was there before us.[2] Christian education is nurture in a peculiar rootage that is profoundly countercultural.

The narrative account of reality stretches wondrously from creation, that daring moment of first light in the midst of darkness, when elemental confusion began to take ordered form that made life possible. The story moves through one of the world's great dysfunctional families (in Genesis) through the slave camp of Egypt, through the desperate hunger of wilderness, all the way to Sinai. And there, out of the very mouth of God, is disclosed an alternative way to order the world. We are perhaps so smitten with historical questions or so keen to produce definitive closure that we grow inattentive to the huge panorama of our past that connects the sweeping vista of creation to the insistences of Sinai. For Sinai is a directive about how to live differently and congruently with a *shalom*-ordered world as God's creation.[3]

That root tradition is marked in a variety of ways that characterize the peculiar perspective of this community:

1. Every facet of Torah tradition is focused on YHWH, the God of Israel. It is the remembering and reciting of the narrative that keeps YHWH as the defining character for all reality:

- It is YHWH who turns chaos to life-giving, life-sustaining creation;
- It is YHWH who turns barrenness to birth and the durable prospect of land;
- It is YHWH who turns barren wilderness to a place of adequate bread;
- It is YHWH who speaks ten times and reorders the world toward well-being.

The Torah is countercultural because it testifies, repeatedly, against every itch toward autonomy and against every anxiety of disorder, for it is YHWH who is the primal subject of every treasured cadence of the root tradition.

2. This YHWH, moreover, is an active agent in transformation, a power, a will, an agency well beyond Israel, who, in the concreteness of daily life, heals, restores, liberates, and makes new. Church education is nurture in the canonical recital of transformations wrought by YHWH,

> who by understanding made the heavens . . .
> who spread out the earth on the waters . . .
> who struck Egypt through their firstborn . . .
> who divided the Red Sea in two . . .
> who led his people through the wilderness . . .
> and killed famous kings . . .
> and gave their land as a heritage . . .
> and rescued us from our foes . . .
> who gives food to all flesh. (Ps. 136:5, 6, 10, 13, 16, 18, 21, 24, 25)

The transformations are given us in a stock recital.

Two things strike me about this recital. First, it is poetry with a recognizable cadence; I have no doubt that church education must teach the cadences of the mother tongue that produces wide-eyed amazement in the primal mode of self-transcending praise. The remembered inventory of transformation impinges upon the imagination of the remembering generations of those who appropriate the tradition. Second, this cadenced recital is not user-friendly, but it shows how this tradition is rooted in violence that implicates both God and people. It is God who struck the firstborn and killed kings—eggs necessarily broken, one might say, for the omelet of emancipation and well-being.

3. This root tradition of doxology represents the transformations in special ways to save the recital from excessive explanation. The tradition does not explain or ask how but accepts transformation as wonder, sign, miracle—that is, happenings beyond any critical scrutiny. Thus in Psalms 136:4, YHWH is hailed as One "who alone does great wonders," acts that evoke not curiosity but awe—in the words of the hymn, wonder, love, and praise. Thus, church education is a practice of the suspension of disbelief and the embrace of innocence before a normative recital that contradicts the reason of this age and of every age. Education is to commit to a miracle-remembering recital.

Indeed, Israel has a full and rich vocabulary to witness to this most elemental claim that can only be voiced and heard lyrically, out beyond controlling reason:

> One generation shall laud your works to another,
>   and shall declare your mighty acts.
> On the glorious splendor of your majesty,
>   and on your wondrous works, I will meditate.
> The might of your awesome deeds shall be proclaimed,
>   and I will declare your greatness.
> They shall celebrate the fame of your abundant goodness,
>   and shall sing aloud of your righteousness. (Ps. 145:4-7)

4. The accumulation of "wonders" that live on the doxological lips of Israel—and that attest, against much critical evidence, to YHWH as the agent of palpable newness in the world—yields a certain narrative world that the faithful inhabit, a world marked by bottomless fidelity.[4] Thus, the mother-tongue cadences of Psalm 136 offer counterpoint to every concrete wonder with the refrain, "for his *ḥesed* ("steadfast love") endures forever." In verse after verse, the psalm offers a characteristic interpretive *novum* that seems commonplace; it is, however, a *novum* that reflects the evangelical idea upon which the entire rootage of Torah rests, namely, that specific, concrete, named transformations ("killed famous kings") lead to

the deep generalizing verdict, "his *ḥesed* endures forever." The second line of each verse of the psalm does not need to follow the first and is indeed something of a leap. It is, however, the characteristic, quintessential leap of Torah faith that produces the doxological sweep and that knows the world to be, at bottom, upheld by cosmic, holy, sovereign fidelity.

The outcome of (a) God as subject, (b) named transformations, (c) understanding as signs and wonders of God's engagement, and (d) rendering a general verdict of doxology attests the world as God's sphere, as a safe place in which and from which and toward which we may live joyously.

Before I leave Torah, one other note is important: As Jews have known for a very long time, the Torah culminates in and is dominated by the commands of Sinai. These commands begin in God's own utterance and then trail off to Moses and to endless interpretive variations because Israel was never finished at Sinai, because the God of Sinai is never finished commanding. Of course, the question of the relation of *narrative* to *commandment* is an old one, and the tradition is profoundly complex. At bottom it is, however, sufficient that the wondrous transformative miracles that make new life possible summon to a particular kind of life in the world and evoke a particular response of glad obedience. The Christian misconstrual of this matter—all the later distortions in the name of "gospel and law" that produced deathly stereotypes of Jews—has been tremendous.

Church education in a therapeutic culture can no longer afford to witness to grace that is so cheap and thoughtless that the miracles are wrongly understood as unconditional gifts without commanding expectations. If the shape of the Torah means anything, it means that one must read straight through to the end of Sinai, that the sustained interpretive energy of the Torah is about an *obedience* that is commensurate with *miracles*. The Sinai traditions mediate an alternative to the demanding world of Pharaoh in which there are many commands but no constituting gifts of miracle. The God of miracle intends an alternative community, initiated by an infinitive absolute in Exodus 19:5, without compromise, a relation of fidelity that summons to fidelity in response.

Thus, church education can imagine a community scripted by a narrative that (a) centers on God, (b) receives transformations, (c) represents its life as miracle, (d) embraces steadfastness, (e) haunts beyond explanation, and (f) summons to obedience. Clearly such a script invites a performance of faith outside the deathly realm of autonomous consumerism.

III

Rootage in tradition is clear and normative; a simple story line is readily followed. Having said that, church education must, I believe, *script the baptized* into an awareness that the root tradition is complex and many-layered, so that the performance of the script requires a knowing, sustained, energetic act of imaginative interpretation. That is, church education must be nurtured in the practice of hermeneutics (even if the word is never used), what Robert Alter terms "a culture of exegesis."[5]

It cannot be doubted that the root tradition of Torah is immensely complex, and serious church education cannot leave the impression that the root tradition is flat, seamless, or spoken in a single voice. The documentation of complexity, or as we now say, multivalence, has been a major aim of historical criticism. It is most unfortunate that the so-called Documentary Hypothesis has been reduced to a scissors-and-paste explanation because, as later tradition history has made clear, the impulse of the Documentary Hypothesis is the recognition that the root tradition consists in layers and layers of interpretation, since the root tradition never arrives at a final interpretation.[6] Each subsequent interpretation, in a new time, place, and circumstance, and from a somewhat altered perspective, must re-say the tradition in a way now seen to be adequate and satisfying. The new interpretation, however, must always know that in due course it also will be found inadequate and unsatisfying, and so subject to "correction" and rearticulation. Thus, the root tradition that evokes the community is the product of the ongoing work of interpretation, no part of which is absolute, but all parts of which together yield a world of bottomless fidelity that evokes responding fidelity.

Although it is hardly necessary to do so, we may point to some clear examples of layered interpretation that exhibit the dynamism of the tradition:

- The two creation narratives of Genesis 1–3 attest that the origin and character of the world as God's creation cannot be voiced in only one way. More specifically, human persons and human community must be renarrated not only as *image* but as *dust,* not only as *dust* but as *image.*
- The self-announcement of YHWH in the pivotal disclosure at Sinai after the golden calf suggests the complexity of YHWH's own internal life (Exod. 34:6-7).[7] In that decisive utterance, God is

known to be utterly faithful and forgiving, all the while punishing to the fourth generation, an enigma of self-giving generosity and self-regarding sovereignty that will not be mocked or trivialized.

- The layered character of the root tradition as a complex act of imaginative interpretation is nowhere more evident than in the traditions of Deuteronomy. It is remarkable, unsettlingly complex, and endlessly interesting that the root tradition of Genesis–Deuteronomy includes Deuteronomy as a covenantal enactment that happened apart from Sinai, at a later time by forty years, at a later place on the Plains of Moab, in a different circumstance now focused on an agrarian economy. As Gerhard von Rad has seen, Deuteronomy exhibits the central hermeneutical dynamic of Israel's Torah: that by interpretation what is old is made new, not once, but in an endless process of today and today and today, a day of liturgy and a day of catechetics, so that the educated believer is always engaged in catching up, by eager interpretation, with the new place where God has put God's people.[8]

This dynamism is evidenced:

- In the introductory formula of Moses in Deuteronomy 1:5: "Beyond the Jordan in the land of Moab, Moses undertook to expound this law as follows." The verb "expound" is difficult; it is in any case clear that Moses in the belated venue of Deuteronomy did not simply reiterate what is remembered from Sinai, but said it over with interpretation.
- In the epitome text of Deuteronomy 5:3: "Not with our ancestors did the LORD make this covenant, but with us, who are all of us here alive today."
- In the offer to the king of a "copy" of the Torah in Deuteronomy 17:18, a *deuteros,* that is, a second version pertinent to the monarchical period.
- In the later effort of Ezra, in what is taken as the founding moment of Judaism, that clearly intends to do yet again all that Moses had done on the Plains of Moab: "Also . . . the Levites helped the people to understand the [Torah], while the people remained in their places. So they read from the book, from the [Torah] of God, with interpretation. They gave the sense, so that the people understood the reading" (Neh. 8:7-8).

It is always *with interpretation*. It is always exposition that takes the written text and connects to the new; and afterward the exposition itself that connects also becomes normative. In the text itself, Deuteronomy was "with interpretation" to Sinai. In Nehemiah 8, Ezra's work is "with interpretation" to Deuteronomy. And beyond the biblical text, Lutherans know that Luther's "with interpretation" became normative; in Reformed circles, moreover, Calvin's "with interpretation" is normative; and, more broadly, the exposition of Martin Luther King Jr.'s "with interpretation" is normative for civil religion in the U.S. at its best. It is only the innocent, the uninformed, and the frightened who imagine that one has the text without interpretation.

An extended scholarly literature shows how Deuteronomy expands and turns the older corpus of the Covenant Code to new use so that strict constructionism of biblical material is manifestly impossible.[9] Beyond expansion we may notice two remarkable and characteristic leaps in the dynamic of the tradition whereby new context evokes fresh Torah: First, in Deut. 17:14-20, the tradition of Deuteronomy offers an entirely new commandment on monarchy that has no explicit rootage at Sinai. The command, moreover, is a venturesome act of imagination, for the text "invents" a notion of kingship whereby kingship in covenant—unlike that all around Israel—is not for self-aggrandizement by way of silver, gold, wives, horses, or chariots, but is for daily, disciplined pondering of the Torah. Thus, the ongoing root tradition conjures a fresh mode of covenantal power eventually exhibited in the royal narrative through the good king Josiah (2 Kgs. 22–23).

Second, conversely, the imaginative, legal corpus of Deuteronomy ends in 25:17-19 with a Mosaic mandate to conduct permanent ethnic cleansing of the Amalekites: "You shall blot out the remembrance of Amalek from under heaven; do not forget." This command is rooted in the old narrative of Exod. 17:8-15, but it has no warrant or precedent in Sinai commands. I cite this text to suggest that the dynamism of the root tradition is not always healthy. The tradition is clearly capable of development that is ignobly negative and in contradiction to the main flow of covenantal imagination; that this particular command stands in the final position of the corpus of commands suggests that it is to be particularly pondered . . . alas!

The complexity of the tradition—with the prime example of Deuteronomy—indicates that Torah education of a canonical variety consists in immersion into the tradition and then the demanding, endless task of interpretation in order always to bring the mandates of the God of Sinai close to the place of contemporary obedience.

IV

This community, rooted in a complex tradition of critical interpretation, evidently must cross the Jordan into the land and into the prophetic canon. *The land* has been the defining project of Israel since the initial promise to Abraham (Gen. 12:1-3) and the invitation to the slaves in Egypt (Exod. 3:7-8). It is *the land* that God will give, that Israel will receive, that is contested by Israel's neighbors, and that is endlessly at risk in the interplay of power and faith. It is *the land* that delivers the Bible and church education from excessive privatism, spiritualism, romanticism, moralism, or otherworldliness. For land is seen in this tradition to be indispensable for life, completely the gift of God, utterly and endlessly contested among the neighbors.[10]

In canonical form, it is Torah that permits Israel to think prophetically about its land. It is the prophetic that brings Torah into the real world. Church education must take up the prophets as a way in which Torah *rereads the world*, to show that the world is not as we thought it is, but it is a quite odd place where the rule of God cannot be outflanked, even if that rule remains hidden. I wish, of course, to disallow the popular notion that the prophetic is simply indignant social action. It is rather rereading the soil of promise through the texts of Torah:

1. The "historical" narrative of Joshua–Kings, called by Jews "Former Prophets," is a sustained reflection on land as gift, land as risk, and land loss according to the mandates of Deuteronomy. While the narrative is complex, I shall instance only one point, namely, that Joshua–Kings is a model of *social criticism,* a narrative critique of social power that masquerades as faith, but that in fact serves narrow political-economic interests.

- The narrative presentation of Solomon is one of high irony in which the glories of Solomon are duly reported, but with a pervasive awareness that in fact Solomon's royal system was a replica of that of Pharaoh (one of his fathers-in-law), and that it was a practice of abusive economic power that amounted to oppression that ended in an Exodus-like tax revolt in the meeting at Shechem (1 Kings 12). Thus the social criticism of Solomon is direct and confrontational.

- The narrative corpus of Elijah and Elisha in the middle of the royal narrative of Kings is not only testimony to the astonishing power of these uncredentialed outsiders sent by God; it is at the same time an exposé that kings, who are their contemporaries, are nonplayers, without power or authority. The prophetic figures characteristically seize the initiative, and the kings (who are anointed to manage the land) are dismissed by default as an irrelevance.
- The brief testimony to Josiah indicates a deep critique of conventional royal power (on which see Jeremiah 22) and asserts the claim that royal power can be practiced acceding to the Torah. Josiah represents a powerful critique of conventional power and an embodiment of an alternative mode of power that could be covenantal.

The sum of this narrative exposé is a script for the faithful in seeing the world with alternative eyes through alternative tradition. What passes for the conventional in an ordinary way is here shown to be a distorted packaging of power in the disregard of truth. I regard this exposé as a critical facet of church education, for without such a sustained church alert, the capitalist power of technology can advance without any critical challenge.

2. In the preexile prophets such as Amos, Hosea, Isaiah, Micah, and Jeremiah—the ones we know best—the combination of *Torah command* and *Torah sanction* (blessing and curse) is transposed into *prophetic lawsuit* of *indictment and sentence*. That is, the uncompromising connection made in Torah between *present obedience or disobedience* and *future life or death* (Deut. 30:15-20) becomes a prophetic assumption. While there are, to be sure, modest invitations offered to repentance, Claus Westermann has seen that the prophetic speech of judgment is the primary mode of communication.[11]

The preexilic prophetic material is a sustained meditation upon the recognition that in a world governed by the God of Torah, Israel's hold on the land is precarious and the land itself is deeply at risk. Note well, it is the land that seemed completely guaranteed that is deeply at risk. The prophets employ the fragile craft of poetry to ponder, probe, and provoke, in the face of the deep ideology of guarantee and certitude. Thus, church education might consider poetry that penetrates certitude, the poetry of Paul Celan, Rainer Maria Rilke, and many more recent poets who by utterance make risk palpable.

In that context of jeopardy, the voices of canon say it like this:

> Hear the word of the Lord, O people of Israel;
>> for the Lord has an indictment against the inhabitants of the
>> land.
> There is no faithfulness or loyalty,
>> and no knowledge of God in the land.
> Swearing, lying, and murder,
>> and stealing and adultery break out;
> bloodshed follows bloodshed.
>> Therefore the land mourns, and all who live in it languish;
> together with the wild animals
>> and the birds of the air,
>> even the fish of the sea are perishing. (Hos. 4:1-3; see Amos 4:1-3,
>> Mic. 3:9-12, and Jer. 5:27-29)

Of course, I have taken the easiest, most obvious case. But imagine, at the center of canon, a *script of jeopardy* in order to ponder how loosely we hold that which we most passionately treasure, aware that in harsh poetic utterance all the certitudes are savagely rendered null and void.

3. With the fruition of covenantal threat and the enactment of prophetic jeopardy in 587 B.C.E.—we do not think it could happen, and they did not think it could happen in Johannesburg or in Moscow—the scene changes abruptly. The savage rhetoric of jeopardy designed to penetrate denial now gives way, for now there is loss and grief, the whole long weeping of Lamentations, the silence of despair, sullen beyond anger. In such a land loss—like the loss of the whole known world of Western, white, male, heterosexual domination—Israel's poets must find new voice, now the *rhetoric of buoyancy* designed to penetrate the despair and give utterance to possibilities for land when there seem none. Church education might ponder the poetry of possibility that we do not usually associate with the prophetic. Except that the prophetic is characteristically a contradiction of the conventional, an alternative voice of the impossible made possible because it is the God of Sarah who vouches for newness that is not possible. Where else are the cadences of possibility to be heard in a mean world of despair, if not through church education in this script that ponders land loss and land yet again to be given? My judgment is that education in hope is now an urgent matter for us, but one not possible until there has been an embrace of the education in loss. In canonical Israel that loss has been accomplished:

- between Isaiah 39 and Isaiah 40 sits the Book of Lamentations;
- between Jeremiah 28 and Jeremiah 29 sits the Book of Lamentations;
- between Ezekiel 24 and Ezekiel 25 sits the Book of Lamentations.

After Lamentations, only after Lamentations, there is the God who will wipe away every tear that is honestly shed over loss. The poets said it in many ways. In all those ways, however, they witness to the same astonishing reality. The present and the future, derived from Torah rootage, are not finally about land loss. They are about land gift that the world—and even Israel—thinks is impossible. The poets are able to give voice to a claim so difficult for the managers. Long before it addresses concrete policy matters, church education is the practice of poetic cadences that refuse to take the world as it seems to be.

4. The former prophets of Joshua–Kings clap with one hand and go beyond loss only in the enigmatic final paragraph of 2 Kgs. 25:27-30. The poets, however, do more and sound the clap of the second hand. Brevard Childs and especially Ronald Clements have shown that the prophetic books (especially the "Big Three") are now editorially, canonically arranged to join together the *rhetoric of jeopardy* and the *rhetoric of possibility,* in order to contradict in turn the denial of Israel about land at risk and the despair of Israel about the land about to be given yet again.[12]

The juxtaposition of *jeopardy* and *possibility* contradicts in turn the *denial* and the *despair* that constitutes the covenantal (some would say "evangelical") shape of prophetic faith. It is possible to think that the Torah that lives outside Pharaoh's world could be a utopian world of otherness that imagines Israel unaffected by the world out there.[13] The prophetic tradition, of course, permits no such misperceived utopianism, for the twin *rhetorics of jeopardy and possibility* are shot through with raw transformative power. Israel must utter, treasure, embrace, and practice prophetic cadences in the real world of imperial danger. The empire is familiar, for all empires (including our own as the most recent) act in the same way. In that familiarity, however, prophetic cadence renders our most known world unfamiliar, made unfamiliar by the hovering, hidden, decisive presence of the God of Torah, who plucks up and tears down, who plants and builds (Jer. 1:10).

The God-given jeopardy that the poet utters is in, with, and under empire.[14] It is Assyria who is for the moment "the rod of my anger" (Isa. 10:5). it is by "the hand of King Nebuchadnezzar of Babylon, my servant," that Jerusalem will be destroyed (Jer. 27:6). Much more astonishing, however, is the utterance that declares that it is by Cyrus the Persian, "my messiah," that Judaism will spring to new life (Isa. 45:1). Just now it is faith making its fragile way in the midst of the global economy.

This is the *real world of familiarity* processed through the *unfamiliarity of YHWH* that yields a strange, new world:

- not Sargon against Samaria without YHWH, but also not YHWH against Samaria without Sargon;
- not Nebuchadnezzar against Jerusalem without YHWH, but also not YHWH against Jerusalem without Nebuchadnezzar;
- not Cyrus to remake Judaism without YHWH, but also not YHWH without Cyrus.

It may be that this double-visioned, bilingual version of reality is already inchoate in the Torah. It is in any case the most characteristic mode of transformative rhetoric in Israel, a *familiar* world made *unfamiliar* by the centrality of YHWH in the rhetoric, not a rash supernaturalism featuring a God of magic, and not a flat naturalism of cause and effect, but an unfamiliarity only possible in poetic, prophetic, covenantal cadence. This is the very cadence upon which rests church education, the very cadence now so difficult in church education because our technological attention deficit disorder has no patience for such flimsy, amorphous rhetoric. But without it, of course, there can only be denial, despair, and surely death.[15] The best procedures of liturgy, preaching, teaching, pastoral care, and diaconal work all belong to the act of rescripting. Only such scripting permits new performances of obedience and praise in the world. Embeddedness in the old scripts of amnesia, autonomy, despair, and self-sufficiency will yield old performances. Victor Borge had a much-used piano routine in which he would play a familiar classical piece by Mozart or Beethoven, but one hand was recalcitrant and in the middle of the number while the other hand kept with the program; that recalcitrant hand reverted always again to "The Third Man Theme." He would grab his hand and bring it back to Mozart, but it refused. Rescripting is like that. We play the new piece, but our bodies revert to the old familiar script, so that rescripting takes great practice, patience, and passion.

We may, however, imagine a great renewal among the baptized. We may reverse the imagery: While the media, the market, and the furies of technological reason seek to induct us into new scripts of autonomy and brutality, our hands are practiced and, will-nilly, revert to our best script of baptism. We are tempted into the narrative of Coke or Nike or Toyota or Budweiser; but our disciplined, baptized hands revert to Miriam:

> "Sing to the LORD, for he has triumphed gloriously;
>> horse and rider he has thrown into the sea." (Exod. 15:21)

Our educated, baptized lips sing with Sarah, defiantly in exile:

> Sing, O barren one who did not bear;
>> burst into song and shout,
>> you who have not been in labor!
> For the children of the desolate woman will be more
>> than the children of her that is married, says the LORD. (Isa. 54:1)

Our enigmatic baptized bodies dance with all the saints:

> "The kingdom of the world has become the kingdom of our Lord
>> and of his Messiah,
> and he will reign forever and ever. (Rev. 11:15)

We will keep learning; but we will not learn the new mantras of control.

- Against the narrative of Coke, we know about wonder;
- Against the narrative of Nike and Toyota, we know about love;
- Against the narrative of Budweiser, we know about praise.

In our resolved baptismal anthems of wonder, love, and praise addressed to God, we know that right after the first commandment comes a second like unto it: "neighbor!" Everything hangs on these two commandments, much more important than all burnt offerings and sacrifices (Mark 12:33). It has been so since Sinai; and it is so for all imaginable futures for which we wait with eager longing.

CHAPTER FOUR

Faith at the *Nullpunkt*

A ncient Israel in the Hebrew Bible/Old Testament is capable of thinking theologically about the future of the world and about the future
destiny of individual persons.[1] Its preferred and most characteristic mode
of thought, however, is done through critical theological reflection about
the community of Israel itself, its situation in the world, its position vis-à-
vis its God, YHWH, and its future amid the vagaries of history.

I

While historical questions about the origin and character of Israel are now
deeply unsettled and disputed, Israel's theological tradition is not ambiguous. Israel understands that it exists in the world as a peculiar people and
as an object of YHWH's peculiar attention precisely because of the initiatory attentiveness of YHWH, who in sovereign power and self-giving love
invests in the life of Israel. This remarkable sense of *origination in gift* is
expressed in two strands of tradition.[2] First, Israel's origin is articulated in
the *ancestral traditions* of Genesis 12–36, wherein YHWH without reason
or explanation addresses father Abraham (and mother Sarah) and summons them to a life of obedience as a carrier of YHWH's blessing for
the world. YHWH's commitment to Israel, moreover, is reiterated in each
new generation as a future is granted, always in the eleventh hour, with the
birth of an heir who can continue the peculiar life of Israel into the next
generation.

The second root of tradition is the *Exodus narrative* (Exodus 1–15),
wherein YHWH intervenes decisively on behalf of an abused and suffering people. YHWH's immense power overrides the oppressive regime of

the pharaoh in Egypt and makes possible an escape from slavery with an alternative life given in a land out of the reach of the oppressive pharaoh.[3] This decisive intervention on the part of YHWH is belatedly articulated in the tradition of Deuteronomy as an act of inexplicable love: "It was because the Lord loved you and kept the oath that he swore to your ancestors, that the Lord has brought you out with a mighty hand, and redeemed you from the house of slavery, from the hand of Pharaoh king of Egypt" (Deut. 7:8). This articulation has the merit of linking the two originary traditions of Genesis and Exodus.[4]

A third, subsequent tale of origin concerns the peculiar commitment YHWH is said to make to the *Jerusalem establishment* of temple and dynasty (Ps. 78:67-71). It is certain that Jerusalem and its theopolitical establishment are no part of Israel's self-presentation of origins. Later power arrangements nonetheless required its incorporation, and so "Zion and David" are also understood as gifts of YHWH's remarkable and inexplicable self-giving that has the capacity to create a *novum,* to bring to be that which has no warrant except the undomesticated resolve of YHWH. All of these traditions attest to the power of newness present in the character and resolve of YHWH.

II

The power of *novum,* discerned in YHWH and characteristically regarded as "unconditional," is nonetheless marked by a proprietary insistence on the part of YHWH. That is, YHWH is not just a giver of gifts, but has a determined and enduring intention for the newness wrought that is Israel. YHWH imposes a will and character upon the newness that is Israel. For that reason, Moses at Sinai hears from YHWH a loud, determined "if" (Exod. 19:5-6).[5] As a people generated out of YHWH's love, Israel is to be responsive and obedient to YHWH who gives it life. That intention of YHWH for Israel, moreover, is deeply and insistently ethical. For that reason, the extended address at Sinai is "Torah," direction, guidance, and instruction for how Israel is to live in the world.[6] The people of promise and of emancipation are immediately and inalienably a community under command.[7] The interface between the tradition of promise and of covenantal demand is a defining and bearable theological tension. In the actual lived life of Israel, however, that tension is not easy to manage or sustain.

III

The "if" of Moses does prevail. It is given a classic expression in Deut. 8:19-20. The same ethical seriousness, however, is endlessly sounded and reiterated by a series of prophets. We may suppose that the prophets arise quite ad hoc and give varied voicing to the ethical urgency of YHWH, arising no doubt from covenantal traditions but also from a felt sense of the failure of Israel. But even if their actions are ad hoc, in the final form of Israel's faith the prophets are all of a piece (see 2 Kgs. 17:13). All of the prophets, in sum, warned and anticipated a dire future for an Israel that refused to come to terms with YHWH's ethical passion. No doubt the privileged in the royal arena had confidence in their own privilege and advantage, reflecting of YHWH's devotion to Israel. The "if" did prevail. The people, the monarchy, the temple, the city—all gifts of YHWH's generosity—were swept away. The promises did not hold and could not hold, given YHWH's ethical urgency.

IV

The great theological reality of the Hebrew Scriptures/Old Testament is the failure of Jerusalem, the end of its hegemony, the deportation of Israel, and the reality of exile, a dismal ending that was the termination of all old faith claims.[8] It is impossible to overstate the cruciality of this fissure in Israel's self-understanding. This was for Israel a genuine and profound ending, the very ending that Amos had anticipated (Amos 8:2-3). The public, institutional life of Judah came to an end. But beyond that Israel made the theological judgment that YHWH had now abandoned Israel and had nullified all the old promises. The *political-military* experience of an ending is effectively transposed into a deep *theological* crisis.

It is this moment of failure that Walther Zimmerli terms "the *nullpunkt*" (in English, variously, "the nadir," "point zero").[9] It is the moment when Israel has two tasks that belong definitively to its faith. The first task—long practiced in Israel's Psalms of lamentation and complaint—is to *relinquish* what is gone, to resist every denial and every act of nostalgia, to acknowledge and embrace what YHWH has ended. The task is reflected in the communal laments of Psalms 44, 74, 79, 137, and in the Book of Lamentations. Jerusalem is gone! Israel will not soon have done with its sense of loss, variously expressed as grief and as rage.

Israel's second task—long practiced in Israel's hymns and Songs of Thanksgiving—is to *receive* what is inexplicably and inscrutably given by YHWH, to resist every measure of despair, to await and affirm what YHWH, beyond every quid pro quo, now gives. The faith of Israel envisions no automatic move from relinquishment to reception; one does not follow necessarily from or after the other. Israel's poets, singers, and speakers of oracles, heard as the very assurance of YHWH's own voice, arise precisely in the *nullpunkt*. Here we are close to the center of our topic and to the deepest issues in biblical eschatology. Amos Wilder had it right, even without having seen the phrasing of Zimmerli:

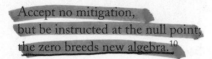

> Accept no mitigation,
> but be instructed at the null point;
> the zero breeds new algebra.[10]

We are here at the center of the mystery of Jewish faith that receives, in Christian perspective, its dramatic enactment in Easter. There is a "breeding," a hidden generativity of newness, just at the zero. The "breeding" at zero is not simply necessity. The "breeding" at zero is not only Israel's act of will for newness or wishful thinking. The "breeding" at zero is not simply buoyant poets in their extreme imagination. Perhaps it is all of these; but beyond these is the wounded but undefeated, affronted but not alienated, shamed but not negated resolve of YHWH to have a people—this people, this same people, this deported people—as YHWH's own people in the world.[11] YHWH will not be "Israel-less" in the world![12] YHWH will be—of necessity, of Israelite insistence, of poetic imagination, of fundamental resolve—the God of Israel. And therefore, it is clear in the canonical text of Jews and Christians, there will be a new Israel, Israel again, Israel reloved, healed, ransomed, blessed, brought home, rejoicing—by no claim of its own but by the nonnegotiable resolve (not yet known in the act of relinquishment)—of YHWH to have Israel.

The rhetoric of hope whereby Israel, in its hopelessness, must receive its new gift from YHWH is given in many voices. Indeed Israel requires endless generativity in order to speak the unspeakable newness from YHWH that is beyond explanation. Here I shall mention three voices that Gerhard von Rad has shown to be decisive and defining.[13]

"The Book of Comfort" collects together all the hopes and possibilities of the Jeremiah tradition (Jeremiah 30–31). The one who *scattered* in exile will *gather* in homecoming like a shepherd gathers the lost, at-risk sheep (31:10). The one who has watched *to pluck up and break down* will now supervise *building and planting* (31:28). This is the God of "everlasting love" who "continued in faithfulness" (31:2), who will "restore the fortunes" of Israel (30:3, 18; 31:23; see 19:14; 32:44; 33:7, 11, 26). This latter phrase, with YHWH as subject, envisions a radical reversal of circumstance wrought by nothing other than YHWH's act of power and resolve.[14] The literature teems with verbs of planting and building and consequent rejoicing. See especially Jer. 30:12-17 and 31:31-34.[15] The deep resolve of YHWH makes possible a new beginning in Israel, such as the shambles of exile would never have suggested.

As the corpus of Jeremiah "rolls" into Judaism, we are able to notice "futuring" that moves toward apocalyptic language, so eager is the wording to witness to a deep and real newness.[16] Indeed, the poetry just before the new covenant has it this way:

> Thereupon I awoke and looked, and my sleep was pleasant to me.
> (Jer. 31:26)

Is it a dream? Is it a fantasy? Or is it a future that the givenness of exile would never permit in wakeful control? It is precisely the dream that would begin to override circumstance, to invite exiles to venture out beyond where they are to where they will yet be. The new place is home beyond exile, where they have never been, a home not derivable from exile, but a new gift bred in the zero hour, conjured by poets, assured by the One who denied home and now wills it.[17]

The second large voice of newness in exile is Ezekiel, in a very different idiom. Hope and new possibility are given extended expression in chapters 33–48, especially in the vision of the new temple and its new divine presence. Here I shall mention only two specific utterances of this future-laden rhetoric. Best known is the visionary statement of "dry bones" in 37:1-14, but for being well known no less important. The key player in the encounter is the "breath" (*rûah*) that comes upon the dead carcass of Israel in the valley of death. The breath is not at the disposal of the prophet and lies beyond prophetic control or understanding. Everything waits for the inexplicable, unsummonable breath. Until it is given, the flesh, skin, and bones of Israel are as nothing, clearly a *nullpunkt*. When the breath is given, there is life anew.

End . . . *nullpunkt* . . . zero hour. And then wind . . . opens graves. The grave is exile. The new life is restoration and homecoming (37:12-14). The grave cannot prevail when the wind comes.

In a very different idiom, 36:22-32 offers newness concrete and relational, but also national. YHWH's declaration is about YHWH's resolve for restoration (vv. 24-27). What interests us, however, is not the promise, but the ground of the promise (vv. 22-23, 32).[18] The ground of newness is nothing about Israel or even about YHWH's inclination toward Israel. It is rather YHWH's self-regard. In an "honor-shame culture," YHWH has been shamed by Israel. The only way the honor of YHWH can be recovered (along with self-regard) is to rescue Israel so that all the watching nations and watching gods can see the fidelity and power of YHWH.[19] Israel's future is a function of YHWH's full Godness. YHWH is so tied to Israel (as in "I shall be your God") that Israel's future is as sure as YHWH's self-regard and self-resolve.

In self-regard, YHWH will make YHWH's own name (reputation, identity) holy as it has been profaned by Israel. The future of Israel is a strategy for enacting and reasserting YHWH's own *sui generis* quality. This motif is then unfolded in the tradition of Ezekiel in terms of holy temple, holy priests, holy city (chapters 40–48).[20] All of these holy accoutrements, however, are only functions of YHWH's own holiness, the propelling power of Israel's future.

The third powerful voice of exilic expectation is Isaiah 40–55 that anticipates the homecoming of Israel to Jerusalem as the power of Babylonian hegemony is broken by YHWH through YHWH's regent, Cyrus (see 45:1). Here I shall mention only one aspect of this rich, promissory literature. Twice the poetry uses the term "gospel" (*basar*) in an intentional way to declare YHWH's transformative presence (40:9; 52:7; see also 41:27; 60:6).[21]

The exile is understood in this poetry either as the provisional defeat of YHWH by the Babylonian gods or, more likely, as YHWH's willing submission to Babylonian negation as a way to enact harsh punishment upon Jerusalem. Either way, YHWH is silent, dormant, and invisible, and Israel is alone in the world without YHWH. Now, in this moment of poetry, YHWH breaks the silence and is again active in the life of the world (42:14-16; see 62:1). The specific formulae of the "gospel" are "Behold your God. . . . Your God rules."[22] YHWH is back in action! YHWH is back in play! This is the same YHWH who seemed feeble and inoperative in the face of Babylon. As exile is the end, so the gospel of homecoming is a new beginning, a "new thing." The life of Israel begins anew, made possible by the reappearance, reemergency, and reengagement of YHWH, no longer dormant, silent, or invisible.

V

The fissure of exile and homecoming in the imaginative, liturgical life of Judaism is defining. The texts of Jeremiah, Ezekiel, and belated Isaiah are the most eloquent in leading Israel—originally and in every subsequent generation—in and through exile to new life.[23] We may observe five general conclusions out of this redescribed history:

1. The turn from exile to homecoming is *lyrical, imaginative, and exuberant*. Israel fully expects that which is not in hand, which it cannot see. Its hope is not reasonable, controlled, or precise. It is wildly beyond the data and cannot be held accountable to circumstance. Israel's rhetoric refuses such sober restraint.

2. Israel's lyrical, imaginative exuberance about the future it will receive from YHWH is informed and shaped by *Israel's memory* of YHWH's previous generosity and fidelity that dominate Israel's remembered past. Indeed, the entire past of life with YHWH is seen as a profound sequence of *ḥasadim*, of miracles of transformative fidelity (as in Psalm 136). Israel is now able and willing to imagine the continuation of this sequence of miracles into its future, miracles that characteristically overpower circumstance.

3. The lyrical, imaginative, exuberant mode of discourse that transposes remembered miracles into anticipated miracles requires discourse that is open to *a myriad of images, figures, and metaphors*. The refusal of discipline and restraint in rhetoric dictates a pluralism of expression. No single imagery is adequate, because such a reduction would turn lyrical expectations into description and prediction, something Israel will not and cannot do.

4. The lyrical, imaginative tenor of hope refuses to be pinned down concretely. And yet these voices of possibility intend and insist that their cadences of hope pertain to *real life in the real world*, dealing with real power and real public possibility. The lyrical pluralism of hope summons Israel away from the closed world of despair sponsored by Babylon or advocated by Israel's deep guilt. Hope is a concrete summons to act in venturesome ways, not only in expectation but in defiant resistance to other construals of reality that give no credibility to YHWH as a defining player. By situating

4) hope in the real world, hope is not merely a passive wait upon God; it is rather a buoyant, sociopolitical, risky practice of a subversive counterlife in the world of geopolitics.

5. The utterance of hope is characteristically in the *nullpunkt*. The null point per se does not "breed" new algebra. The new algebra of life, peace, and joy is found in the hidden, determined ways of YHWH. That is, hope 5) is *theocentric, YHWH-centric*. It is the irreducible conviction of Israel that YHWH is not a victim of observed or predicted circumstance. This is an unfettered "thou" who works newness, either out of compassionate fidelity or out of uncompromised self-regard. YHWH, so Israel imagines, is never held at the *nullpunkt*.

VI

In both its depth and its lyrical buoyancy, the troping of life as exile and homecoming is decisive for Israel. It is through this troped experience that Judaism knows itself to be the at-risk, protected people of YHWH; it is, moreover, through this troped experience that the church comes belatedly to its Friday-Sunday certitude of YHWH and its life as the Easter people. The old slogan, "God acts in history," surely means that the community of faith characteristically attests to what it knows in and through the givenness of its own lived life, for hope from anywhere else is of only second-range importance.

But of course Israel did not linger exclusively in its reflection upon its own life. It was able, through its own life and by appeal to the great imperial liturgies all around it, to think and believe imaginatively about the life of the world . . . hence "creation theology."[24] When Judaism thought, believed, and sang about the life of the world, it was able to admit negatively and affirm positively in parallel to its own lived life. As exile-homecoming, with its strange texture of continuity and discontinuity, is defining for Israel, so the rubric of "creation-chaos-new creation" tells the story of the world as YHWH's creation, wherein *chaos* may be seen as a close cognate to *exile*.[25]

Given the enigmatic grammar of Gen. 1:1-2, it is commonly agreed that creation in the Hebrew Scriptures/Old Testament is characteristically not *ex nihilo*, but it is an act whereby the creating God imposes a life-generating order upon an extant chaos, a chaos about which the scriptures themselves exhibit no curiosity.[26] The imposition of a life-giving order that makes the world a safe, joyous, peaceable place is due cause for celebration. Israel celebrates the wonder and goodness and beauty and reliability of creation even as it celebrates the wonder of its own life in the world as a gift of YHWH (see Gen. 1:1—2:4a; Psalm 104).

The world is YHWH's creation. It is not self-made or self-sustaining. It prospers at the behest of YHWH. For that reason, in a context of shattering and dismay, the tradition of Jeremiah can envision the complete *undoing* of the world (4:23-26). This heavy judgment is a counterpoint to the liturgy of Genesis 1; point by point it foresees the dismantling of creation and the regression of the world into its primal chaos. Thus the "waste and void" of verse 23 is the same power of negation as "formless void" in Gen. 1:2. Everything will return to a precreation state of disorder in which the generative powers for life are not available and cease to function. The daring imagery of this poem—subsequently escalated in apocalyptic imagery—is as decisive and massive as any current scientific scenario of the undoing of the world.[27]

It may be that this poem in Jeremiah in the context of the late seventh century is a parabolic way of speaking of Israel. That is, the poet employs "limit language" to give voice to the radical undoing of Israel and all its lived context. The vision of world-dismantling, however, cannot be completely subsumed into or explained as the dismantling of Israel. Israel is able to ponder and contemplate the end of the world of generativity precisely because it does not confuse creation with the creator who is its only source of future.

As a seventh-century poet at the threshold of the failure of Jerusalem can envision a failed world, so a later poet, perhaps at the threshold of restored Jerusalem, can envision a restored creation (Isa. 65:17-19a). It is surely instructive that "new heavens and a new earth" are intimately connected to "Jerusalem as a joy," for Israel's imagination stays fixed upon its own homecoming. It is no doubt correct to see new creation here as a function of new Jerusalem, restored Judaism. And yet the creation imagery cannot be domesticated out of its cosmic scope.

Israel is able to imagine that as YHWH in the *nullpunkt* of exile will fashion homecoming, in parallel fashion Israel knows that in *tôhû wabôhû*, the *nullpunkt* of a failed creation, the creator of heaven and earth can and will form a new creation that is ordered, secure, joyous, and peaceable. Israel's cosmic imagination is not of a world ordered and settled or of a world failed and ended, but of a more perfect world about to come to be, solely by the God who "calls into existence things that do not exist" (Rom 4:17). This is indeed "hoping against hope," engaged in lyrical imagination rooted in memories of miracle but pushing beyond them in an act of hope that summons to an alternative kind of life in the world.

VII

As Israel is able to think through its own life of *exile and homecoming* to a cosmic framing of *chaos and (new) creation,* so Israel was able to think through its own life of *exile and homecoming* to a personal destiny of *trouble and new life.*

It is a truism of scripture study that these ancient texts, on the whole, did not entertain any notion of "life after death." Only two texts—Isa. 19:26 and Dan. 12:2—seem to be clear attestations of life after death, and they are commonly regarded as quite late, cast in apocalyptic language, and influenced by the entry of Judaism into a world of Hellenistic thought. While these two texts clearly give a ground for personal hope beyond death, they are so atypical that not much of a claim can be made.

The conventional truism of scholarship—given classic theological formulation by Oscar Cullmann—has been frontally challenged.[28] First, Mitchell Dahood (along with his student Nicholas Tromp), in a formidable study of the Psalms especially informed by cognates in Ugaritic, has proposed that many Psalms attest to life after death.[29] In his summary of his argument, Dahood considered "life" as "eternal life," "the future" as "future life," banqueting as an image of eternal life, beatific vision, and a summons to "awake, awake" as a summons to life after death.[30]

It is important that our discussion should take notice of the suggestions of Dahood, Tromp, and Barr. But because the dominant opinion of scholarship has not embraced their arguments, we may consider the theme of personal hope in a different mode shaped as *lament/complaint and praise.* Israel's voiced life with YHWH, in all its intimacy, is expressed in laments and complaints. Such speech characterizes with urgency to YHWH situations of need and then petitions YHWH in demanding imperatives that YHWH intervene promptly and make things new.[31] While the troubles of the Psalms seem characteristically to be illness, prison, or social isolation, the rhetoric of laments and complaints is the hyperbolic language of death, so that every need is portrayed as ultimate, as warranting YHWH's immediate and decisive intervention (Pss. 6:4—5; 7:4-5; 13:3-4; 22:14-15).

The remarkable feature of the pattern of these poems, as Claus Westermann has made clear, is that they characteristically end in resolution and praise (Pss. 6:9-10; 7:17; 13:5-6; 22:21a-22).[32] The rhetorical structure of "plea-praise" affirms that an urgent petition evokes YHWH's responsive intervention. YHWH comes into the *nullpunkt* of personal life—death in a myriad of forms—and acts decisively to make a new life of joy and well-being possible. It is not necessary to follow Dahood into literalism to see that the movement of *complaint-praise* is the ground of hope for personal life in Israel. The Psalmists voice their urgent petition precisely as acts of hope, in complete confidence that when YHWH hears and is moved to act, newness is given. It is at the nadir of human misfortune that the individual believer prays. It is toward the individual person in a variety of forms of death that YHWH comes to give new life.

VIII

We may from our analysis draw five conclusions concerning hope in ancient Israel:

1. The three spheres of life—communal, cosmic, and personal—are practiced in parallel fashion in the faith of Israel:

> communal: exile . . . homecoming;
> cosmic: chaos . . . new creation;
> personal: complaint . . . praise.

The three negative states of *exile/chaos/complaint* are roughly synonymous, all bespeaking a circumstance without resource, seemingly beyond the reach of YHWH's good resolve. The remarkable affirmation of Israel's text, however, is that the *nullpunkt* (exile, chaos, complaint) is characteristically transformed by the responsive initiative of YHWH who makes new life possible where none seemed available. The triad of *exile-homecoming, chaos-new creation, despair-doxology* is defining for Israel with YHWH. The move from point *A* (the negative) to point *B* (the new positive) is not the automatic or guaranteed.

It is in between the two, at the *nullpunkt*, that Israel does its hoping. It is characteristically impossible for Israel to keep silent in the *nullpunkt* or to entertain the thought that there will be no second element of gift from YHWH. It is this impossibility that makes Israel's hope definitional. Israel counts on a response of newness, not derived from circumstance, but from the same responsive, transformative God so thick in Israel's past circumstances of need. Thus the practices of hope for Israel, for the world, and for individual persons are of a piece.

2. The grounding of future expectation is rooted in *memories of past miracles of fidelity.* While this appeal to the past is evident in many places, it is nowhere clearer than in Lam. 3:21-23. The speaker has lost hope (see v. 18). It is memory that revives hope. And the memories that matter concern the great terms of covenantal fidelity: *ḥesed, raḥam, 'amûnah.*[33] Israel is incapable of imagining any future in which YHWH's known and characteristic fidelity is not operative. Israel cannot imagine a communal displacement, a cosmic distortion, or a personal abandonment that lies beyond the reach of YHWH's fidelity.

3. This reservoir of past fidelity moves Israel, in the *nullpunkt,* to offer *a variety of expressions* of hope. Here I notice only the tension between the covenantal (Dtr.) tradition of Jeremiah and the holiness (Priestly) tradition of Ezekiel. The ground of hope for Jeremiah is YHWH's *deep love for Israel* that not only endures through crisis but is revivified in crisis (Jer. 31:20). In a very different idiom, the tradition of Ezekiel has nothing to say of such moving, tender compassion. Here it is all the *cold holiness* of YHWH's self-regard (Ezek. 39:25-27). The wonder of hope at the *nullpunkt* is that Israel, in its urgent utterance, did not opt for one of these voicings, but knew that every voicing counts. The voicings arise in deep need and therefore are rich and varied, shrill and insistent, desperate and trusting. All of them count and continue to reach from Israel's need to YHWH's ear.

4. Informed by Ernst Käsemann, Hans Heinrich Schmid has shown that the themes of justification, creation *ex nihilo,* and resurrection of the dead are already offered together as synonyms in the Hebrew Scriptures/Old Testament.[34] That insight is crucial for our argument. If we may judge that these three theological schemata are congruent with our three spheres of hope, we may see that hope in the *nullpunkt* for Israel, creation, and individual persons is all of a piece. Hope in all three spheres invites the needy and desperate to look beyond circumstance to appeal to the God who presides over the *nullpunkt,* who can move into it and through it and beyond it.

The quintessential case in Christian parlance of course is Easter. Easter, however, is no isolated event. It belongs to Israel's wide and deep practice of hope that appeals to a long recital of parallels but finally stakes everything on the unfettered "Thou" who is not in thrall to the reasonableness of any *nullpunkt*. All *nullpunkt*, in every sphere, have common properties. In the end what counts is the capacity of this "Thou" to intrude into the *nullpunkt* and override it. The theological formulae of justification, creation *ex nihilo*, and resurrection from the dead are choice ways to speak about this singular claim for YHWH.

5. Following Hans Joachim Begrich, it is widely held that it is the "salvation oracle" uttered on behalf of YHWH by an authorized human speaker that turns the plea to praise in Israel's complaints and laments.[35] The point is not more than a hypothesis. But it does account for a decisive turn in Israel's sense of its own situation.

According to the hypothesis, the salvation oracle has at its heart the phrase, "Fear not" (Isa. 41:10, 14).[36] The assurance, taken as YHWH's announcement of presence, is the ground of hope and the harbinger of the newness only YHWH can give. The *nullpunkt*, in its many forms, is enough to evoke deep and raw fear. The exile offers a fear of *abandonment*. The pressure of chaos invites fear of *obliteration*. The immediacy of death bespeaks nullification and *nonbeing*. The *nullpunkt* carries the prospect of total nullification. Into that is spoken, "Do not fear." The antidote seems modest in the face of the threat. Unless, of course, the antidote is uttered by one who is trustworthy. Everything depends upon that. The future always depends for Israel upon the trustworthiness of the One who characteristically hovers somewhere between the fear so palpably grounded and faith so fragilely embraced. It is the pivot point of hope: "Do not fear!"

II.

The Word
Redefining the Possible

CHAPTER FIVE

The City
in Biblical Perspective

Failed and Possible

The city is not a primal or intentional theme in the Bible. It is an incidental theme that surfaces only as a byproduct of other issues. Moreover, it is not likely that what is said about any ancient city, concrete or anticipatory, is directly pertinent to our urban issues. More specifically, the Bible finally cares only about Jerusalem. In order to make the linkage to the urgent issues facing our cities today, then, it is necessary to take "Jerusalem" as a free-ranging metaphor for all of our cities.[1]

I

At the outset, the city in the Bible is a Canaanite phenomenon, looked upon resentfully and fearfully by the Israelites who are a peasant, hill-country enterprise. The term "Canaanite" is not an ethnic one, but it is an ideological term referring to those adversarial to Israel's covenantal faith and communitarian social practice (Num. 13:27-28; Josh. 6:16-21, 26; 12:7-24). The Israelite commission is to destroy the Canaanite city-kings and their cities, and the socioeconomic systems they support.

Inquiring about this profound antipathy toward cities requires a bit of social analysis. While the following categories are no doubt imposed anachronistically, they surely are broadly correct. The city is a place of

- division of labor, with different social roles and consequently different social classes;

- stratification of power, with kings and their entourages on top of the heap;
- surplus value, in which the "upper class" urban elites lived off the produce of the peasants who themselves lived hand-to-mouth, produce taken either by shrewd commercial transactions or by imposed, coercive taxation. The economy of the city was no longer aimed at use value, but at surplus that provided a cushion from the vagaries of life—a cushion for some, produced by the labor of others.

The city-king system dominated the landscape so that power was arranged in concentric circles with a fortified city at the center, administering peasant lands as far as a sphere of influence could be extended and sustained. The city was at the pinnacle of a monopolizing system. Israel had framed its primal narrative such that its initial experience in Egypt was not different from its experience in the land:

> Therefore they set taskmasters over them to oppress them with forced labor. They built supply cities, Pithom and Rameses, for Pharaoh. But the more they were oppressed, the more they multiplied and spread, so that the Egyptians came to dread the Israelites. The Egyptians became ruthless in imposing tasks on the Israelites, and made their lives bitter with hard service in mortar and brick and in every kind of field labor. They were ruthless in all the tasks that they imposed on them. (Exod. 1:11-14)

The Exodus narrative is about the monopolistic practices of Egypt with Pharaoh as the effective and symbolic administrator. Thus, Israel's founding story concerns emancipation from urban practices of exploitation. The move from Egypt to Palestine, from Moses to Joshua, is only a change in venue, from Egyptian city to Canaanite city; it is all the same when seen from the underside.

The perspective of resentment is termed by a number of scholars (not without dispute) a "peasant movement," a claim that receives important but ambiguous archaeological and demographic support.[2] That peasant perspective was at least communitarian and, to some extent, egalitarian (even though we must not romanticize). That is, the goods belonged to and were shared by the entire community, with a minimum of social stratification, only modest division of labor, and certainly no surplus value. The only economic value was the immediate use value that is characteristic of every peasant economy.

Thus, the origin of the social conflict of the Old Testament, seen in this context, is a clash of systems, urban and peasant, in which the peasants knew themselves to be endlessly exploited by urban centers. It is suggested, notably by George Mendenhall and Norman Gottwald, that the Bible originated in the midst of a peasant revolt of tribes. The revolt was fueled and evoked by YHWH, who urged the peasants to withdraw from the urban economy they supported but from which they profited very little, in order to reconfigure their own social power and social relationship in very different ways.

II

Out of the work of Joshua, Samuel, and the judges, the tribal apparatus of Israel gained genuine freedom and considerable stability. As the movement evolved, however, the peasant arrangement was felt by some to be less than adequate and too much ad hoc, hence the question of kingship, that is, the establishment of a permanent urban leadership in order to give Israel stability.[3]

The dispute about kingship (a cipher for an urban power structure) is highly visible in 1 Samuel 7–15. The key resistance to monarchy is found in 1 Sam. 8:11-17, which asserts that kings are "takers" who will tax you to death; and so there is resistance. As it turned out, David became a transitional figure—not a king but a chief—a genius who managed to hold things together in this disputatious and unsettled agenda.[4]

David managed that tension in many brilliant stratagems, but here I will mention only one. He had two priests! A priest, in a royal apparatus, serves primarily to legitimate theological-ideological tradition. It is like keeping Billy Graham permanently in the White House. One priest was Abiathar (1 Sam. 21:1-6; 22:14-23). His father, Ahimelech, and the entire priestly family was slaughtered by Saul. But David protected the only one of the family, Abiathar, who fled for his life (1 Sam. 22:22). Abiathar, it is clear, represents and embodies the old tribal configuration, the old peasant, communitarian tradition that, when attached to Yahwism, becomes the covenantal tradition of Sinai and the prophets.

The second priest of David, Zadok, is not so easy to understand. He is abruptly listed as one of the royal bureaucrats. Unlike Abiathar, there is no narrative about how he got there. He is simply there in prominence. Such a silence about origin gives scholars room for speculation. A dominant hypothesis is that Zadok was a Canaanite priest in the old shrine of Jebus, which became the city of David: Jerusalem.[5] When David conquered that city, Zadok was already there as an established priest of the Canaanite religious apparatus. According to the hypothesis, David did not disrupt the city or its shrine, but became its king, that is, king of a Canaanite city, a Canaanite city-king. So it is proposed that David exercised two different roles, king over the Israelite tribes and king over a Canaanite city-state, that dual role signaled in the dual priesthood of Abiathar and Zadok.[6] David is a charismatic figure and provider of protection, and so keeps it all in balance.

We know less than we would like to know about these two priests. Without any precision, we may take the two priests of David as symbols and metaphors of public power: Abiathar as the voice of Torah neighborliness, Zadok as the voice of palace and dynasty privilege. David was an agile juggler, the kind of juggler that effective public power must always require.

III

The balance between Abiathar and Zadok, between Torah neighborliness and pragmatic aggrandizement, could not be maintained in Israel beyond David. When he died, deep conflict arose, requiring that new decisions be made. Two of his sons, Adonijah and Solomon, competed for succession to the throne; Solomon won and the rest of the story of Jerusalem is history. The competition was not just between two brothers who wanted power, but between two parties, two bodies of opinions, two visions of urban reality. Allied with Adonijah were Joab the military man and Abiathar the priest. Adonijah lost. Allied with Solomon were Benaiah, the number-two military man, Nathan the prophet, and Zadok the priest. Solomon won. He immediately killed his brother Adonijah and Joab (1 Kgs. 2:28-35). It was not allowed to kill a priest, so he banished Abiathar to his home village of Anathoth, and there kept him under surveillance (1 Kgs. 2:26-27). Zadok (along with Solomon) won and monopolized the priesthood, the high priest of urban pragmatism. I propose, speaking metaphorically, that the banishment of Abiathar, the voice of Torah conscience, was the decisive twist in the future of the city, for a city without the voice of Torah conscience will pursue its own way to its own self-destruction.

The story of Solomon is well known. He was a big operator—big triumph, big harem (300 wives and 700 concubines), big military apparatus, big commercial enterprise, big wisdom, big money, big power (1 Kgs. 4:20-21). The queen of Sheba said of him in admiration: "Happy are your wives! Happy are these your servants, who continually attend you and hear your wisdom!" (1 Kgs. 10:8). Big happiness. And we may presume that the priest—Zadok—never said a mumbling word!

But the story of Solomon's Jerusalem is not only one of success. Its ending is told theologically three times:

- In 1 Kgs. 11:29, an unknown prophet called Ahijah appears and dramatically announces that the king's family would lose its royal territory because it had not kept Torah.
- In 1 Kings 12, things fall apart in a labor dispute, for the peasant people were weary of owing their lives to the urban elite.
- In 1 Kgs. 12:10, Rehoboam is urged on by his "young men" to make even heavier tax demands on the peasants for the sake of their own ease and comfort, indicating that the dynasty had remembered little and had learned nothing.

The text subtly suggests that Jerusalem, under Solomon, kept up its appearances. But all around the edges, for those who noticed, there were ominous hints of inadequacy, failure, and subversion.

IV

The city, along with its monarchy and temple, continued four hundred years—a very long time by modern standards—as an enterprise of privileged urban elites. For that four hundred years, the Zadokite priests of pragmatic utilitarianism presided over *pro forma* success, imagining all the time that this beloved city would be safe forever. The entire long period of the Davidic dynasty focused on the city and the administration of the countryside in order to sustain the urban enterprise. That city was remarkable.

- It possessed the governance where messianism was seeded.
- It possessed the temple that offered YHWH's guaranteed presence.
- It possessed an ideology of king and temple that made it immune to the vagaries of history.
- It monopolized Israel's imagination and faith so that those who wanted to thank and trust YHWH had to thank and trust Jerusalem.

These marvelous claims for the city were profoundly reinforced in 701 B.C.E. when the city was miraculously rescued from Assyrian assault, "for the sake of my servant David" (Isa. 37:35). Nothing bad could ever happen here!

But the city, for all its persuasive power, could never silence the arrested voice of Abiathar, expelled to village life in Anathoth. What Abiathar represented inside, which was then excluded, is reiterated outside by the prophets, those deeply subversive voices amid the ideological claims of the city.

Two instances of this ancient and definitional voice of Torah conscience are worthy of particular mention.

1. About 715 B.C.E., Micah, a villager from Gath, a voice of the peasants, came to the city and delivered a poetic threat.[7] He contributed to the danger of the urban elites in several ways:

- He assaulted the norms of acquisitiveness that violated the tenth commandment:

    Alas for those who devise wickedness
        and evil deeds on their beds! . . .
    They covet fields, and seize them;
        houses, and take them away. . . .
    Therefore thus says the LORD:
    Now, I am devising against this family an evil
        from which you cannot remove your necks;
    and you shall not walk haughtily,
        for it will be an evil time. (Mic. 2:1-2)

Micah saw clearly that when acquisitiveness displaces neighborliness, bad things happen. It invites an evil time.

- He spelled out the future of the city. He did not say, "I have a dream . . ."; he said, "I have a nightmare":

    Therefore because of you
        Zion shall be plowed as a field;
    Jerusalem shall become a heap of ruins,
        and the mountain of the house a wooded height. (Mic. 3:12)

The city stands under this massive, irresistible "therefore" of YHWH, anticipating that the city will be void of habitation.

- He imagined new village leadership that was not inured to expansive urban living. Significantly, the new leader will come from Gath or Bethlehem or some such place with communitarian tradition:

> But you, O Bethlehem of Ephrathah,
>   who are one of the little clans of Judah,
> from you shall come forth for me
>   one who is to rule in Israel. . . .
> And he shall stand and feed his flock in the strength of the LORD. . . .
>   And they shall live secure. . . . (Mic. 5:2-4)

The village leader, so says the village poet, will withstand even the threat of Assyria.

2. A hundred years later comes Jeremiah. He, too, is an outsider who is regarded as a traitor to the city and who undermines the war effort. In his most famous comment, he dared to assert that the jingoism of urban propaganda—royal or temple—would never succeed. Security would come only from the ancient Torah practices of neighborliness:

> Amend your ways and your doings, and let me dwell with you in this place. Do not trust in these deceptive words, "This is the temple of the LORD, the temple of the LORD, the temple of the LORD."
>   For if you truly amend your ways and your doings, if you truly act justly one with another, if you do not oppress the alien, the orphan, and the widow, or shed innocent blood in this place, and if you do not go after other gods to your own hurt, then I will dwell with you in this place, in the land that I gave of old to your ancestors forever and ever. (Jer. 7:3-7)

Jeremiah asserts a huge "if" over the future of the city, an "if" he had learned from Moses, the "if" of aliens, orphans, and widows. His daring comments got him arrested. He was put on trial, in a scene that anticipates the trial of Jesus. He was opposed in the trial by the entire power structure of the city, especially the religious types, and was about to receive a death sentence. However, the civil leadership resisted the aggressive religious leadership that was surely derived from Zadok the pragmatist. The issue was turned when some "elders of the land," some of the leaders of village life who had come to the city for the occasion, with their odd perspective reminded the assembly of Micah's denunciation (26:17-18).[8] The village leaders saved his life because they cited the poet Micah. They remembered that prophets must be heard and honored when they care about the city.

Surely, the Zadokites, wanting to execute him, did not welcome such a disruption of court by appeal to old village tradition. Their distaste for the intrusion of "the elders" must have been acute, for we notice that Jeremiah, the one who spoke of the deathly future of the city, is "of the priests who were in Anathoth in the land of Benjamin" (1:1). He comes from Anathoth and from a priestly family. He belongs to the line of Abiathar. Abiathar had been banished, but his voice could not be silenced. And now, Abiathar speaks yet again, against the self-deceiving arrangements of an urban elite that neglects the neighbor commands of the Torah. The city is not safe when it denies the demands of the neighbor.

V

Eventually the city failed. The Jerusalem establishment of temple and monarchy, and the ideology of self-importance and self-sufficiency and self-security, turned out to be false. It may have fallen because of the external pressure of Babylon, or because of the internal failure of bad leadership (see Ezekiel 34), or because of the spent quality of YHWH's love and patience, exhausted by the endless recalcitrance of the city. But for whatever reason, the city failed.

In my opinion, this is the same pregnant moment in which we find ourselves in urban America. I speak of course metaphorically and imaginatively, but here, too, the royal city that specializes in acquisitiveness, that has banished the countervoice of Abiathar, has failed. The failure of communal relations and the failure of consensus meaning are evident. The power of acquisitiveness can sustain itself only for a while, perhaps a long while; but it does so without moral credibility. And so I suggest that in its public imagination, the church and its pastors must situate themselves at this pregnant moment of failure and loss.

This moment is most dramatically expressed in Ezekiel. For reasons that are not clear, YHWH has caused Ezekiel to be unable to speak. But God promises that when the city falls, he can speak again (24:25-27). Then:

> In the twelfth year of our exile, in the tenth month, on the fifth day of the month, someone who had escaped from Jerusalem came to me and said, "The city has fallen." . . . So my mouth was opened, and I was no longer unable to speak. (33:21-22)

The loss of the city is the moment of the recovery of voice, when those numb with despair are able and dare to tell the truth. Thus, there is a deep linkage between the failure of the city and the power of recovered speech.

In this season of loss, I want to identify what I think are three major moves that belong to urban failure.

VI

First, the lost city must be grieved. We require a public and intentional assertion that the urban world we have treasured is no more. It is gone, and its loss evokes grief, rage, sadness, and hurt. It takes public grief to shatter the numbness and denial that are sponsored by those who want to pretend business as usual.

Two blocks of scripture show displaced Jews in grief. The first is the long collection of five poems in the book of Lamentations. This poetry was likely performed in response to the destruction of Jerusalem. The first four poems are alphabetical acrostics; grief is thereby complete from A to Z. The poetry speaks of a great reversal; at the same time it celebrates what was and it acknowledges how it is now:

> How lonely sits the city
>> that once was full of people!
> How like a widow she has become
>> she that was great among the nations! (1:1)

Tod Linafelt points out that the city is offered as a dying, forlorn widow, not dead, but endlessly dying, vulnerable, exposed, ravaged, raped, abused, and helpless.[9] She keeps dying in order to keep the pain available, seemingly forever.

The refrain is that there is "none to comfort" (Lam. 1:2, 9, 17, 21). YHWH had been a comforter to those who suffered loss, but now YHWH is not available. YHWH is no longer interested in the city, and therefore not available, not attentive. Jerusalem is completely bereft of support. And therefore,

> Gone is my glory,
>> and all that I had hoped for from the Lord. (3:18)

The poetry ends in 5:19-22. These lines move quickly through a doxology (v. 19) and then into a complaint that dares to use the harsh terms "forgotten, forsaken" with reference to YHWH:

> Why have you forgotten us completely?
>> Why have you forsaken us these many days? (v. 20)

Israel still has energy for a petition, "Restore us to yourself, O Lord," but the petition breaks off in wonderment: "unless you have utterly rejected us, and are angry with us beyond measure" (vv. 21-22). The poet does not know. Nobody knows. It is the moment of deep loss when the faithful do not know. It is an astonishing way to end a book of the Bible; but that is how it is with the failure of the city.

The second cluster of grief poetry is in the songs of communal lament in the Psalter. In these poems of wretchedness, Israel tells the truth to YHWH about the city. It is the enemies who have done it to the city, but the enemies could only act because YHWH has been absent or negligent:

> Your foes have roared within your holy place;
>> they set up their emblems there.
> At the upper entrance they hacked
>> the wooden trellis with axes.
> And then, with hatchets and hammers,
>> they smashed all its carved work.
> They set your sanctuary on fire;
>> they desecrated the dwelling place of your name,
>>> bringing it to the ground. . . .
> How long, O God, is the foe to scoff?
>> Is the enemy to revile your name forever?
> Why do you hold back your hand;
>> Why do you keep your hand in your bosom? (Ps. 74:4-7, 10-11)

The poem seeks to get YHWH to act by a grand doxology, reminding YHWH about how glorious it used to be (vv. 12-14), but then comes a petition, one that is not yet answered:

> Rise up, O God, plead your cause;
>> remember how the impious scoff at you all day long.
> Do not forget the clamor of our foes,
>> the uproar of your adversaries that goes up continually. (vv. 22-23)

Israel can only wait, for in the psalm there is no answer. But in this prayer of protest and petition, Israel has told the truth about the city and about YHWH, about misery and need.

Of course Psalm 137 is difficult, but it also is about the loss of Jerusalem:

> If I forget you, O Jerusalem,
>> let my right hand wither!
> Let my tongue cling to the roof of my mouth,
>> if I do not remember you,
> if I do not set Jerusalem
>> above my highest joy. (vv. 5-6)

Israel, in its loss, is fixated on the good old days. Grief that can be starchy piety here moves to rage, and dares to focus bitterness on the proximate cause of the loss. Perhaps YHWH has abandoned the city in its recalcitrance. But the one we can see—YHWH as agent being invisible—is Babylon. Grief turns to rage, irrational, unarguable rage. That is what loss does:

> O daughter Babylon, you devastator!
>> Happy shall they be who pay you back
>> what you have done to us!
> Happy shall they be who take your little ones
>> and dash them against the rock! (vv. 8-9)

I cite these psalms because I believe church and synagogue must practice the liturgy of loss, grief, and rage, in order to relinquish a city that has failed. Israel knew that loss unacknowledged is paralyzing. Conversely, loss voiced emancipates from ancient anger, liberates from cherished rage, and permits new waves of God-given constructive energy. The city cannot afford a loss ungrieved, because loss ungrieved produces fatigue and brutality.

VII

Suffering produces hope (Rom. 5:3-5), but not just any suffering. Suffering that is recognized, admitted, voiced, and enacted produces hope. We do not know why, but it is so. Suffering denied and unarticulated produces numbness and irrational rage. Israel knew that. And so, I propose a second response to the failed city of Jerusalem, second not first. It is a season of rich, exuberant, imaginative hope for a restored, new Jerusalem. But the new one requires the complete relinquishment of the one that is gone.

I make this linkage by two utterances in Second Isaiah, the exotic voice of hope for a new city.

1. In Lamentations 5:20, Israel had said: "Why have you forgotten us completely? Why have you forsaken us these many days?" Second Isaiah picks up this motif and echoes it: "Zion said," presumably in the liturgy, "The LORD has forsaken me, my lord has forgotten me" (Isa. 49:14). The prophet uses the same verbs as Lamentations 5:20. And then the poem offers prophetic resolution:

> Can a woman forget her nursing child,
> or show no compassion for the child of her womb?
> Even these may forget,
> yet I will not forget you. (49:15)

The mother God is beyond mothers who forget. For this mother God attends, remembers, goes back, suckles, so that the lament is embraced, received, and overcome. This God will be the mother of all restorers.

2. The key phrase of Lamentations is "none to comfort" (1:2, 9, 16, 17, 21). There is no prospect of divine intervention. It is precisely in response to that reiterated deficit that we get these well-known words:

> Comfort, O comfort my people,
> says your God.
> Speak tenderly to Jerusalem, and cry to her
> that she has served her term, that her penalty is paid,
> that she has received from the LORD's hand,
> double for all her sins. (Isa. 40:1-2)

Hope grows out of suffering. Hope answers suffering. Hope turns the lost past toward the expected future.

There is only one moment of hope in the grief of Lamentations. The poet has said, "Gone is my glory, and *all that I had hoped* for from the LORD" (3:18). But then:

> But this I call to mind,
>   and therefore I have hope:
>
> The steadfast love of the LORD never ceases,
>   his mercies never come to an end;
> they are new every morning;
>   great is your faithfulness. . . .
>   "therefore I *will hope* in him." (3:21-24)

Israel remembers the three great words of piety: love, mercy, compassion. When it breaks the pattern of numbness, silence, and denial, Israel remembers accounts of fidelity from YHWH that have characterized Israel's life. Israel in loss dares to turn that inventory of fidelity to the future, to affirm that YHWH's fidelity will shape the future in ways the past has never been shaped.

And there is, in exilic Judaism, a flood of promises for a new city. It is as though the canon has gathered together all the candidates for the Martin Luther King award. They have learned to say, in distinct, harmonious tones:

> I have a dream,
> I have a dream,
> I have a dream . . .
> the long nightmare of loss is over.

The loss is real; the city as we know it is defeated and failed. Nobody believes that poverty or homelessness or crime or any of the other maladies can be answered. And indeed, they never will be, given the categories of imagination now operative. There are simply no categories of imagination that can mobilize public will.

It is amazing to me that the great hopers of the exile did not talk policy.[10] They did not make recommendations. What they offered was poetry that shattered the categories that precluded newness. They reimagined the city, reimagined it in a matrix of exile, in which YHWH was the key player. YHWH had been eliminated from that ancient world, even as YHWH is not at the table in our cities. YHWH has always and only been present in poetic scenarios.

So Jeremiah speaks of a new covenant rooted in forgiveness (31:31-34), moving then to a vision of rebuilding that includes the whole valley of dead bodies and ashes (31:38-40).

Then this statement of resolve, a resilience not subject to veto:

> For I surely know the plans I have for you, says the Lord, plans for your welfare and not for harm, to give you a future with hope. Then when you call upon me and come and pray to me, I will hear you. When you search for me, you will find me; if you seek me with all your heart, I will let you find me, says the Lord, and I will restore your fortunes and gather you from all the nations and all the places where I have driven you, says the Lord, and I will bring you back to the place from which I sent you into exile. (29:11-14)

So Ezekiel, once he gets to speak again, proclaims YHWH as the good shepherd (34:11-16). The text is a welfare program that specializes in neighborliness. He announces an outpouring of generative grace that will heal the contrariness that makes human, urban life impossible:

> I will take you from the nations, and gather you from all the countries, and bring you into your own land. I will sprinkle clean water upon you, and you shall be clean from all your uncleanness, and from all your idols I will cleanse you. A new heart I will give you, and a new spirit I will put within you; and I will remove from your body the heart of stone and give you a heart of flesh. I will put my spirit within you, and make you follow my statutes and be careful to observe my ordinances. Then you shall live in the land that I gave to your ancestors; and you shall be my people, and I will be your God. (Ezek. 36:24-28)

The poet imagines a new ecological system no longer marred by war and famine (34:26-27a, 36:29b-30). Restoration will be like an Easter:

> "I am going to open your graves, and bring you up from your graves, O my people; and I will bring you back to the land of Israel. And you shall know that I am the Lord, when I open your graves, and bring you up from your graves, O my people. I will put my spirit within you, and you

shall live, and I will place you on your own soil; then you shall know that I, the LORD, have spoken and will act," says the LORD. (37:12-14)

This is spirit-driven Easter, when all the powers of death are overcome. Back in Psalm 74:22, Israel had prayed, "Rise up, O God." And now there is a rising to Easter faith and Easter imagination.

Second Isaiah, the supreme hoper of ancient Israel, envisions a return home, along a way no longer administered by the categories of scarcity and brutality derived from Babylon. The poet dares to say to the ones who have lost the city, "Fear not" (Isa. 41:10, 13, 14; 43:1; 44:1, 8). The basis for the new possibility is the resolve of God:

> For my thoughts are not your thoughts,
>   nor are your ways my ways, says the LORD.
> For as the heavens are higher than the earth,
>   so are my ways higher than your ways
>   and my thoughts than your thoughts. (55:8-9)

And then the possibility: "You shall go out in joy, and be led back in peace" (55:12). This is a homecoming, but not to the old city, to a home, an urban home, a city as a true home. It is promised, and therefore it is possible. It is made possible by the lips of poets who have been through grief and rage and loss, the ones who now "sustain the weary with a word" (50:4).

VIII

Suffering produces hope. And hope does not disappoint. The reason hope does not disappoint is that it issues in determined, resolved action, my third needed response. Poetry does its work, but not on our schedule. So in the Old Testament, the poetry worked until finally it evoked those two great urban redevelopers, Ezra and Nehemiah.

The links between *suffering* and *hope* and *action* are not clear. But consider the amazing scenario in Nehemiah 1. Nehemiah has been a cup bearer among the Persians, a high office. He hears of the debacle of Jerusalem, and he weeps (1:4). He prays that there will be a Persian foundation to give money for urban redevelopment (1:5-11). And then he secures the support of Persia, a mandate to rebuild, with financial backing (2:7-9). He is a shrewd man, driven by a vision.

We can identify four actions that make the new city possible:

1. Ezra does *Torah* (Nehemiah 8). The drama has theological authorization. It is the recovery of a self-conscious identity that gives energy for the new city.

2. Nehemiah institutes severe *financial reform* that pertains to the rich charging interest to the poor (Nehemiah 5). There will be no new city until there is a neighborly form of debt management.

3. Ezra insists on *sabbath* (Neh. 13:15-22). The sabbath observation goes deep to root identity and asserts that the new city is not about acquisitiveness; the community in sabbath is disengaged from the production-consumption game.

4. Ezra condemns *mixed marriages* (13:23-27). Without commending his action, we do need to appreciate his single-minded, disciplined embrace of a dream, large enough to include, concrete enough to enact. Restoration requires discipline.

IX

I finish with three conclusions.

1. Israel's faith offers an alternative narrative of the city. The conventional narrative of the city is a thin tale of acquisitiveness and scarcity that produces violence. In that tale, there is no break, no going back, no alternative. That tale is a tale so well and so often told that it seems a given. But it is not. It is an ideological construal, grounded in scarcity and brutality, that in principle admits of no alternative tellings of the city. It is the task of church and synagogue to tell an alternative account of the city, that concedes nothing to the claims of an ideological telling that, in light of the gospel, is false. The pastoral task is to wean all of us away from that false tale of the city.[11]

2. This scenario is, of course, incomplete. The city hoped for is not yet built or given. At the end of the canon (Revelation 21), the faithful still wait and still hope. I suggest that we should not be given to too much long-range hope without attention to more immediate engagement. In the great recital of Hebrews 11, we have a celebration of our ancestors in faith:

> If they had been thinking of the land that they had left behind, they
> would have had opportunity to return. But as it is, they desire a better

country, that is, a heavenly one. Therefore God is not ashamed to be called their God; indeed, he has prepared a city for them. (vv. 15-16)

They sought a city. But then, in a remarkable bid to the present generation, the chapter concludes:

> Yet all these, though they were commended for their faith, did not receive what was promised, since God had provided something better so that they would not, apart from us, be made perfect. (vv. 39-40)

Our ancestors in faith did not receive the promise. Their getting it right depends upon us. "Apart from us," this faith is not complete. While the church has Revelation 21 for the long term, the immediate claim of Hebrews 11 is crucial. Present action fulfills past faith, an incredible summons to concrete engagement in the hopes of our ancestors.

3. Finally, a parable. I spoke with a Presbyterian layperson in Atlanta about the city. He told me that in growing up, his father had a shop downtown, next to Rich's department store. After school, he often went to his father's shop, and often the two of them went to Rich's for a Coca-Cola. It was a wonderful happening, even more wonderful in memory.

But now Rich's is gone, replaced by a bank. The old city that centered in Rich's is no more. And he said, "When I see it or think of it, I am enraged and sad at the loss." We talked about relinquishing a city that is no more. Out of much thought and prayer, he told me, one day he drove down and parked across the street from where Rich's and his father's shop had been. He sat in the car and cried. Cried long, cried bitterly, cried for what was and is not, cried over a city now reduced to banks and exploitative labor, cried a lost shop and a lost family and a lost world.

And then, he told me, he started his car. He drove to his suburban church. And for the first time, he signed up to work the soup kitchen, to contribute modestly to a new urban possibility.

Whoever has ears, let them hear!

CHAPTER SIX

Evangelism and Discipleship

The God Who *Calls*

The God Who *Sends*

I begin with four affirmations that I will exposit in some detail:

1. The God of the Gospel is *a God who calls* persons and communities to God's own self, to engage in praise and obedience.

2. The God of the Gospel is *a God who sends* persons and communities to claim many zones of the world for God's governance of "justice, mercy, and faith" (Matt. 23:23).

3. The God of the Gospel lives among and *in contestation* with many other gods who also call and send, but whose praise and obedience are false, precisely because there is no commitment to "justice, mercy, and faith."

4. Consequently, the persons and communities called by this God for praise and obedience and sent by this God for justice, mercy, and faith, also live among and *in contestation* with other gods, other loyalties, other authorities. Inescapably, the ones called and sent are always yet again deciding for this one who calls and sends. This endless process of deciding again is accomplished in freedom from all other calling gods and all other sending loyalties. That endless deciding, moreover, requires great passion, imagination, and intentionality.

I

The God of the Gospel *calls* to praise and obedience. That is because, so we confess, that is the one true God who is the giver of all life, and who intends that all life should gladly be lived back to God. It is God's rightful place to invite and expect such a turn back to God in joy and well-being. The characteristic response to the creator by all creatures is to give praise (that is, exuberant, self-ceding gladness to God), and obedience (that is, active engagement in doing God's will and making the world to be the creation that God intends). The call of God, in short, is to discipleship, that is, to follow God's presence and purpose and promise with the disciplines necessary to the project.

1. The God to which *the Old Testament bears testimony* is a God who calls, who disrupts the lives of settled people, who gives them a vocation that marks life by inconvenience and risk. The ground of the call is the good news of the Gospel that God has a powerful intentionality for the world that, when enacted, will make a decisive difference for good in the world. Of the many calls to the disciplines of praise and obedience in the OT, I will mention only two.

a. The story of Israel begins in the abrupt address that the God of the Gospel makes to *Abraham,* an address that is decisive and that is delivered without any forewarning. Abraham is addressed in an imperative, "go"; Abraham's life is radically displaced. He is caught up in a world of discourse and possibility about which he knew nothing until addressed, a world of discourse and possibility totally saturated with God's good promises for him and for the world through him (Gen. 12:1). By this call Abraham is propelled into an orbit of reality that completely preempts his life, and removes him completely from any purpose or agenda he may have entertained for himself before that moment. In the answer of Abraham, father of faith, to the address of God, we are told very little. We are told only that he was surely responsive to God's new initiative in his life. The text says only, "So Abram went" (Gen. 12:4). Later this response is interpreted as a supreme act of faith:

> By faith Abraham, when put to the test, offered up Isaac. He who had received the promises was ready to offer up his only son, of whom he had been told, "It is through Isaac that descendants shall be named for you." He considered the fact that God is able even to raise someone from the dead—and figuratively speaking, he did receive him back. (Heb. 11:17-19)

b. Parallel to Abraham, this same God also calls *Moses* by meeting him in the burning bush (Exod. 3:1-6). The call itself consists in three elements:

- God calls him by name, "Moses, Moses." This address evidences God seizing the initiative in the life of Moses. He is known from the outset in elemental ways by God and is called to engage the mystery of God.

- Moses is warned that he is standing on holy ground. That is, his locus is not what he thought, not simply a place for the struggle for social justice in which he was already engaged, but a zone inhabited by demanding, addressing holiness. The call is an abrupt act that displaces Moses for a world of conflict propelled by God's holiness.

- Moses is resituated in the tradition of God's people, as God recalls God's identity from the book of Genesis, "God of Abraham, God of Isaac, God of Jacob." Moses is thereby wrenched away from what he might have thought was the circumstance of his life and decisively relocated in a larger narrative about which he knew nothing until that moment of confrontation.

2. The same God, in the life and in the utterances of Jesus, makes the same claim in the New Testament. In each case the call, an authorizing imperative, is a disruption that sets lives on totally new trajectories that had not previously been in purview. The simple, uninflected imperative is "follow me," an imperative that sets people on a new path of obedience, trailing along the path that Jesus himself walked in obedience:

- In Mark 2:16-20, immediately upon announcing the nearness of the kingdom (vv. 14-15), Jesus comes upon the four fishermen who abandoned their old life for this new following.

- In Mark 8:34-38, just after announcing his own death and resurrection (v. 31), he issues a call to the disciples:

> "If any want to become my followers, let them deny themselves and take up their cross and follow me. For those who want to save their life will lose it, and those who lose their life for my sake, and for the sake of the gospel, will save it." (vv. 34-35)

The "following" is on the road to Jerusalem, a path that culminates in a cross, a reality that contradicts all the hopes and promises of the world into which he goes, that is, into the world of settled legitimacy and power.

- In Mark 10:17-22, Jesus offers a call to the man who had kept all the commandments:

> Jesus, looking at him, loved him and said, "You lack one thing: go, sell what you own, and give the money to the poor, and you will have treasure in heaven; then come, follow me." (Mark 10:21)

In all these cases, it is clear that Jesus enacts a major claim upon people's lives that places their lives in crisis, the same sovereign claim that is so uncompromising in the narratives of Abraham and Moses.

3. Of course, it is a huge leap from these biblical summons to *our own time, place, and circumstance*. Except that in parallel fashion, we imagine that the same calling God calls "people of all ages, tongues, and races" into his church.[1] The call is not to join an institution or to sign a pledge card; it is rather to sign on for a different narrative account of reality that is in profound contrast to the dominant account of reality into which we are all summarily inducted.

When we ask about the call or of our sense of the God who calls, it is clear that this God of the Gospel calls men and women away from the bad news of the world, away from the dominant, dehumanizing values of commodity and brutality that are all around us. Conservatives tend to think it is a displacement about sexuality, and liberals incline that it is a displacement concerning economics. But clearly the common point shared by all is that the calling God means for us to disengage from the postures, habits, and assumptions that define the world of power and injustice that is so devoid of mercy and compassion in every arena of life. The call is away from ordinary life, ordinary possessions, and ordinary assumptions to a way of life that the world judges to be impossible. Thus the call is, indeed, to an impossibility.

Discipleship is no easy church program. It is a summons away from our characteristic safety nets of social support. It entails

a. a resolve to follow a leader who himself has costly habits,

b. in order to engage in disciplines that disentangle us from ways in which we are schooled and narcoticized into new habits that break old vicious cycles among us, drawing us into intimacy with this calling God. Discipleship requires a whole new conversation in a church that has been too long accommodationist and at ease in the dominant values of culture that fly in the face of the purposes of God.

It is right to conclude, in my judgment, that the God who calls is the God of discipleship, the one who calls people to follow, to obey, to participate in his passion and mission. Such disciplines—in the Old Testament, in the New Testament, now—insist that there is no more business as usual. Such disciplines intend and permit a drastic reorienting of one's life, an embrace of new practices, and, most particularly, a departure from other loyalties that have seemed both legitimate and convenient.

II

The God who calls is *the God who sends*. This God sends because (a) this God has compelling authority to issue imperatives that anticipate ready acceptance and (b) this God has a compelling passion for what is to be effected and enacted in the world over which this God is governor.

1. The sending of *Abraham (and Sarah)* is perhaps the overarching missional dispatch in all of Scripture. God issues to Abraham an initial imperative, "go." Then God makes extravagant promises to Abraham concerning land, name, and blessing. But the sending culminates in 12:3 with this responsibility entrusted to Abraham:

> By you all the families of the earth shall be blessed.

We may begin with a focus upon the notion of blessing. Israel exists to cause a blessing that is to be widely shared. It is important to recognize that "blessing" is not a religious or moral phenomenon in the world of Israel, but is a characteristic feature of creation that is fruitful and productive. Thus blessing is that the world should be generous, abundant, and fruitful, bespeaking effectiveness in generative fertility, material abundance, and this-worldly prosperity. Perhaps our best way to speak of this mandate is to think of "shalom" in the broadest scope. Israel's life is to make the world work better according to the intention of the creator. That is an immense mission given to this one man and his family!

It has been noticed by scholars, moreover, that Gen. 12:1-3 functions as a hinge to what follows, on the one hand.[2] The passage looks forward toward the entire family of Abraham that exists in order to evoke blessing in the world. More stunning, on the other hand, is the awareness that this mandate looks back to Genesis 3–11, that is, to all the nations of the world that are under curse . . . Adam and Eve, Cain and Abel, the flood, and the tower. All of these narratives tell of the families of the earth being alienated from God and living in contradiction to the will of God. It is the missional mandate of God to Abraham that Abraham should exist so that the general condition of curse in the world is turned to a general condition of blessing, life, and well-being. The condition of curse is popularly linked to "original sin" and "the fall." One does not need to use such harsh and belated labels, however, to appreciate that Israel's mission is *to mend the world* in all its parts. That is Israel's raison d'être in the midst of creation.

The mandate is not specific about how Israel is to effect such systemic change, though many narratives in Genesis suggest a variety of means, all of which seek to break the vicious cycles of alienation by positive acts of conciliation that may take many variant forms.

Concerning this initial sending of Israel on behalf of the nations, it is important that Paul quotes this very text from Genesis in his urging that the Gospel pertains to the Gentiles:

> And the scripture, foreseeing that God would justify the Gentiles by faith, declared the gospel beforehand to Abraham, saying, "All the Gentiles shall be blessed in you." (Gal. 3:8)

The wondrous phrase of Paul, "Gospel beforehand," is a recognition that from the outset the good intention of the creator God cannot be limited to any ethnic or racial or national enclave. Here is the warrant for a vision of a community of *shalom,* rooted in God's own vision of the creation, that repudiates every death-bringing distinction and every leverage of some over against others. It is to be noted, moreover, that the mandate in Genesis is not to make the nations over into Israelites, nor even to make them Yahwists. The focus is kept upon the improvement of the quality of life as willed by the creator God.

2. The issue of sending is rhetorically the same in the Exodus narrative, though the effect is very different. *The sending of Moses* is almost a humorous rhetorical act. In the rhetoric of Exod. 3:7-9, YHWH issues a series of first-person resolves, all concerning what YHWH intends to do in the face of Pharaonic oppression:

> Then the Lord said, "I have observed the misery of my people who are in Egypt; I have heard their cry on account of their taskmasters. Indeed, I know their sufferings, and I have come down to deliver them from the Egyptians, and to bring them up out of that land to a good and broad land, a land flowing with milk and honey, to the country of the Canaanites, the Hittites, the Amorites, the Perizzites, the Hivites, and the Jebusites. The cry of the Israelites has now come to me; I have also seen how the Egyptians oppress them." (Exod. 3:7-9)

But then verse 10 comes as a surprise. YHWH might then have said, "I will go to Pharaoh." That, however, is precisely what is not said next. Rather it is,

> So come, *I will send you* to Pharaoh to bring my people, the Israelites, out of Egypt. (v. 10)

It is of immense importance that the most difficult, most dangerous task in emancipation is not undertaken by YHWH as divine deliverance. Rather, emancipation is a human task to be undertaken amid the risky problematics of Pharaoh's political reality.

The mission of Moses is nothing less than the confrontation of political power that no longer has anything of a human face. More than that, Moses' mandate is to confront exploitative economic power that is understood to be an embodiment of false theology, so that the task of liberation and transformation of the empire is deeply rooted in a theological conflict between the lord of liberty and the gods that endorse and legitimate exploitative economics (see Exod. 12:12).

It cannot be overstressed that the mission is, indeed, a human mission, with YHWH cast in a crucial, but supporting role. There is here an offer of God's transformation of the slave economy, but only in and through direct, risky human engagement. And, of course, Moses immediately senses the problem and the risk of the call; consequently, Exodus 3 and 4 offer five points of resistance that Moses makes to the call from YHWH (Exod. 3:11—4:17). Moses does not want the mission. The mission is to transform the functioning social system of Egypt from working according to the vision of the pharaonic superpower and to bring that economy in line with a covenantal vision of reality. The mission concerns the way in which power is practiced in the world. YHWH's role is to legitimate, authorize, and support the human mission by shows of presence and power that are only available in the midst of alternative human action.

After so much resistance on the part of Moses concerning his inability to utter the right words, YHWH answers with dismissive contempt for Moses' reluctance:

> Then the anger of the lord was kindled against Moses and he said, "What of your brother Aaron, the Levite? I know that he can speak fluently; even how he is coming out to meet you, and when he sees you his heart will be glad. You shall speak to him and put the words in his mouth; and I will be with your mouth and with his mouth, and will teach you what you shall do. He indeed shall speak for you to the

people; he shall serve as a mouth for you, and you shall serve as God for him. Take in your hand this staff, with which you shall perform the signs." (Exod. 4:14-17)

3. The *sending of the disciples of Jesus* concerns both walk and talk. I take Matt. 10:5-15 to be a model for Christian mission. The initial mandate to the twelve is to *talk:*

As you go, proclaim the good news, "The kingdom of heaven has come near." (v. 7)

The kingdom of heaven—the rule of God—has come near. The sentence is terse and does not last long enough to say, ". . . has come near in the life and person of Jesus." It is the insistence of the Synoptic tradition that in the actions of Jesus—acts of healing, cleansing, feeding, forgiving—it is unmistakably clear that a new governance is in effect. The Kingdom comes near when the creation begins to function according to the blessed intention of the creator. That is the news, the basis of all that follows in missional theology. God has drawn near to effect a new reality that is to be enacted and effected by human missioners who act boldly on the basis of the proclamation that they themselves accept as true and as the basis for an alternative life in the world.

The second part of the mandate to the disciples is *the walk:*

Cure the sick, raise the dead, cleanse the lepers, cast out demons.
(Matt. 10:8a)

The imperative to act is fourfold:
- Cure the sick, because the sick have fallen under power that wish them ill;
- Raise the dead, enact the power of life where the spiritual force of death prevails;
- Cleanse lepers, make the unclean ritually acceptable;
- Cast out demons, break the power that is against the new governance.

And then the conditions for effectiveness are stated:

You received without payment; give without payment. Take no gold, or silver, or copper in your belts, no bag for your journey, or two tunics, or sandals, or a staff; for laborers deserve their food. (Matt. 10:8b-10)

The condition for mission is about money, resources, and supplies. The mandate is to "travel light." No comment is made, but surely we are to conclude that the capacity to effect these transformative wonders requires complete reliance on the news of the new ruler; and the negative counterpoint is the shunning of the resources of the status quo that will rob the disciples of power to be effective.

The mission is dangerous. The next paragraph concerns the risk inherent in the mission, risky because God's will for the world is in deep tension with the way the world is organized:

> See, I am sending you out like sheep into the midst of wolves; so be wise as serpents and innocent as doves. Because of them, for they will hand you over to councils and flog you in their synagogues; and you will be dragged before governors and kings because of me, as a testimony to them and the Gentiles. When they hand you over, do not worry about how you are to speak or what you are to say; for what you are to say will be given to you at that time; for it is not you who speak, but the Spirit of your Father speaking through you. (Matt. 10:16-20)

The mission is profoundly conflictual because the present population of the sick, dead, lepers, and demon-possessed is not an accident. Rather, the present system works as it does precisely because a certain "quota" of lives have been "handed over" to anti-human forces, and the system prospers on their backs. The attempt to draw those "handed over" back into the realm of the human will evoke deep hostility, wolves that may be viciously ravenous, but who will work by legal means under the guise of respectability. The normal state of the missioner is to be in trouble with the authorities who are characteristically defenders of systems that deny humanness. (It occurs to me that the promise of words given by the spirit in appearance before the authorities is precisely parallel to the promise of God made to Moses who also must speak words beyond his capacity in the face of authority [Exod. 4:10-17].)[3]

All of that is about the mission. But verse 24 picks up on our other theme of discipleship:

> A disciple is not above the teacher, nor a slave above the master; it is enough for the disciple to be like the teacher, and the slave like the master. If they have called the master of the house Beelzebul, how much more will they malign those of his household! (Matt. 10:24-25)

The people among whom Jesus is sent do not like him; so they will not like you either as his disciples. Clearly the mission is done by those under discipline. And then in verses 26-28, we have perhaps the ultimate discipline:

> So *have no fear* of them; for nothing is covered up that will not be uncovered, and nothing secret that will not become known. What I say to you in the dark, tell in the light; and what you hear whispered, proclaim from the housetops. *Do not fear* those who kill the body but cannot kill the soul; rather fear him who can destroy both soul and body in hell. (vv. 26-28)

4. Much of the same scenario is given in Luke 10, only now it is seventy sent on a mission. The same components of the sending are given, this time in a different sequence:

- A warning about risk:
  Go on your way. See, I am sending you out like lambs into the midst of wolves. (v. 3)

- A mandate to travel light:
  Carry no purse, no bag, no sandals; and greet no one on the road. (v. 4)

- An imperative for acting (walk):
  cure the sick who are there. (v. 9a)

- An imperative for utterance (talk):
  and say to them, "The kingdom of God has come near to you." (v. 9b)

The *walk* is to cure, the restoration of broken humanness to full creaturely well-being. The *talk* is to assert the nearness of the new rule. The later point is to be said—out loud and without shame. But Jesus knows about resistance to the mission. And so his climactic statement to the seventy is that "*you know* [. . . even if they refuse to know . . .] the kingdom of God has come near" (v. 11). That much is known by the church whenever it draws close to Jesus who enacts his own wonders about which the church is to testify. Jesus, moreover, authorizes the church's enactment of wonders that replicate the wonders of Jesus. The *talk* makes the *walk* possible, and the *walk* is to heal, to break all vicious cycles of diminishment that violate the intention of the creator.

This double mandate of "cure" for the twelve in Matthew 10:8 and for the seventy in Luke 10:9 permits me to call attention in a general way to the Jewish phrase "*Tikkun 'olam*," "to mend the world." It is an old rabbinic phrasing that Israel's work in the world is to repair creation so that it may function again fully and abundantly; more specifically the same phrase is used by Michael Lerner in his important journal, *Tikkun*, a publication that is as important for Christians as for Jews. Lerner's work has begun with a sustained Jewish critique of the policies of the state of Israel. More recently, however, Lerner has organized a "*Tikkun* community" of Jews and others who are about "mending the world." It is clear, without any theological slogans, that the whole creation has fallen under the rule of alien powers disguised in various ideologies. It requires at-risk human bodies acting in obedience to the alternative to break that alien ruler, to make restoration of life possible.

5. Our talk of mission must, of course, pay attention to the conclusion of *Matt. 28:16-20*, verses that are commonly understood as decisive for our theme of mission. Now, as Matthew ends his account of the Gospel, there are only eleven followers remaining. The imperative of the risen Lord to them is clear and firm:

> —Go;
> —make disciples;
> —baptize;
> —teach.

- *Go:* The formula is so familiar that we do not notice. The post-Easter company of disciples, the inchoate form of the church in this most churchy Gospel, is *sent*. Its task is to recruit others into the counter-community of Jesus.
- *Making disciples* means to bring others under the disciplines that mark the followers of Jesus. It is assumed in such an enterprise that the primal core of disciples is indeed under discipline themselves, so that they can instruct new recruits into the practices and habits that will sustain life and mission in the counter-community.
- *Baptism,* reflecting a more ecclesial assumption on the part of Matthew, has become the rite of initiation into an alternative community. Clearly, in the earliest church, baptism was a decisive, dramatic transfer of life into a new community with new disciplines, new

loyalties, and new obligations. It is likely that the letter to Ephesians represents and reflects that dramatic turn of life at baptism:

> You were taught to put away your former way of life, your old self, corrupt and deluded by its lusts, and to be renewed in the spirit of your minds, and to clothe yourselves with the new self, created according to the likeness of God in true righteousness and holiness. (Eph. 4:22-24)

> Put away from you all bitterness and wrath and anger and wrangling and slander, together with all malice, and be kind to one another, tenderhearted, forgiving one another, as God in Christ has forgiven you. (vv. 31-32)

- *Teaching* is fundamental to the missional church that is sent. Trinitarian reality as the primal curriculum of the church's teaching pivots on the twin claims (a) that the historical person of Jesus is the embodiment and disclosure of God's true character, and (b) that Jesus' spirit continues to infuse this community (and the world) after his departure from the earth. This mandating text at the close of Matthew already recognizes, in the earliest church, that knowledge of the tradition is fundamental to mission; ignorance of the tradition will make mission either impossible or undertaken for the wrong reasons.

6. The difficult and demanding task is to complete the sequence from Old Testament to New Testament to early church by trying to line out what the *sending* now may mean to us in our circumstance. It is clear that the sending is not to another place on the assumption that some places have already been "won over" and other places remain to be "taken." That, of course, was the old assumption of mission that was characteristically "foreign" mission, as it was uncritically assumed that the home base was "secure" for the Gospel. Rather, the sending means to be dispatched as *alternative in every place* where anti-creation powers rule, dispatched there to talk the talk and to walk the walk, to talk and walk the truth that the legitimate power of governance belongs to the One who authorizes restoration of what belongs rightly—at the outset and at the finish—only to God in any case. That is, the sending is to be understood as *alternative community* in the midst of conventional communities.

- To enact alternative community in the midst of conventional communities is *highly conflictual* as it was for Moses and for Jesus in his own life, as indeed it was for the early church. The powers of the conventional have acute antennas for the ways in which status quo reality is thwarted and called into question by any alternative.
- Enactment of alternative community requires *intentionality* sustained by carefully embraced and regularly practiced disciplines, so that discipleship is a *sine qua non* for mission.
- This counter-community has as its core task the *naming and confrontation of alien spiritual powers* that govern conventional society into which we are all, in many ways, inducted.[4]
- These alien spiritual powers, however, characteristically are manifested as *socio-political-economic powers,* so that religious and political-economic issues are always "both-and," both spiritual and political-economic, never "either-or." This "both-and" reality in turn means that the old quarrel between evangelism and social action is a cheap, misinformed argument. It is precisely the talk of the evangel that matches the walk of action in the world on behalf of the new governance that is proclaimed in the evangel.
- Most of us recruited into the alternative community who seek to recruit others into the alternative community are ourselves *profoundly ambivalent* about the matter; we . . . liberals and conservatives . . . vacillate in every way we can that is not too obvious or too shameful. We try to keep the ambiguity in our own lives hidden, discrete, and well-mannered, but the acknowledgment of that double-mindedness is likely the beginning point for both discipleship and evangelism.

Having said all of that, I submit that the news of a restored creation is *counter* to a system of meaning and power that I term technological, therapeutic, military consumerism that in our society unrelentingly offers a total worldview that comprehends all and allows no opening for any alternative. This dominant mode of power and meaning is a way of rendering reality that silences "the news" and voids the One who is the subject of our "news":

- *technological,* the reduction of life's choices to technological options in which critical voices of alternative are screened out and eliminated as thinkable alternatives. Thus techno-speak can allow no room for the slippery, dramatic Character who is at the core of the church's news.

- *therapeutic,* the assumption that our goal in life is to live a pain-free, stress-free, undisturbed life of convenience. It is worth noticing that most of the ads on television are aimed at this elusive and impossible goal that stands deeply opposed to any news that has a cross at its center.
- *military,* the deployment of immense forces, funded by massive resources, to protect an entitled advantage in the world that is committed to an unsustainable standard of living. Such militarism, moreover, saturates the image-making of our society, all the way from ads to military cinema that creates an environment in which imagination is aimed at entitled privilege protected by brutal force that entertains not a shred of self-doubt.
- *consumerist,* the deep and unexamined assumption that "more" of whatever will make us safer and happier, a claim difficult to maintain when one ponders the outcome of massive consumerism that is matched by pervasive unhappiness and profound insecurity.

I submit that to characterize our culture as marked by an ideology of technological-therapeutic-consumerism—to which all of us subscribe in some serious way—is to mark a primal mission context for the evangel. In that world, the mission to be enacted by those under discipline is to cure, raise the dead, cleanse, and cast out demons, make disciples, teach, and baptize.

So consider:

> The calling God calls.
> The sending God sends.

This God calls and sends because God the creator intends that the world will again be free and able and competent to be God's abundant creation. That prospect, however, requires breaking the grip of alien powers that impede the fullness of creation. It is the intention of the creator, we confess, that the kingdom of this world should become the kingdom of our God who is the creator. The New Testament version of that claim is of course that the coming rule of our God will be the coming rule of his Messiah (Rev. 11:15).

I submit that the called and sent in our time have a mandate not unlike that of Abraham, Moses, and not unlike that of the disciples of Jesus, because the task of the talk and the walk is in every time and place fundamentally the same.

III

This lining out of biblical material now permits some clarity about our twin themes. First it allows us to identify theological presuppositions for discipleship and evangelism:

1. That God calls and sends with authority attests to our common conviction that this God is entitled to such imperatives among us, that is, acts with appropriate authority in calling and sending.

2. The God who calls and sends is the God of the good news, the one who created the world and calls it "good," the one who in Israel is manifested through wonders of emancipation and sustenance, wonders that constitute the dazzling miracles of Israel's doxologies, the one evidenced in Jesus of Nazareth who caused the blind to see, the lame to walk, the lepers to be cleansed, the dead to be raised, the poor to rejoice (Luke 7:22). The God who calls and sends has a long history of miracles of transformative goodness.

3. This God of creation and redemption, of newness and transformation, is a God with a concrete intent for the world, an intention of well-being that is articulated in quite concrete mandates and commandments, one who will be obeyed by those who offer praise.

4. This God who calls and sends is the originator, sponsor, and advocate for *shalom* in all the world, and summons creatures of all sorts to join in the enactment of that *shalom*.

5. It is clear that this God of the Gospel, evidenced in miracles and voiced in imperatives, is a counter-force in the world, a counter to all of the powers of death and negation that operate in every zone of creaturely reality. God calls that we should disengage from those powers to which we have tacitly sworn allegiance and sends us to confront, struggle with, and defeat those powers for the sake of God's counter-will in the world.

6. The calling and sending of God place us regularly in crisis, because (a) we do not want to disengage from the powers of negation to which we are deeply inured, and (b) we do not want to struggle against those mighty powers. Thus a willing response to God's call and sending, in praise and obedience, entails sustained, disciplined, concrete intentionality.

It is the character, reality, will, and purpose of God that propels us into a crisis of discipleship and evangelism. It is to be noted that the dominant script of our society wants to silence the voice of this God of miracle and imperative. Where the dominant script of our time and place can eliminate God, moreover, the possibility of discipleship and the capacity for evangelism evaporate, because it is only the option of the good news that produces ground and opportunity for either discipleship or evangelism.

The preceding discussion of biblical material also allows us to reconsider the terms that concern us, discipleship and evangelism, more deeply in the church in our time and place.

Discipleship. It is clear that discipleship is not just a nice notion of church membership or church education, but it entails a resituating of our lives. The disciples of Jesus are the ones who follow their master and who are able to follow their master because they have been instructed in his way of life, both his aim and his practice of embodying that aim. Note well that the disciple is one who is in sync with the master-teacher, a profoundly undemocratic notion, for the relation consists in yielding, submitting, relinquishing to the will and purpose of another.

Discipleship fundamentally entails a set of disciplines, habits, and practices that are undertaken as regular, concrete, daily practices. Such daily disciplines are not very exciting or immediately productive, but like the acquiring of any new competence, require such regimen, not unlike the learning of a new language by practicing the paradigm of verbs, not unlike the learning of piano by practicing the scales, not unlike the maintenance of good health by tenacity in jogging, not unlike every intentional habit that makes new dimensions of life possible. The church is a community engaged in disciplines that make following the master-teacher possible and sustainable.

There is no clear inventory of such workable disciplines, but let me name a few. We may begin with the constants of the early church in the book of Acts:

> They devoted themselves to the apostles' teaching and fellowship, to the breaking of bread and the prayers. (Acts 2:42)

The four disciplines of the early church are undertaken immediately upon baptismal entry into the alternative community, and become the basis for the startling missional activity in the narratives that follow. Thus the disciplines stand exactly between the entry of baptism and the mounting of mission. The practices are the following:

- *Teaching:* instruction into the tradition. We know from 1 Cor. 11:25, according to Paul, that the tradition to be learned and transmitted concerns especially the practices of the Eucharist and the most succinct assertion of the crucifixion and resurrection of Jesus. A baptized church is a studying church.

- *Fellowship:* The church is a face-to-face community of people who are together for good stretches of life, for whom company with other believers is enjoyable and important. The pragmatic reason for this practice is that resistance and alternative are not possible alone, a point long known in the twelve-step programs.

- *Breaking of bread:* Nothing is so elemental as solidarity in eating, where we are bodily engaged with each other.

- *Prayer:* Prayer is the regular communal act of ceding one's life and our common life over to the Real Subject of the "news." We may imagine, further, that these prayers of the church include table prayers, the church's most intimate practice of creation theology wherein we marvel at the inscrutable production of bread, a gift freely given to us.

A second version of early church discipline is "prayer and fasting" (see Mark 9:29). I have already mentioned *prayer.* It may interest us that some manuscripts on this narrative of Jesus couple, along with prayer, *fasting,* as a precondition of the power to heal and transform. Fasting is essentially an alien notion in much of our Reformed tradition, because we shun visible spiritual practices and because we affirm the goodness of life. If, however, we think of fasting as a breaking of the vicious addictive cycles of loyalty to a consumer society, we may think again about prominent forms of addiction—notably television—that may admit of disciplined disengagement.

To these I would add that in current discussion, the *recovery of Sabbath* as a day of disengagement from the power of production and consumption may be important. I have noted of late connections made by Jewish scholars between Sabbath and stewardship—Sabbath as relinquishment of control over my life and stewardship as a recognition that life is not our own.

The most characteristic *neighbor practices* of the Christian life are to be understood as acutely countercultural, especially *generosity, compassion,* and *forgiveness.* The daily commitment to such practices is grounded, I have no doubt, in study, prayer, and fellowship. The practices themselves, however, are profoundly countercultural in a society that is deeply lacking in the elemental ingredients of common humanness. These practices amount to a deep challenge to dominant assumptions in our culture. No one has written more eloquently on such disciplines than has Wendell Berry. In his most recent novel, *Jayber Crow*, Berry writes of Troy, a young man on the make who has completely swallowed the dominant ethic of self-promotion and self-sufficiency. After presenting Troy in all his shamelessness, Berry contrasts him with his old-fashioned parents-in-law, Della and Athey, of whom he writes:

> They were a sight to see, Della and Athey were, in their vigorous years. They had about them a sort of intimation of abundance, as though, like magicians, they might suddenly fill the room with tomatoes, onions, turnips, summer squashes, and ears of corn drawn from their pockets. Their place had about it that quality of bottomless fecundity, its richness both in evidence and in reserve.[5]

This old couple practiced the disciplines of abundance and generosity that had become second nature to them. These disciplines are crucial in the world that Troy inhabits, for Berry says of Troy, "He thought the farm existed to serve and enlarge him."[6]

I make two additional points on disciplines: First, it is clear that these disciplines, if taken seriously, are immensely inconvenient. But of course that is part of their purpose in a culture that imagines it need never be inconvenienced. The disciplines function to inconvenience us enough that we become conscious, self-conscious, and intentionally aware of who we are and what we are doing with our lives. In writing of Jewish practices of Sabbath, kosher, circumcision and the other marks of Jewishness, Jacob Neusner concludes that the reason Jews engage in such practices is in order that they may every day imagine that they are Jews.[7] Neusner judges that if Jews fail to engage in such concrete acts of imagination, they will soon cease to be Jews. *Mutatis mutandis,* it is now the case that Christians in our society must, in a like way, engage in such imaginative acts or we shall in our culture soon cease to notice our baptism. I submit that only those who are inconvenienced enough to be intentional will have any energy for mission.

Second, even in a consumer society (or perhaps especially in a consumer society), discipline is not unknown, even if we avoid such a demanding label for it. It is the purpose of the dreary repetitions of TV ads to "brand" us in loyalty. Thus, for example, in Atlanta it becomes a discipline, a regular act of bodily loyalty, to drink Coke and to shun the evil seductions of Pepsi. Or for myself, the discipline of watching *The West Wing* is enough that I organize my day, even my week, to honor that commitment with regularity. The point is, of course, that disciplines that cohere with dominant cultural assumptions do not seem like demanding disciplines, but are only the "givens" of convenience. It is, on the contrary, the disciplines of counterculture that seem to us demanding, because they break deliberately with the seeming givens of dominant faith.

Evangelism. The term "evangel" is a rendering of "Gospel" that is in turn a rendering of "news, good news." The most succinct usages of the term in the Old Testament are in Isaiah:

> Get you up to a high mountain,
>   O Zion, *herald of good tidings*;
> lift up your voice with strength,
>   O Jerusalem, *herald of good tidings*,
>   lift it up, do not fear;
> say to the cities of Judah,
>   "Here is your God!" (Isa. 40:9)

> How beautiful upon the mountain
>   are the feet of the messenger who announces peace,
> who *brings good news*,
>   who announces salvation,
>   who says to Zion, "Your God reigns." (Isa. 52:7)

In both of these cases, the phrasing, "Here is your God," "Your God reigns" is gospel talk. The two statements assert that the God of Israel whom Babylon had silenced and voided is back in play. The evangel asserts the revivification of this God long dormant:

> The Lord is the everlasting God,
>   the Creator of the ends of the earth.
> He does not faint or grow weary;
>   his understanding is unsearchable. (Isa. 40:28)

> Now after John was arrested, Jesus came to Galilee, proclaiming the good news of God, and saying, "The time is fulfilled, and the kingdom of God has come near; repent, and believe in the good news." (Mark 1:14-15)

The talk of Gospel is a summons to notice the announcement of new governance. The walk of Gospel is to act *as though* the new rule of God were in effect, though there continues to be much data to the contrary.

Thus *the talk* and *the walk* of the news constitute an act of resistance and the embrace of an alternative, even when the ground for the alternative is readily doubted in dominant culture. The "as though" proviso is an act of defiance and refusal, as in these texts:

> *Though* the fig tree does not blossom,
>   and no fruit is on the vines;
> *though* the produce of the olive fails,
>   and the fields yield no food;
> *though* the flock is cut off from the fold,
>   and there is no herd in the stalls,
> *yet* I will rejoice in the Lord;
>   I will exult in the God of my salvation. (Hab. 3:17-18)

> I mean, brothers and sisters, the appointed time has grown short; from now on, let even those who have wives be *as though* they had none, and those who mourn *as though* they were not mourning, and those who rejoice *as though* they were not rejoicing, and those who buy *as though* they had no possessions, and those who deal with the world *as though* they had no dealings with it. For the present form of this world is passing away. (1 Cor. 7:29-31)

As discipleship is not simply church membership, so evangelism is not simply church recruitment of new members. Evangelism is the invitation and summons to resituate our talk and our walk according to the reality of this God, a reality not easily self-evident in our society. The call of the gospel includes the negative assertion that the technological-therapeutic-militaristic-consumerist world is phony and is not to be trusted or obeyed, and the positive claim that an alternative way in the world is legitimated by and appropriate to the new governance of the God who is back in town.

We should not be too grandiose about the alternative. There are indeed occasional times appropriate to spectacular evangelical assertion. On most days in most places, however, the talk and the walk of good news become the slow, steady engagement with and practice of God's will for *generosity, compassion,* and *forgiveness* in a world organized against those practices. Such practices are undertaken (a) in the conviction that such acts on the spot make an important difference to the condition of the world and (b) on the further conviction that the effect of such testimonial living is cumulative and will prevail, because such practice is rooted in the reality of the Messiah of whom we confess,

> Christ has died,
> Christ is risen,
> Christ will come again.

Does it strike you as it does me—?

Does it strike you that *denominational structures and programs* tend to be remote from such deeply rooted, biblical notions of discipleship and evangelism? Well, yes. We have been a long time getting this way, gathering power over time, so that much denominationalism has become a defense of old patterns of power, ill suited to the realities of our faith. The mandate then is for denominations, in structure and in program . . . and in the lives of those who shape such structures and programs, to ponder the extent to which our practices witness not to the God crucified and risen but to the constraints of technological, therapeutic, militaristic consumerism.

Does it strike you that *congregational life* for the most part is remote from such deeply rooted, biblical understandings of discipleship and evangelism? Well, yes. Much congregational life has so fuzzied the claims of the Gospel in order to accommodate to culture that the church, only with difficulty, can be a truth-teller in the face of denial and a hope-teller in the face of despair.

It is clear now, is it not, that this is a new time in the church. It is a time when many people, with deep ambiguity, want an alternative with a deep sense that dominant patterns of life in our society simply are not working. There is a hunch and a wish, guarded to be sure, that the church should let the news, with all its implications, have its say. Such a say depends upon preachers who risk, supported by congregations who will stand by in solidarity.

Does it strike you that *theological seminaries* are remote from the deeply rooted biblical understanding of discipleship and evangelism? Well, yes. Seminaries have spent a long time getting as they are, paying heed to the entire intellectual tradition of the Enlightenment in its conservative-scholastic mode and in its liberal-evolutionary mode, lusting after university prestige, too geared to "ideas" and not to practices. This is a time, however, when seminaries are at the brink of relearning, not to dumb down, but to see learning rooted in the news, and teaching linked intimately to practice.

There are many things about which to despair concerning denominations, congregations, and seminaries. That ground for despair, to be sure, has nothing to do with the liberal-conservative disputes now so vigorous in the church, because the same accommodations have been embraced across the theological spectrum, by both conservatives and liberals. We have, in all these quarters, been careless enough in submission to dominant powers to engage in self-indulgence to the addictions of the technological, therapeutic, militaristic, consumerist society.

That we meet to think about these demanding themes is itself a sign among us. To be *called out* is a countercultural summons; to be *sent back* is a countercultural practice. It is a two-way deal, always called *to disengage* and *to embrace,* always sent to risk in *praise* and *obedience.* This is not easy stuff; it is nonetheless the true stuff, the stuff about the true God and our true selves before that God.

The call is a summons, but a summons away from a world too hard. Listen to the call that is a genuine alternative to life in a distorted world that can produce joy or well-being:

> "Come to me, all you that are weary and are carrying heavy burdens, and I will give you rest. Take my yoke upon you, and learn from me; for I am gentle and humble in heart, and you will find rest for your souls. For my yoke is easy, and my burden is light." (Matt. 11:28-30)

The sending is risky and to be celebrated. Lest we congratulate ourselves too much on being sent, here is Jesus' word on the return of the evangelists who report success:

> The seventy returned with joy, saying, "Lord, in your name even the demons submit to us!" He said to them, "I watched Satan fall from heaven like a flash of lightning. See, I have given you authority to tread on snakes and scorpions, and over all the power of the enemy; and nothing will hurt you. Nevertheless, do not rejoice at this, that the spirits submit to you, but rejoice that *your names are written in heaven.*" (Luke 10:17-20)

The outcome of the news is that the ones under discipline have their names written in heaven . . . utterly safe, utterly loved, and utterly treasured, where moths do not consume and where thieves do not break in to steal. This is a good destiny offered and promised to the ones called and sent.

Options for Creatureliness

Consumer or Citizen

A remarkable turn has happened in the theological interpretation of the Christian Old Testament. Through the first part of the twentieth century, theological interpretation was dominated by an accent upon "God's Mighty Deeds in History," together with an intentional disregard of the theme of "creation."[1] This one-sided account—instigated indirectly by Karl Barth and given primary impetus by Gerhard von Rad—was in response to the brutalizing ideology of German National Socialism with its distorted "theology of creation" expressed in its "Blood and Soil" mantra.[2] In that crisis situation, it was relatively easy to find a warrant for "history against nature" in the more ancient polemic of Israel against "Canaanite fertility religion." That polemical contrast came to dominate Christian (especially Protestant) theological interpretation. It is not necessary to polemicize against such an interpretive practice but only to appreciate the great extent to which that interpretive angle, like every interpretive angle, is context-determined.

It was not until the 1970s that interpretation, led by Claus Westermann, Frank Cross, and Hans Heinrich Schmid, began to break free of the older German church struggle and to move in new directions, with explicit reference to creation as a primal theme of theology in the Christian Old Testament.[3] The reason for this interpretive turn are many and complex, but it is at least indirectly related to the emergence of a feminist hermeneutic and to a growing awareness of an environmental crisis. In what follows I will explore some dimensions of a freshly articulated creation theology and consider the ways in which this fresh interpretive accent may be drawn closely toward the contemporary crisis of society and of interpretation.

I

"Creation theology" must of course begin with reference to the Creator, the generative Agent of the world who is known, named, confessed, and celebrated in the doxologies of Israel. Attestation to this God in Israel's ancient text is known, of course, in Genesis 1–2, and more powerfully and poignantly in the Psalms and in exilic Isaiah, even though these several texts are not as popularly known as the opening chapters of Genesis.

The Creator, attested by Israel, is the one who wills and enacts the world as an ordered place of life, and who endows the world with the power for life and well-being, *shalom*.[4] The Creator, in will and in act, combines unrivaled power and immeasurable goodness to evoke an ordered world of well-being that is not possible without that will and that is endlessly sustained by and dependent upon that will.

The characteristic way by which Christian theology speaks of this initiatory, sustaining power of life is "providence," a will and purpose that faithfully works in, with, and under the world for the good of the world.[5] While that will for the good of the world is hidden from view, it is nonetheless decisive for the life and future of the world, and so is brought to speech in Israel's most extravagant doxologies. The term "providence," as Karl Barth has nicely observed, derives from *pro-video*, to see for, to see before, to "provide" in prospect all that the world might require for its joyous life and secure well-being.[6] Thus creation faith is an affirmation that the world lives, is sustained, and prospers because of God's capacity to *provide* all that is needed.

Now that large theological theme of providence comes to be concrete when we ask what it is that God provides for the well-being of the world. While we may readily say that God provides "all that is needed," we may say more specifically that the Creator God is a nurturer and nourisher who provides food that the creation and all its creatures may have daily sustenance of food that the earth gives for all the creatures.[7] The elegant liturgy of Genesis 1 asserts that all kinds of growing things produce food, "each according to its kind." Indeed, God has formed and ordered the world so that it is a gift that keeps on giving:

> For as the rain and the snow come down from heaven,
> and do not return there until they have watered the earth,

> making it bring forth and sprout,
> giving seed to the sower and bread to the eater. . . . (Isa. 55:10)

The deep claim of creation and the large theme of providence come down to the daily amazement that the earth produces and all of the creatures—including human creatures—eat the bread of life that is always gift and never production.

The wonder of food, moreover, is matched by the culminating festival of sabbath in Gen. 2:1-4a, a liturgic cessation of all productivity so that the creatures, in imitation of God, may be at peaceable rest. They may be on the receiving end of the generosity of the Creator, unanxious about sustenance, unconcerned about food, trustfully at east in God's good, providential abundance.

This creation faith, I suggest, comes to the specificity of the daily act of eating:

- Israel's doxologies are endlessly amazed at the gift of food that the creation keeps providing:

> You cause the grass to grow for the cattle,
>   and plants for people to use,
> to bring forth food from the earth,
>   and wine to gladden the human heart,
> oil to make the face shine,
>   and bread to strengthen the human heart. (Ps. 104:14-15)

Israel names the staples of human existence: food, wine, oil, bread.

- Israel's doxologies in praise of the Creator sound like table prayers, the gladness of creation come to rest in daily food:

> These all look to you
>   to give them their food in due season;
> when you give it to them, they gather it up;
>   when you open your hand,
> they are filled with good things. *ḥesed* . . . (Ps. 104:27-28)

> The eyes of all look to you,
>   and you give them their food in due season.

> You open your hand,
>> satisfying the desire of every living thing. . . . (Ps. 145:15-16)

- The church, in its most elemental prayer, engages in creation theology, knowing that life in the world is not autonomous and is not automatically guaranteed:

> Give us this day our daily bread. . . . (Matt. 6:11)

- The church, in its most characteristic sacramental sign, partakes of the gifts of creation and finds God's presence peculiarly and concretely in bread and wine—the staples of peasant food—bread and wine blessed and broken.

The faith of Israel and of the church is given its most elemental, daily, concrete, material articulation in the act of eating. The faithful, moreover, never touch bread or wine or any food, except it is known to be the strange generosity of God's providence come to abide at our very table.

II

My theme, however, is *creature*. I have spoken of the faithful, generous, sustaining, nourishing work of the Creator in order that I might consider the creature who is *the one fed*. My entry into "creature" as the one *who is fed* is in two quite distinct ways. First, I want to consider some texts in the book of Deuteronomy with reference to creatureliness. That I can begin here is a sign of the profound change in interpretive perspective that I have already mentioned, because Deuteronomy is a book of Torah linked to Moses and rooted in Sinai, all some distance, scholarship has thought, from creation. It is astonishing to notice, however, that the corpus of the commandments of Moses in Deuteronomy 12–25 is framed by creation theology, for the commands of Deuteronomy are intended for the new land of promise that flows with milk and honey, that is a specific land that bears all the generative, generous marks of God's abundance. In Deuteronomy 8, as one introduction to the commandments, we find a reflection on *land* as God's generative *earth;* we are treated to critical creation theology.[8]

In vv. 7-9, the text celebrates the rich abundance of the new land that is filled with sustaining resources:

> For the LORD your God is bringing you into a good land, a land with flowing streams, with springs and underground waters welling up in valleys and hills, a land of wheat and barley, of vines and fig trees and pomegranates, a land of olive trees and honey, a land where you may eat bread without scarcity, where you will lack nothing, a land whose stones are iron and from whose hills you may mine copper.

And then in v. 10, Moses offers the great triad of verbs that are to guide Israel's receptivity and response as creatures:

> You shall *eat* and *be full* and *bless* the LORD your God for the good land that he has given you.

- *You shall eat.* You shall exercise your most elemental, God-given function. Eating is an act of receptivity that acknowledges that creatures, especially Israelites, are not self-sufficient, but must be given food.
- *You shall be satiated.* Eat all you want! There is nothing parsimonious about the gift of the new land or the intent of the gift-giving Creator. There is more than enough! Israel in the new land will be fully satisfied with the produce of the land, with no unmet need or desire.
- *You shall bless* the LORD your God for the good land that he has given you.

This third verb, after "eat," "be satisfied," is quite remarkable. "Eat" and "be satiated" focus upon Israel's well-being. The action, however, is not completed until the third verb that turns Israel's satiated attention back to the Creator God. Israel is fully satisfied by the second verb, but is not so satiated as to refuse the Creator.

"Bless the LORD your God" is an odd phrase, because we usually think God blesses Israel. How does Israel, the receiver, "bless" God, the giver? We say it familiarly and without thinking,

> Bless the LORD, O my soul, and all that is within me, bless his holy name. . . . (Ps. 103:1)

We may take the term "bless" to mean in a generic sort of way to "praise, thanks, acknowledge, rejoice in," all adequate enough. Likely there is in the term "bless" a more dynamic notion that means to transmit energy from one life to another, so that Israel—fed and satiated—is to give back to the Creator in gladness something of the life-force that God first grants. (On the matter of Israel giving to YHWH, Ps. 50:9-13 suggests offerings are unwelcome; yet Ps. 51:19 commends them. Ps. 22:3, moreover, suggests that Israel's praise supports YHWH's divine throne.) The articulation of the three verbs together cannot be over-appreciated. Israel, in its anticipated prosperity in the new "earth" (land), knows that "eat and be satisfied" are not completely without a turn to the giver, a turn that fends off every illusion of self-sufficiency.

The verbal sequence in slightly emended form is reiterated negatively in vv. 12-18. The first two verbs are in proper sequence in v. 12:

> When you have *eaten* and are *satisfied* . . .

So far so good. These verbs are explicated by filling out the coming satiation in detail:

> When you have built fine houses and live in them, and when your herds and flocks have multiplied, and your silver and gold is multiplied, and all that you have is multiplied. . . . (vv. 12b-13)

Satiation is not just about eating, but concerns the entire range of economic prosperity.[9] But then Moses proposed a substitute third verb:

> Do not *exalt* yourself, *forgetting* the LORD your God. . . . (v. 14)

The verbs "exalt yourself" and "forget" are reinforced in v. 17:

> *Do not say* to yourself, "My power and the might of my own hand have gotten me this wealth."

This text knows that the first two verbs, "eat and be satiated," set up an immense seduction, the chance to imagine autonomy, self-sufficiency, and self-congratulation. The available third verb may not "bless" but "*exalt self, forget, say* to self," all self-absorbed self references that invite no turn back to the creator with "bless." The negative options for a third verb, here named and immediately rejected in the text, have caused the proper third verb to be held in abeyance until v. 18:

> But *remember* the LORD your God. . . .

Here the third verb is not "bless," as in v. 10, but its very rough cognate "remember." Eating and satiation may lead to self-regarding amnesia. But not in faithful Israel. In Israel *eating* and *satiation* lead to *remembering,* naming, and referencing the God who makes life possible as creator.

In the positive sequence of v. 10 and the more complex negative sequence of vv. 12-18, the first two verbs are consistent: *eat* and be *satiated.* That is what the Creator intends and what the creature enjoys. Everything turns on the third verb, either *bless and remember* or *exalt self, forget, say to one's self.* The creature has the deep chance of glad, grateful *responsiveness* to the Creator or *self-sufficiency* in which the Giver of food and satiation is disregarded in a spasm of self-regard.

This challenge of creation theology, at the beginning of Deuteronomy, is matched at the end of the book in 31:20:

> For when I have brought them into the land flowing with milk and honey, which I promised on oath to their ancestors, and they have *eaten* their *fill* and *grown fat,* they will turn to other gods and serve them, despising me and breaking my covenant.

The first two verbs are the same: *eat* and *be satiated.* But the third verb, now an indictment of failed Israel that has rejected creatureliness, is "*grown fat.*" This is satiation pushed to an extremity of self-indulgence that becomes a narcotic against acknowledged, responsive creatureliness. The outcome of such numbed self-absorption is a turn away from the Creator God who is no longer blessed or remembered, a "turn to other gods" in violation of the Creator's one requirement, a turn that leads to the *despising* of the creator and the *violation* of a covenantal relation of generosity and gratitude.

It is likely that Deuteronomy 31 is a belated reflection upon Israel when Israel has forfeited its blessed, luxurious land, so says this text, because of its failure to take the land as gift. The outcome is a systematic abandonment of Sabbath in an endlessly restless self-securing that inevitably ends in loss of self, loss of land, and finally loss of viable creatureliness. Moses concludes:

> For I know that after my death you will surely act corruptly, turning
> aside from the way I have commanded you. In time to come trouble
> will befall you, because you will do what is evil in the sight of the LORD,
> provoking him to anger through the work of your hands. (31:29)

The three verbs are an immense affirmation of the creator and of the status
of the creature. An emended third verb, however, leads to loss of the very
provisions the Creator intends for Israel.

III

My second access point to creatureliness is from a very different angle,
remote from Deuteronomy. On November 1, 1972, Mike Royko, that irascible Chicago theologian, wrote a column about the Vietnam War.[10] The
point of his essay was that U.S. people are so preoccupied, as he put it, with
"pro football, baseball, the Wide World of Sports and the late movie" that
they neglect the bold war critics like Sen. William Fulbright, Sen. Wayne
Morse, and Dr. Benjamin Spock, and follow like sheep the easy slogans of
John Wayne and Bob Hope.[11]

What interested me in particular about the column is that Royko contrasts the book of Jacqueline Susann, *The Valley of the Dolls*, that he terms
"lurid trash" with the books of Bernard Fall that are, he says, "brilliant
studies of Vietnam and the war."

The sales of Susann's book reached ten million copies and one of Fall's
only as much as 55,000, indicating where public attention has been focused.
Warning against such preoccupied cynicism and self-indulgence, Royko
also takes early aim at Ralph Nader:

> It's interesting that during all those years, the one person who could
> rock the national boat and not be hated was Ralph Nader. That's
> because he didn't ask about the blood that was being shed in Vietnam.
> He questioned whether the color TV sets on which we saw it being
> shed were worth the money we paid.[12]

And then he says of the Nader of that era:

> He treated us as "*consumers*" and demanded that we get our money's
> worth, and we liked that. But those who treated us as *citizens,* with all
> the responsibilities that involves, were told to shut up and stop causing

trouble. It's more comfortable being consumers, and patting our bellies, than being citizens and having to flex our brains.

That was in 1972. Since then the heat of Vietnam has long cooled (I think), Jacqueline Susann is mostly forgotten and displaced by Danielle Steele, and Ralph Nader has moved on, perhaps to serious citizen questions. What lingers for me is Royko's nice contrast between *consumers* who "pat our bellies" in self-indulgence and *citizens* who "flex our brains." (I understand that the term "citizen" is an anachronism in the political frame of the Old Testament, but the word pair is an adequate articulation for the rhetoric of Deuteronomy already mentioned.)

- *Consumers* are those who, after they "eat and are satiated," use as a third verb variously "exalt self, forget, say to self, grow fat, serve other gods," a collage of self-sufficiency, self-indulgence, self-congratulation, self-reference—autonomous and automatic—an ocean of self, characteristically growing fat.
- *Citizens* are those who, after they "eat and are satiated," have as a third verb "bless, remember," that is, they turn life and satiation back to the Giver in order to acknowledge the gift, the return of given life to the giver of life, to situate self in the world of gift and demand well beyond self. In that transaction of return, the self has a role to play but never autonomous, never automatic, never guaranteed, never taken for granted, always engaged with the reference beyond self who commands, creates and guarantees.

I cite Mike Royko because his word pair, "consumer/citizen," is an effective way of providing contemporary contact to the most elemental options for creatureliness that are available, options that are as early as Moses and as recent as Ralph Nader. The option is one made liturgically and explicitly, ordinarily and implicitly, politically and intentionally, a great either/or about one's locus in a creation that is rooted in generosity, experienced as abundance, uncompromising in limit and in demand. Nowhere is that gift of abundance and generosity more palpable than in our present, unprecedented U.S. economy that we are pleased to call "global." Consequently, nowhere is the option of "consumer or citizen" more urgent and inescapable than in this very economy that in abundance outruns the best doxological dreams of ancient Israel.

IV

Keeping in mind creatureliness—having received life from a creator of abundance, generosity, and fidelity—and focusing on Royko's nice pair of "consumer/citizen," I want now to line out the ways in which *options for creatureliness* appear everywhere in the Old Testament. I engage in this exercise because I believe that options for creatureliness pertain precisely to the crisis in our society that is manifest economically, that has deep theological rootage in the reality of creatureliness, and that has immediate resonance in a practice of spirituality that stands strong against the powers of scarcity and anxiety. My point is to exhibit the claim that a biblical understanding of creatureliness is a reference from which to rethink the deep crisis of the emerging global economy. That rethinking for some will be because the biblical text is authoritative revelation that compels attention. For others, that biblical text summons by its *gravitas* as a lingering voice from the depth of our cultural past. Either way, this text tradition invites an engagement.

A. The signature, defining moment in the life of ancient Israel is *the meeting at Mt. Sinai.* Everything in the Torah is arranged to move toward the mountain and to move from the mountain. The God who meets Israel at the mountain, moreover, is the creator of heaven and earth. Indeed, in Israelite discernment, the story of God's life is the trek from the creation doxology of Gen. 1 to the meeting with Israel at Sinai. This God at Sinai affirms as Creator, "The whole earth is mine" (Exod. 19:5).

At Sinai, however, the creator of heaven and earth came to do a very particular thing, namely, to make covenant with Israel, to bind God's own life to this particular people, to give God's own life for the sake of this community, and to draw Israel in obligation and in obedience so that Israel's whole life would be lived toward God, creator of heaven and earth.[13] In that strange binding at Sinai, something happened in the story of God and in the story of politics that has never happened before in the entire history of the world, a political community created with a loyalty to a holy God who makes all other political loyalties penultimate. That ultimate authority, moreover, makes demands upon Israel. In the end, however, it is clear that at Sinai the self-giving risk of a God who takes a new way in the world far outruns the demands that this God makes upon Israel.

This covenant emerges as an alternative practice of power. Perhaps you know that scholars have spent great energy locating antecedents to the covenant of Sinai, perhaps as early as Hittite political treaties or later in

Assyrian documents.[14] There are indeed antecedents to the covenant at Sinai and those antecedents are all political. It is, however, this hidden transaction at the mountain that permits an extrapolated political formulation to take on the ultimacy of theological definition. That ultimacy places God at the center of the political process as a critical principle against every absolutism.

It is not yet proper at Sinai to term Israelites "citizens," as they are still subjects and not citizens, making Royko's terms still premature. The development of this covenant, moreover, is complex and partly hidden, but we may notice two dramatic derivative developments. The first of these concerns the traditions of Calvinism with particular reference to Heinrich Bullinger (1504–1575), Zwingli's successor in Zürich. It is Bullinger who, in 1534, in the heat of the Reformation, wrote the treatise that transposed the biblical notion of covenant into a political theory, who advocated a federalism of power and who prepared the way for the coming revolutions of the modern period that made "citizenship" a proper term for a participant in the political community.[15] It is of course a long stretch from Sinai to Zürich and on to Paris, but the continuities are important so that we may see that "citizenship," with all the responsibilities pertaining thereto, has old covenantal rootage in Israel.

A second move, via Bullinger, is the fact that Robert Bellah not so long ago characterized the at-risk condition of U.S. society under the rubric *The Broken Covenant*.[16] Bellah's theory is that U.S. society is deeply rooted in a theological conviction, expressed as "civil religion," in which its members are committed in elemental ways to participate with each other in the development of what he later has called *The Good Society*.[17] The "brokenness" of that covenantal arrangement attests, even if negatively, to covenantal rootage. Thus Sinai, rooted in the giving of God, sets in motion the political vision of an alternative form of public power.

The God who meets Israel at Sinai is, to be sure, still something of a despot. But even that despotic propensity on the part of Israel's God shows up well when contrasted with Pharaoh, the tyrant of Egypt, antecedent ruler of Israel in the slave camp. Sinai is fundamentally a break with the Egyptian slave camp. It is to be observed about Pharaoh that there is in his Egypt no covenantal restraint, no self-giving on the part of Pharaoh in order to make covenantal bonding possible, no inchoate sense of citizenship; he is the quintessential consumer. He devours all the land and its produce. He devours the Nile, turning that river of life into a death canal

(Exod. 7:24).[18] He devours the slave community. Unfettered consumerism, absent citizenship, devours not only the produce of creation, but the sources of produce until the land is reduced to waste. Israel's departure from Egypt is risky and costly, and some immediately wanted to return to slavery. Every departure from consumerism to citizenship is a risky, costly one, the renunciation of a chance for indulgence. The Creator presides over both Egypt and Sinai, and creatureliness came to be expressed in two sharply contrasting ways in these contrasted venues. The covenantal choice is one way of being creature, a creature beloved by the Creator who loves and obeys in response.

B. The key event at Sinai is the sound of YHWH's own voice ten times in *the giving of commands*. This is, as Martin Buber says, "the commanding voice of Sinai." Israel is under command and its true mode of existence is obedience that preempts all other loyalties. That is why, at Sinai, one cannot speak yet of "citizen," for Israel is subject.

That holy action of God at Sinai, however, should not surprise. Because the one who speaks at Sinai to command Israel is the creator of heaven and earth who from the beginning commands, for creation is the realm of God's rule. Indeed God's first utterance in the Bible is command: "Let there be light," and the creatures scurry to obey (Gen. 1:3). God's first word to human creatures is command:

> Be fruitful and multiply, and fill the earth and subdue it; and have dominion over the fish of the sea and over the birds of the air and over every living thing that moves on the earth. . . . (Gen. 1:28)

In the second narrative God orders that the human creatures shall "till and keep" the garden (Gen. 2:15). Immediately after this mandate to care for the earth, God uttered to them a characteristic "thou shalt not" that anticipate the "thou shalt nots" of Sinai. God's ordering of creation is with limit, boundary, and restraint in order to make life possible:

> You may freely eat of every tree of the garden; but of the tree of the knowledge of good and evil you shall not eat, for in the day that you eat of it you shall die. . . . (Gen. 2:16-17)

It had never occurred to me before that God limits the consuming propensity of the human creatures. "Thou shalt not eat." The human creatures cannot eat everything they want to eat. They cannot indiscriminately devour the earth. For in "Thou shalt not eat," it is asserted by the Creator, "Thou shalt not be autonomous, thou shalt not be like god and pretend to have your own food supply, thou shalt not have endless indulgence."

This holy, commanding voice hardly misses a beat between the "thou shalt not" of creation and the "thou shalt not" of Sinai. For at the Sinai the Creator God speaks again.

- "Thou shalt not make graven images," a refusal to be commodified, a denial that the free rule of God can be turned into a market fetish to be bought and sold, a refusal that holiness should be reduced to manageable handleable, salable goods (Exod. 20:4).
- That same commanding voice, after declaring the holiness of God and the sanctity of the neighbor (kill, adultery, steal), culminates with the tenth assertion, "thou shalt not covet" (Exod. 20:17). This command against coveting is not a little psychology lesson about envy. It is rather the Creator's curb of acquisitiveness, the endless temptation to reduce social relations to market transactions. The specificity of the utterance concerns "your neighbor's wife, your neighbor's house," that which the neighbor treasures and which gives social standing and security, because communal transactions must respect social reality of neighbors and the *gravitas* of the community.

The Creator who prohibits *endless eating* in the garden is the voice of Sinai who curbs the *endless devouring* to which Israel is tempted as the human creatures in the garden are tempted. The Sinai term "covet" is taken up in the prophetic cadences of Israel:

> Woe to you who join house to house,
> who add field to field,
> until there is room for no one but you. . . . (Isa. 5:8)

> They covet fields and seize them;
> houses, and take them away;
> they oppress household and house,
> people and their inheritance. . . . (Mic. 2:2)

> Like a cage full of birds,
> their houses are full of treachery;

therefore they have become great and rich,
they have grown fat and sleek . . .
they do not judge with justice the cause of the orphan, to make it
    prosper,
and they do not defend the rights of the needy. . . . (Jer. 5:27-28)

It is remarkable that coveting as the consuming of the life of another is a trope that shows up, much later, in the teaching of Jesus:

- The well-known prodigal is condemned by his brother: But when this son of yours came back, who has *devoured* your property with prostitutes . . . (Luke 15:30).
- Jesus condemns the social leaders: They love to be greeted with respect in the marketplaces and to have the best seats in the synagogues and places of honor at banquets. They *devour* widows' houses . . . (Luke 20:46-47).

What a convergence: "market, synagogue, and banquets," public places of trading, worship, and eating, and all a cover for devouring without limit.

Think of the holy commands of Sinai as a decisive curb on consumerism, not yet citizenship but on the way there. The one who speaks these commands is the same one who, between Eden and Sinai, issues a command to Pharaoh: "You shall send my people free." It is a command even though we familiarly translate otherwise, an imperative that Pharaoh will not honor. This command to economic emancipation issued by YHWH to Pharaoh prepares us to think of Pharaoh's counter-commands. He is the lord of Egypt, the lord of all consumption, busy devouring and storing up, using political leverage for indulgence on the backs of nameless peasants.[19]

His commands, filtered through his bureaucracy, go like this (Exod. 5):

Get to your labors! (v. 4)
Let heavier work be laid on them. (v. 9)
Go and get straw yourselves, wherever you can find it; but your work will not be lessened in the least. (v. 11)
Complete your work, the same daily assignment as when you were given straw. (v. 13)
Make bricks! (v. 16)
Go now, and work; for no straw shall be given you, but you shall still deliver the same number of bricks. (v. 18)

The imperative of Pharaoh to the slaves is relentless. It knows no limits, no restraint, no boundary. The devouring of Israel is the command of a disordered world wherein the intent of the Creator has been voided and consumption runs wild, dependent only upon slave labor. Sinai is an alternative command en route to citizenship wherein social relations cannot be reduced to the accumulation of good. The commands of YHWH and Pharaoh offer a radical either/or to the creatures in Egypt, Pharaoh and slaves, both creatures under the command of the Creator.

C. The commanding voice if Sinai, at the center of this ten-fold utterance, issues one other command concerning *sabbath:*

> Remember the sabbath day, and keep it holy. Six days you shall labor and do all your work. But the seventh day is a sabbath to the LORD your God; you shall not do any work—you, your son or your daughter, your male or female slave, your livestock or the alien resident in your towns. (Exod. 20:8-10)

At the center of YHWH's alternative intention for creation is sabbath rest already made the defining mark of creation in Gen. 2:1-4a. Indeed, the Sinai command specifically alludes to the creation and holds together creation and covenant:

> For in six days the LORD made heaven and earth, the sea, and all that is in them, but rested the seventh day; therefore the LORD blessed the sabbath day and consecrated it. (Exod. 20:11)

Imagine! Work stoppage at the center of a theopolitical arrangement, work stoppage on behalf of ex-slaves who are to enjoy a covenantal existence that contrasts with the endless brick quotas of former days!

Out of that elemental rule for work stoppage came an entire calendar of humaneness in ancient Israel.[20] After a *seven day pause* came a *seventh year of release,* whereby poor people have a firm limit placed on their debt (Deut. 15:1-18). Moses intends that there should never form in Israel a permanent under-class. And beyond that comes *seven times seven, a Jubilee year* of land reform, for Moses intends that none in the community of the emancipated should be landless, or placeless, or homeless in a covenantal society (Leviticus 25). Covenantal times are organized in order to commit the economically advantaged to a common future with the economically marginated.

It is easy enough to discern the intent of the sabbath provision for ex-slaves. But the sabbath is also intended for ex-pharaohs. Pharaoh, it turns out, is as pressure-ridden as the slaves, feverishly engaged in accumulating and devouring, propelled by an anxiety that he does not yet have enough even though he has all.[21] Sabbath is work stoppage, but sabbath is also stoppage of the anxiety of scarcity that drives to endless accumulation and wild acquisitiveness. Moses intends to break the vicious cycles of irrational consumption, to create pause from consumption that genuinely refreshes, and that invites a return to sanity. Imagine that Sinai is precisely a political vision that breaks the devouring patterns of pharaonic consumption.

Sabbath was of course good news to the slaves and ex-slaves. It must have been a stunning surprise to Pharaoh, for there was no sabbath in Egypt, never had been, no work stoppage, no easement of quotas, no lessening of the pressure to produce. There was no pause in production for neighborly public life . . . not for slaves, but also not for Pharaoh. Pharaoh could (would?) take no break from his eating, from his acquisitiveness, because his devouring was not grounded in need or in hunger, but in an anxiety rooted in an old nightmare of scarcity: scarce resources, scarce food, scarce bricks, scarce labor pool, scarce pyramids, scarce granaries, scarce time . . . hurry, gather, save, coerce, manipulate (see Gen. 47:13-26).

The very sabbath that is good news for ex-slaves is a worrying disruption for quintessential consumers, as Amos understood so well:

> Hear this, you that trample the needy,
> and bring to ruin the poor of the land, saying,
> "When will the new moon be over
> so that we may sell grain
> and the sabbath, so that we may offer wheat for sale?" (Amos 8:4-5)

The options for creatureliness perhaps come most clearly onto focus around the sabbath, an option for yielding or controlling, for receiving or seizing, for thanking or hustling. Oddly, as Amos saw from the pages of Moses, the most strenuously propelled to nonstop work are not the hungry or the needy, but the satiated busy in selfhood of an autonomous variety.

D. One of the primary forms of participation in covenantal politics is the *capacity to cry out* in need, to address power with pain, to move those in power to attentiveness, and to expect a response of redress. This is an extraordinary feature of the social vision of Sinai, one against conventional social vision that imagines social order and social power from the top down. But then this alternative power arrangement is covenantal, deeply interactive, in which it is insisted that the powerful and the powerless are engaged in a common future. It is provided, moreover, that the voice "from below" can initiate newness, so that those in power are charged with attentive, responsive listening.[22]

In the initial extrapolation from the ten utterances at Sinai, Moses offers two specific commands for the covenantal enactment of power. The first, in Exod. 22:21-24, begins with two "thou shalt nots" that echo the ten: "You shall not wrong or oppress a resident alien, for you were aliens in the land of Egypt. You shall not abuse any widow or orphan." The prohibitions themselves put us quickly on notice that participation in this politics is very different. But then the mandate from Moses entertains the prospect of disobedience that involves oppression and abuse of the vulnerable. In light of such anticipated disobedience, a special warning is used: "If you do abuse them, when they cry out to me, I will surely heed their cry; my wrath will burn, and I will kill you with the sword, and your wives shall become widows and your children orphans." The abused and oppressed cry out. Their shrillness may reach the ear of the Holy One who is especially attuned to such a cry. The cry will lead to divine intervention that will cause the demise of the abusers. Remarkably, it is the cry of the resident alien, the widow, or the orphan that triggers YHWH's decisive engagement.

The second provision, in Exod. 22:25-27, offers protection for debtors from exploitative creditors; creditors who, we may assume, want to foil the communal process in their accumulation of surplus wealth. This provision has three directives:

1. Do not act like a creditor, for this is not a debtor but a neighbor.
2. Do not exact interest on the loan.
3. Do not keep a coat in collateral overnight.

All three provisions are designed to re-situate the economic reality of debt in a neighborly context.

Again the provision entertains disobedience to the requirements and, as in the previous case, authorizes a cry from exploited debtors: "And if your neighbor cries out to me, I will listen, for I am compassionate." The relation of debtor and creditor is reshaped by the attentive reality of YHWH, the Great Equalizer as partisan to the debtor. But that Great Equalization is triggered by the cry from below.

This social theory of power organized by cry is engaged on large scale in the narrative of Exod. 2:23-25: "After a long time the king of Egypt died. The Israelites groaned under their slavery, and cried out. Out of the slavery their cry for help rose up to God. God heard their groaning. . . ." This is the same cry from the slave camp that evokes YHWH's exodus activity. In this transaction, Pharaoh is the abusive neighbor against whom YHWH intervenes savagely and decisively. (The language and activity of YHWH on behalf of Israel indicate violent brutality; while problematic, in context such language and action are means of YHWH's passionate commitment to Israel.)[23]

I scarcely need to say that YHWH's covenantal attentiveness to "below" is an alternative to Pharaoh who is the great practitioner of the politics of silence. The power arrangements of empire are intended to insulate power from pain, order from cry. When power no longer hears pain, then power may be as brutal as can be. It is the case that unbridled consumerism—as we have seen in the case of Pharaoh—is a narcotic that numbs to the cry from below. Thus it is likely that the raw power of Pharaoh is reinforced by such devouring. It is no wonder that when Moses addressed Pharaoh on behalf of the peasants that Pharaoh did not for a long time compute that the cry of the peasants is dangerously subversive because it evokes holy power. The linkage between overeating and numbed silence seems fully predictable. But Pharaoh, like many after him, learned that there is no adequate insulation from the cry that binds peasant and holy Hearer.

E. As the cry is the defining mark of the new citizenship, the cry as protest of pain has its positive counterpoint in an *assurance of common justice* to which the body politic is pledged. That is, these covenantal "citizens" are able to look beyond their own appetites to the unmet needs of neighbors whose needs will and must be met.

This positive commitment to a redress of injustice includes at least two dimensions. First, there is the affirmation from the old Torah traditions, derivative from Sinai, that *widows, orphans, and alien residents* are the special focus of social well-being. The entire body politic is drawn to that social reality.[24] This three-fold formula of "widow-orphan-resident alien" no doubt arose from concrete needs of those marginated from power and so put at risk. In the ongoing tradition, this triad has come to be representative for all those who are without entitlement, perhaps unproductive, and if unproductive surely unvalued and unappreciated.

In addition to Exod. 22:21-27 already cited, see the typical statement of Deut. 24:17-22:

> You shall not deprive a resident alien or an orphan of justice; you shall not take a widow's garment in pledge. Remember that you were a slave in Egypt and the Lord your God redeemed you from there; therefore I command you to do this. When you reap your harvest in your field and forget a sheaf in the field, you shall not go back to get it; it shall be left for the alien, the orphan, and the widow, so that the Lord your God may bless you in all your undertakings. When you beat your olive trees, do not strip what is left; it shall be for the alien, the orphan, and the widow. When you gather the grapes of your vineyard, do not glean what is left; it shall be for the alien, the orphan, and the widow. Remember that you were a slave in the land of Egypt; therefore I am commanding you to do this.

It is clear of course that when creatures opt for only consumerism and forget that larger reach of citizenship, the need and entitlements of widow, orphan, and illegal immigrant evaporate in an ocean of self-preoccupation. Thus the positive expectations of Sinai are matched by the harsh condemnations of the prophets upon a political economy that has become cynical and indifferent:

> Everyone loves a bribe and runs after gifts.
> They do not defend the orphan,
> and the widow's cause does not come before them. (Isa. 1:23)

> If you do not oppress the alien, the orphan, and the widow, or shed innocent blood in this place . . . then I will dwell with you in this place. (Jer. 7:6-7)

> The alien residing within you suffers extortion; the orphan and the widow are wronged in you. (Ezek. 22:7)

The second dimension of this assurance of justice is the *deep, revolutionary hope of Israel,* already implicit in Sinai, that as YHWH has overturned Pharaoh, so YHWH will overturn every unjust social arrangement and displace it with a new arrangement that will conform to YHWH's intention for creation. In general, the prophetic promises of "in that day" and "behold the days are coming" are acts of poetic imagination that are designed to give hope for a new politics coming soon. Most concretely the peasant dream of equity is voiced in the anticipation of a new distribution of land in which the usurpers will receive no share, for finally land reform is the concrete antidote to rapacious consumerism:

> Therefore you will have no one to cast the line by lot in the assembly of the LORD. (Mic. 2:5)[25]

In larger political vision, it is anticipated that a coming Davidic king, faithful to Torah vision, will enact justice for those who cannot seize it on their own:

> May he judge your people with righteousness,
>   and your poor with justice.
> May the mountains yield prosperity for the people,
>   and the hills in righteousness.
> May he defend the cause of the poor of the people,
>   give deliverance to the needy,
>   and crush the oppressor. (Ps. 72:2-4)

And in even larger scope, it is known in hope that God will act directly to redress the injustice:

> I myself will be the shepherd of my sheep, and I will make them lie down, says the Lord GOD. I will seek the lost, and I will bring back the strayed, and I will bind up the injured; and I will strengthen the weak, but the fat and strong I will destroy. I will feed them with justice. (Ezek. 34: 15-16)

The Torah vision and the prophetic hope are only words, only texts, only poetry. That is all. Against that, Pharaoh offers memos and production schedules. In the horizon of Pharaoh, the quintessential consumer, there is no notice of the unproductive, the unentitled, like widows, orphans, and outsiders. All that counts is production; if they do not produce, they do not exist! In Pharaoh's horizon, moreover, there are no subversive expectations of land redistribution because the land is held as it is to perpetuity. No notice of the little ones, no projection of newness, and above all, no poems.

A political economy of consumption thrives on quotas, memos, ads, and slogans, but no poems. Art withers because it leaves too much open. Poets are silenced because they disclose too much of what must remain hidden. Where art withers and poems fade, predictably, devouring may be without critique. How odd in such hostile circumstance that poems do sound and are heard, rhythms of the little ones, cadences of newness, listeners not so overfed but to hear and to heed.

F. Covenantal alternative everywhere! From Sinai to everywhere, with no place immune. I have been lining out a peculiarly Jewish vision taken up by Christians. The vision is local and modest, nothing so large and grand as Plato and that whole critical tradition of equilibrium.

Notice, however, at the edge of this modest vision, yet a poem about Jewish option opened to the experience of Gentiles:

> In the days to come
>> the mountain of the LORD's house
> shall be established as the highest of the mountains,
>> and shall be raised over the hills;
> all nations shall stream to it.
>> Many peoples shall come and say,
> "Come, let us go up to the mountain of the LORD,
>> to the house of the God of Jacob;
> that he may teach us his ways
>> and that we may walk in his paths."
> For out of Zion shall go forth instruction [Torah],
>> and the word of the LORD from Jerusalem.
> He shall judge between the nations,
>> and shall arbitrate for many peoples;
> they shall beat their swords into plowshares,
>> and their spears into pruning hooks;
> nation shall not lift up sword against nation,
>> neither shall they learn war any more. (Isa. 2:2-4)

The vision is of all nations en route to Jerusalem for Torah that leads to disarmament. Not a stress to submit to David, not even to become Jewish. But Torah, the theopolitical vision of Moses, the opening of alternative citizenship into the numbed arenas of consumerism, a vision modest in origin, lean in scope, but on offer to the nations.

V

I have lined this out in detail because the third verb of Deuteronomy after "eat and be full" is very much undecided . . . a turn toward citizen or toward consumer. Creation is a promise of abundance, generosity, and fidelity; but the response among us is not a done deal. I have stated the either/or starkly, but the practice is not easy. I finish with three texts:

A. The fate of an uncaring, unresponsive, disobedient consumer society is summed up in the ancient curse of Lev. 26:26: "though you eat, you shall not be satisfied." That old curse, moreover, is reiterated in the harsh judgment of the prophet Hosea: "They shall eat, but not be satiated" (Hos. 4:10). This is a remarkable statement, because in all these texts we have considered, "eat and be satiated" come together awaiting a third verb. It has been assumed that satiated follows of course after eat. But now even the first verb "eat" does not lead to the second, "satiated." One cannot eat enough to be full if one eats the junk food of alienation! Attention to creatureliness may cause us to wonder if we have arrived at that place of alienation where no amount of consumption can possibly satisfy, because the hunger is finally for neighbor justice and not for private devouring. We may be left to ask in our scarcity-driven, anxiety-consumed society:

> How much to satiation?
> How much money?
> How much power?
> How much oil?
> How many cars, how big?
> How much beer?
> How much sports, entertainment, shopping, sex?
> How many endowments, or students, or publications?

How much when the true mystery of satisfaction is elsewhere, totally misconstrued by a pharaonic culture with Pharaoh's heart disease of hardness?

B. A countertext from a very different context may be an antidote to the old curse: "Go, eat your bread with enjoyment, and drink your wine with a merry heart; for God has long ago approved what you do" (Eccles. 9:7). At first glance this saying sounds like a permit for consumerism and hedonism, for it is all approved ahead of time. Except that Elsa Tamez, in her shrewd way, observes of the verse:

> God is happy and approves of the work of God's creatures. The word
> "to approve" or "take pleasure" can refer to the past, present, and future.
> That God has already approved the works of humans (v. 7) does not
> mean that everything people do, have done, or will do is agreeable to
> God; rather, God accepts people by grace, and they freely enjoy God's
> gifts. This is an exceedingly liberating message, in the context of the
> rigors of the temple during Qoheleth's time. . . . We must remember
> that this proposal for everyday life is not coming from an individual-
> istic, isolated person who avoids all company but that of the woman
> he loves. Qoheleth argues strongly for unity with others; relationships
> of solidarity give strength and enable people to resist hostility (cf. 4:9-
> 12). Here he is proposing a rhythm of life that favors people as human
> beings, against one that favors economic, political, or social institutions.
> . . . Qoheleth's invitation is not to suicide, cynicism, or resignation; it is
> rather to affirm material and relational life, where we can feel the palpi-
> tations of the heart. It is to enjoy, share, and work, without complexity
> or anxiety: with purity of heart.

The fullness of festival here envisioned is not as private one for the privileged. It is rather a deep joy in a communal practice that cares for all and
shares with all.[26]

The contrast between the "not satiated" of Hos. 4:10 and the "merry
heart" of Eccles. 9:7 is an endless option. Creatureliness leaves open popular chances for death, but also a preferential option for life.

C. Finally, I finish with the testimony of Paul in his word to the church
in Ephesus:

> I coveted no one's silver or gold or clothing. You know for yourselves
> that I worked with my own hands to support myself and my compan-
> ions. In all this I have given you an example that by such work we must
> support the weak, remembering the words of the LORD Jesus, for he
> himself said, "It is more blessed to give than to receive." (Acts 20:33-35)

Paul, he says of himself, did not covet. Rather, in his work on behalf of the
community, he set an example for the support of the weak. He finishes
with a zinger that he attributes to Jesus: "It is more blessed to give than to
receive."

Creatureliness consists in giving and in receiving. Creatureliness marks
us as having already received (see 1 Cor. 4:7). The vocation is giving, in

imitation of the giving Creator. *Citizens* of the new politics are givers and so blessed. The old politics of *consumers* is about receiving and taking and having and owning and eating. It is not a blessing . . . and we creatures keep redeciding.

Ecumenism as the Shared Practice of a Peculiar Identity

Classic ecumenism in the twentieth century has had to do with partnership and cooperation among established denominational traditions. These denominational groupings have tended to reflect centrist, mainline churches that, in their own particular spheres, exercised some theological hegemony. Thus, ecumenism tended to focus upon churches finding each other in the midst of their pronounced socio-politico-economic accommodation to context. Important questions about the locus of such churches in their more-or-less compromised social contexts were not raised. One of the practical effects of such quests for unity and cooperation—without serious self-criticism—was the exclusion from the horizon of churches that did not participate in such centrist hegemony, for example, churches in the left-wing reformation and Pentecostal traditions.

The ecumenical work that is now to be done is no longer among hegemonic denominations and church traditions, as though the largest animals were posturing in front of each other in the forest. Our current context requires that we recognize that unity among Christian churches is not very urgent or important unless it is unity found in an *odd identity* for an *odd vocation* in a world deeply organized against *gospel oddity*. The Lima document prepared the way for this embrace of common oddness, taking baptismal identity and vocation as the starting point for common life. But now, given where the churches find themselves, a common life in baptism is not a matter of agreeing on formulae, classical or otherwise, but on *common praxis* deriving from a shared odd entity.

It is not clear in what way an Old Testament teacher can contribute to these conversations, given our propensity to traffic in old church formulae. The present essay seeks to think through Israel's odd identity in the Old Testament, an identity of course adjusted to different circumstances, but always in deep tension with hegemonic power all around. Increasingly the church in the west is in an analogous situation to that of ancient Israel, no longer hegemonic itself but pressed by powers that are indeed hegemonic.[1] The characteristic locus of ancient Israel as a marginalized community in the midst of hegemonic power (either indifferent or hostile to that odd identity) may be a useful place from which to re-read the text and rethink a shared identity in the church.

I

In the world of ancient Israel in the period of the Old Testament, it is not difficult to identify the ruling groups who we may suppose constructed and maintained dominant values. The list of superpowers that dominated the landscape of that ancient world includes, in sequence, Egypt, Assyria, Babylon, and Persia.[2] From an Israelite perspective one can make some differentiations in their several modes of hegemony, so that it appears that Assyria was the most consistently brutal, and Persia appears to have operated in a more benign or enlightened way; but those differences likely were strategic, or at least the Israelite perception and presentation of them are likely strategic. Without fail, the impinging superpower intended to dominate the political landscape, to control military power, and to preempt the authority to tax. The control of military power, moreover, included the right to draft manpower, which issued in forced labor for state projects.

On the whole these concentrations of power tolerated little deviation in matters of importance to them. To ensure compliance, moreover, the political-economic-military power of hegemony is paired, characteristically, with imperial myths and rituals, liturgical activities that legitimated power realities. It is not too much to conclude that the interface of political and liturgical efforts intended to generate a totalizing environment outside of which were permitted no political forays and, where effective, no deviant imagination. Such hegemony maintained both a monopoly of violence and a monopoly of imagination that assured for its own young privilege, certitude, and domination; it invited into its universal horizon those who stood outside the primary benefits of that monopoly, but who had come to terms with its visible and unquestioned privilege, certitude, and domination.

From an Israelite perspective, the totalizing capacity of hegemony is perceived, characteristically, as arrogant and threatening.[3] Thus, with ancient memories of oppression still palpable, Ezekiel can have pharaoh assert: "My Nile is my own, I made it for myself" (Ezek. 29:3). And in the Isaiah tradition, Assyria gloats:

> Has any of the gods of the nations saved their land out of the hand of the king of Assyria? Where are the gods of Hamath and Arpad? Where are the gods of Sepharvaim? Have they delivered Samaria out of my hand? Who among all the gods of these countries have saved their countries out of my hand, that the lord should save Jerusalem out of my hand? (Isa. 36:18-20)

Babylon is not different: "I shall be mistress forever. . . . I am, and there is no one beside me. . . . No one sees me" (Isa. 47:7-10).

We may register only two footnotes to this parade of totalizing superpowers. First, in the early part of the monarchic period in Jerusalem, emerging in a brief pause from imperial interference, the Davidic-Solomonic regime was not beholden to any external power. And yet the evidence we have, admittedly from a certain (Deuteronomic-prophetic) perspective, is that the Jerusalem regime practiced the same totalizing efforts, surely to be "like all the other nations."[4] Both the relentless prophetic critiques and perhaps especially the Rechabite alternative of Jeremiah 35 indicate that even this regime is no exception to the pattern of hegemonic rule.

Second, in addition to the standard line-up of imperial powers, we may mention a prophetic concern about Tyre, especially in Isa. 23:1-18 and Ezekiel 26–28. What interests us is that Tyre's significance is not military and political, but economic. Indeed, Isaiah suggests that Tyre is the epicenter of a world economy that features opulence, self-indulgence, and general social disregard, so that Tyre can be imagined as saying: "I am a god; I sit in the seat of the gods, in the heart of the seas" (Ezek. 28:2).

This recital of hegemony, focusing on political power but ending with a recognition of commercialism, provides a window on our own current consideration of character ethics. I submit that in our time and place the hegemonic power of international corporate capitalism, driven of course by United States technological power, creates a totalizing environment that imposes its values, its field of images, and its limits of vision upon all comers. Theodore von Laue speaks of *The World Revolution on Westernization,* and more recently Charles Reich terms this phenomenon "the money government."[5] It is self-evident that this community of ruthless expansionism and those allied with it do not need to expend any energy in inculcating their own young into practices of privilege, certitude, and domination. I imagine, moreover, that our modest reflection upon character ethics in such a totalizing environment is not unlike that of Israel in the ancient world, deeply perplexed about how to sustain any vision or practice of life that is not swept away by the force of hegemony. This deep vexation concerns those of us who live at the center of the hegemony, who are implicated in it and benefit from it. But there is also deep vexation among those in the less privileged places that we are pleased to term "under-developed," as they wonder how to maintain any local, rooted identity in the face of invasive, seemingly irresistible Coca-Cola.

II

In its relentless imperial matrix, ancient Israel had only a slight chance and thin resources. It is clear, nonetheless, that a central preoccupation of the Old Testament, surely a discernment assembled and transmitted out of a passionate ideological perspective, is to maintain the scandal and liberty of particularity in the face of totalizing threat. I shall suggest that the maintenance of a self-aware, self-conscious alternative identity in the face of totalism is precisely the practice of character ethics that aims to generate and authorize liberated "agents of their own history"; such practice depends upon the great "thickness" of the community that makes possible such liberated agents on a day-to-day basis.

I will organize my efforts around an easy scheme of superpowers: Egypt, Assyria, Babylon, and Persia. (I am of course aware of the historical-critical qualifications concerning the literature, but I will deal with the literature in terms of its presentation. Texts, for example, that deal with the ancient pharaoh of the exodus period will be read without the critical qualifications of later dating.)

Israel as an intentional counter-community practiced relentless, dense memory as an alternative to the coopting amnesia of the empire.

1. Concerning Egypt. The Exodus liturgy (Exodus 1–15) dominates the imagination of Israel and continues to be decisive for Israel's identity. Three aspects of the narrative pertain to what we may roughly regard as character formation. First, three times, the passover provisions

pay attention to intentional instructing: "When your children ask you, 'What do you mean by this observance?'" (Exod. 12:26; cf. 18:8, 14). This liturgy is a launching pad for conversation. The prescribed response to the child's question is a narrative reiteration of a peculiar world with YHWH at its center.

Second, the entire passover provision of Exodus 12–13 is quite specific and self-conscious about liturgical detail. It is clear, nonetheless, that the primary intention of the narrative and the liturgy is to construct a counter-world whereby pharaoh's totalizing power and totalizing explanation of reality are regularly defeated. The Israelite boy or girl is invited to live in a social reality where pharaoh's abusive power does not prevail.

Third, the narrative makes clear that the recital offers a curriculum for the young:

> Go to Pharaoh; for I have hardened his heart and the heart of his offi-
> cials, in order that I may show these signs [plagues] of mine among
> them, and that you may tell your children and grandchildren how I
> made fools of the Egyptians and what signs I have done among them—
> so that you may know that I am the Lord. (Exod. 10:1-2)

The concern—to make this defining memory operative to the third and fourth generations—is crucial for our subject.

2. Concerning Assyria. Critical judgment suggests that the book of Deuteronomy is to be understood as an instrument of resistance against Assyrian totalism, perhaps influenced by Assyrian forms of treaty documents.[6] Pivotal to Josiah's reform is the celebration of the passover (2 Kgs. 23:21-23). The focus on passover, of course, draws resistance to Assyria into the world of passover resistance to Egypt found in Exodus 12–13. It is the disciplined, intentional retelling of the exodus-seder narrative that provides ground for alternative existence outside Assyrian hegemony. The passover festival recalls Israel's root identity of emancipation and covenant; but it also brings that counter-identity, always contemporary, into the Assyrian crisis.

Passover is one of the three defining festivals that will give liturgical, dramatic, and narrative articulation to Israel's distinctiveness, the other two festivals being weeks and booths (Deut. 16:1-8, 9-17). Thus the danger and the rescue from Egypt are transposed into an Assyrian world. The provision of 16:1-8 mentions Egypt three times; the following provision for the festival of weeks moves more directly to an ethical derivation: "Rejoice before the Lord your God—you and your sons and your daughters, your male and female slaves, the Levites resident in your towns, as well as the strangers, the orphans, and the widows who are among you" (16:11). And then the imperative: "Remember that you were a slave in Egypt" (16:12).

3. Concerning Babylon. The great danger for Jewish exiles in Babylon was assimilation into the totalizing world of Nebuchadnezzar, with the commensurate abandonment of the particular identity of Judaism. It is common to recognize that Second Isaiah is a message to Jews that they will be liberated to go home to Jerusalem. In my view, however, prior to going home geographically, Israel must go home to Jewishness, emotionally, liturgically, imaginatively. Consider this counsel: "Look to the rock from which you were hewn, and to the quarry from which you were dug. Look to Abraham your father and to Sarah who bore you" (Isa. 51:1-2).

I do not follow John van Seters in his notion that these traditions of the ancestors were first formulated in the exile.[7] But there is no doubt that the promissory narratives of Genesis received enormous attention and were found to be pertinent in this context. It is when all seemed lost in the face of the totalizing empire that Israel is driven deep into its narrative past, in order to have an identity apart from the offer of Babylon.

And while there are important historical-critical issues, we may here mention Daniel 1, wherein the self-aware Jew Daniel negotiates his way through the civil service of Babylon by a refusal of the rich food of the empire and a reliance upon the simplicities of a Jewish diet. The refusal of junk food from the empire is linked to his being embedded in a particular sense of identity. The Daniel narrative is an echo of the challenge of exilic Isaiah.[8]

> Ho, everyone who thirsts,
> come to the waters;
> and you that have no money,
> come, buy and eat!
> Come, buy wine and milk
> without money and without price.
> Why do you spend your money for that which is not bread,
> and your labor for that which does not satisfy? (Isa. 55:1-2)

4. Concerning Persia. The issues with Persia are very different: antagonism has yielded to supportive imperial patronage (Neh. 2:5-8). Nehemiah operates with the credentials of Persia. Nonetheless, when that community

of Jews engages in an act of reconstitution, the public liturgical activity is not Persian. It is Torah-based, linking Jews to the oldest memories of Moses (Neh. 8:1-12) and culminating in the festival of booths wherein Israel reengages its memory of vulnerability and inexplicable receipt of well-being (Neh. 8:13-18). A primary dimension of "re-booting" is that Torah was read for seven consecutive days.

Thus in the face of every empire that sought to comprehend Jewish identity, one can see this community intentionally staking out public, liturgical space to reenact and reclaim its own distinctive identity. That liturgical act is surely an act of faith. It is at the same time an act of resistance, of propaganda, of nurture, whereby the community asserts to its young in direct ways that its existence is not comprehended in the totalizing reality of the empire.

III

As an intentional counter-community, Israel practiced liberated, imaginative possibility as an alternative to the circumscribed limiting world of imperial administration.

A totalizing empire is primarily interested in tax revenues, civil order, and due compliance with imperial expectations and quotas. Such hegemony, however, cannot be sustained unless it is supported by poetic legitimation that seeks to define appropriate social hopes and expectations and inescapable social fears and threats. The empire can never resist seeking control of the emotional life of its subjects, for in emotional life are generated dreams and visions that may be subversive of current order.

Israel, as a community with a peculiar destiny, resisted the preemption of its hopes and fears by imperial confiscation. It did so by maintaining a liturgical, instructional claim that its life was not under the control of the empire but under the governance of the Holy One of Israel who rightly and with great authority denied the effectiveness of legitimacy of imperial claims. Israel's insistence upon such YHWH-driven possibility is not made on the basis of the "nuts and bolts" of political and economic life, but on the basis of dramatic enactment that refuses to be domesticated by "nuts and bolts." Israel regularly invites its young into a liturgically constructed counter-world of Yahwistic possibility.

1. Concerning Egypt. The entire exodus liturgy serves the sense of Israel's exceptionalism. YHWH, as a character in a narrative that Egyptian

epistemology would never accept, makes possible for the slave community precisely what pharaoh had declared impossible. The very enactment of the plagues—which make pharaoh a fool—is the assertion that there is emancipatory power at work beyond the reach of pharaoh.

More than that, the liturgy is replete with the protection of Israel, singled out from the massive destruction of the empire:

> Thus I will make a distinction between my people and your people. (Exod. 8:23)

> All the livestock of the Egyptians died, but of the livestock of the Israelites, not one died. (9:6)

> The hail struck down everything . . . Only in the land of Goshen, where the Israelites were, there was no hail. (9:26)

> There will be a loud cry throughout the whole land of Egypt . . . but not a dog shall growl at any of the Israelites . . . so that you may know that the Lord makes a distinction between Egypt and Israel. (11:7)

There are matters possible for Israel that Pharaoh will never permit.

2. Concerning Assyria. The link between liturgical reconstrual and a radical alternative ethic is most clear in Deut. 15:1-18, which places next to Passover the year of release, whereby Israel resists the emergency of a permanent underclass. Both Jeffries Hamilton and Moshe Weinfeld have suggested that this provision of Torah is the quintessential mark of Israel's distinctive ethic.[9] The practice of debt cancellation stands in deep opposition to the imperial economy, which is a practice of hierarchical power and social stratification. This provision stands at the center of Deuteronomy, a script designed to distinguish Israel from Assyrian possibility.

This provision is more than simply a legal regulation. It is a remarkable exploration of a social possibility that is clearly unthinkable in the empire. The empire stands or falls with the administration of debt, for it is debt that distinguishes the powerful and the have-nots.[10]

Deuteronomic resistance to Assyrian impingement, however, is not simply liturgical. It is also the dreaming vision of an alternative economy that imagines neighbors living with generous, palpable concern for each other. And the energy for such subversive activity is, predictably, grounded in memory: "Remember that you were slaves in the land of Egypt; the

Lord redeemed you; for this reason I lay this command upon you today" (Deut. 15:15). Assyria or any other empire would regard this social posture as impossible because Assyria has, as yet, no exodus memory.

3. Concerning Babylon. The challenge of Second Isaiah is to create imaginative space for Jewishness. The danger is that Israel in exile will give everything over to Babylonian definitions of the possible. So the assertion: "My thoughts are not your thoughts, nor are your ways my ways, says the lord" (Isa. 55:8). This assertion is not a generic invitation to repent of sin; it is rather a concrete assault of Jewish readiness to accept Babylonian definitions of the possible. YHWH has another way, another thought, another possibility. Babylon offered food that is not bread, and labor that does not satisfy, but YHWH offers wine and milk and bread without money and without price (Isa. 55:1-2). Babylon thought to keep everything frozen and everyone in place to perpetuity. But YHWH anticipates in exultation: "You shall go out in joy and be led back in peace" (Isa. 55:12).

Babylon had become an arena for abandonment and the absence of God. But now YHWH asserts: "With great compassion I will gather you. . . . With everlasting love I will have compassion on you" (Isa. 54:7-8). The world that 2 Isaiah imagines is not a world from which YHWH has been forcibly eliminated. YHWH is still there. For that reason, Babylonian designations of reality are not finally effective.

4. Concerning Persia. The relation between Israel and Persia is different from the relation to previous hegemonic powers. And yet, even with Persia the Jews knew their life was deeply circumscribed by imperial pressures and realities. This sense of limitation and pressure is evidenced in the great prayer of Ezra in Nehemiah 9. The prayer moves between Israel's wickedness and God's mercy. The final petition, however, lets us see, beyond the intensity between YHWH and Israel, a third party:

> Here we are, slaves to this day—slaves in the land that you gave to our ancestors to enjoy its fruit and its good gifts. Its rich yield goes to the kings whom you have set over us because of our sins; they have power also over our bodies and over our livestock at their pleasure, and we are in great distress. (Neh. 9:36-37)

The reality of restriction is evident. The text nonetheless suggests two facets of emancipated possibility that remained outside Persian administration. The first of these is an act of imagination in the form of prayer. The prayer is a bid for reality that lies beyond the control of Persia, a bid that

shows this intentional community not yet conceding everything to hegemony. The second is the solemn community covenant that follows the
prayer (9:28—10:39); the leaders of the community vow to act in solidarity concerning economic matters, a solidarity that echoes the old year of
release.

The text is saturated with communal, liturgical, and imaginative practice in which a zone of social possibility, outside of imperial regimentation
because it is rooted in YHWH, is maintained, celebrated, practiced, and
made visible.

IV

Israel as an intentional counter-community articulated a covenantal ethic
of neighborliness as an alternative to the commoditization of social relationships it sensed in imperial practice.

I do not want to over-emphasize the ethical dimension here, since it
seems to me that the liturgical-imaginative effort to create and protect
alternative space is more important. Israel, however, cannot entertain or
imagine alternative human space, sponsored as it is by YHWH, except as
space that is saturated with ethical urgency, ethical possibility, and ethical
requirement. Indeed, it is the practice of Torah obedience to the rooted
claims of the community that is the instrument and guarantee of liberated life beyond imperial reductionism: "I will keep your law continually,
forever and ever. I shall walk at liberty, for I have sought your precepts.
I will speak of your decrees before kings, and shall not be put to shame"
(Ps. 119:44-46).

1. Concerning Egypt. As the exodus narrative is the paradigmatic
assertion of community beyond the reality of totalizing power, so the Sinai
recital is the paradigmatic articulation of neighborly ethics that counters
the ethic of pharaoh. In its completed tradition, Israel understood that
emancipation from Egypt was not for the sake of autonomy, but for the
sake of the counter-service of YHWH. And while we may focus on a variety of commands that epitomize such an alternative ethic rooted in liturgy,
we may settle for the first command: No other gods than YHWH, the
God of the exodus, who delegitimates every other loyalty. While the commands of Sinai are demanding and abrasive, they would never be confused
with pharaoh's commands, for they are in general aimed at a communitari-
anism that makes "hard labor" impossible.[11]

The link between the holiness of YHWH and the concreteness of neighborliness is wondrously voiced in Deuteronomy:

> For the Lord your God is god of god and Lord of lords, the great God, mighty and awesome, who is not partial and takes no bribe, who executes justice for the orphan and the widow, and who loves the strangers, providing them food and clothing. You shall also love the stranger, for you were strangers in the land of Egypt. (Deut. 10:17-19)

It is precisely the God who commands lords, gods, and pharaohs who loves immigrants and displaced persons, who provides them food and clothing. This ethic arises from the memory and from the possibility of an alternative to Pharaoh.

2. Concerning Assyria. As a contrast program, Deuteronomy makes one of its foci "widows and orphans," that is, the paradigmatic powerless and vulnerable in society. The Israelite ethic urged here, alternative to imperial rapaciousness, is precisely concerned for those without resources or leverage to maintain and protect themselves.

> Every third year you shall bring out the full tithe of your produce for that year, and store it within your towns; the Levites, because they have no allotments or inheritance with you, as well as the resident aliens, the orphans and the widows in your towns may come and eat their fill. (Deut. 14:18-29; cf. 16:11, 14; 24:17, 19-21; 26:12-13)

This social horizon, moreover, is rooted and made available in exodus memories: "Remember that you were a slave in Egypt, and diligently observe these statutes" (Deut. 16:12; cf. 24:18, 22). Against Assyrian amnesia, which permits exploitative neighborly relations, Israel's narrative embedment in the exodus tradition will energize the radical economics of Deuteronomy.

3. Concerning Babylon. The vision of Second Isaiah, rooted in exodus imagery, broadly understood Israel's life to be a practice of justice (42:1-4), light (42:6; 49:6), and covenant (42:6; 49:8)—generalities that envisioned a differently ordered economy. In Third Isaiah, however, albeit beyond the Babylonian period, the visionary ethics of Second Isaiah continued to ferment and evoke ferocious dispute in the community concerning ethical possibility. Thus, Isa. 56:2-8 raises a powerful voice for inclusiveness, and 58:6-7 names the quintessence of covenantalism as a precondition for YHWH's presence in the community:

Is not this the fast that I choose;
 to loose the bonds of injustice,
 to undo the thongs of the yoke,
to let the oppressed go free,
 and to break every yoke?
Is it not to share your bead with the hungry,
 and bring the homeless poor into your house;
when you see the naked, to cover them,
 and not to hide yourself from your own kin?
 (Isa. 58:6-7)

This issue of inclusiveness is not easily settled in the years immediately after the exile. Nonetheless, the peculiar social vision of Israel continued to summon and empower, even when the community had limited resources and feared for its own survival.

4. Concerning Persia. The lyrical anticipations of the Isaiah tradition came to concrete implementation in the reform of Nehemiah. Though authorized by the Persians, it is clear that Nehemiah and Ezra, in the reconstitution of an intentional community of Torah, had to struggle mightily for a neighborly ethic rooted in Israel's peculiar tradition.

Most spectacularly, in Nehemiah 5, Nehemiah addressed the economic crisis whereby some Jews were exploiting other Jews in a way that created a permanent underclass.[12] Nehemiah's demanding alternative vision is rooted in the exodus memory, alludes to the old Torah, is aware of Israel's distinctiveness, and requires concrete, costly economic decisions:

> As far as we were able, we have brought back our Jewish kindred who have been sold to other nations. The thing you are doing is not good. Should you not walk in the fear of our God, to prevent the taunts of the nations our enemies? . . . Let us stop this taking of interest. Restore to them this very day their fields, their vineyards, their olive orchards, and their houses, and the interest on money, grain, wine and oil, that you have been exacting from them. (Neh. 5:8-11)

In every imperial context, Israel's peculiar ethic is kept alive, each time rooted in old liturgical memory, but each time brought to bear upon concrete social history in a way that requires the covenant community to act peculiarly against the common definitions of imperial social reality.

V

I want finally to reflect upon this sequencing of memory, possibility, and ethic through the several imperial hegemonies under which ancient Israel lived.

The practice of an ethic rooted in an intentional and particular communal narrative suggests a community characteristically at risk in the face of a seemingly irresistible imperial pressure toward homogenization. The pressure of triage, of the elimination of surplus people, worked massively against the Israelites, if not in terms of physical violence then through ideological violence that sought always to eradicate Israel's sense of itself and of YHWH's reality.[13] I think it impossible to overstate the enduringly ominous threat of elimination that required a liturgy, a socialization, and an ethic that had to be understood as resistance.

This resistance pertains to Jewishness in a most concrete sense, for which I will cite two instances in the long history of marginality. The Maccabean revolt against Roman homogenization in the second century B.C.E. is of course a pivotal point for the intertestamental period. Roman triage was not directly violent, but was determined to eliminate Jewish oddness. According to the brief notation in 1 Macc. 1:11-15, "renegade Jews" sought a "covenant with the Gentiles"; "So they built a gymnasium in Jerusalem, according to Gentile custom, and removed the marks of circumcision, and abandoned the holy covenant. They joined with the Gentiles and sold themselves to do evil."[14] The pressure of a "universal identity" is always a threat to a particular identity; assimilation is ever a clear and present danger.

That pressure of homogeneity and threat of triage by assimilation was directly asserted in an advertisement in the *New York Times* that took the form of a litany urging:

> We prayed for Israel when its survival was threatened in 1967 and 1973.
>> Our prayers were answered.
> We prayed for the redemption of Soviet Jewry during the dark years of Communism.
>> Our prayers were answered.
> We prayed for the release of Syrian Jewry, hostages to a most aggressive regime.
>> Our prayers were answered.
> Now it is time to recite a prayer for ourselves—an embattled American

Jewry. . . . Our birthrate is too low and our rate of intermarriage too high. The real question is will we survive?[15]

I make no judgment about this ad or its ideology. I simply note that the issue of a distinct community of character recurs among the heirs of ancient Israel.

Our ultimate concern in this essay, however, is for the distinctive ethic of the Christian church. The end of Christendom in western Europe and in the United States is likely a good thing. The question remains, however: How shall we practice a distinctive ethic of humanness in a society massively driven by the forces of the market economy toward an ethic of individualism that issues in social indifference and anti-neighborliness? It is obvious that the position of the church in the United States directly parallels neither the position in the empire of ancient Israel nor the dangerous exposure of current Judaism. Still, what might have passed for a "Christian ethic" in the period of Christendom has now been thoroughly permeated by secularism in both its liberal and conservative modes. Therefore, attentiveness to peculiar narrative identity seems to me an urgent practical enterprise for a religious community that is often so bland that it loses its raison d'être. The issue is to practice a peculiar identity that is not craven in the face of the moralisms of the right or the left.

An ethic of resistance was regularly needed in ancient Israel; it is, in my judgment, needed now by a depositioned church in the west; it is also needed to combat the power of corporate capitalism, supported as that is by military and technological power as part of the westernization of the world. Around the globe, local communities with peculiar identities and destinies are profoundly under threat from "the money government" that has no patience with or regard for rooted communities. Thus, the issue of ideological triage and the capacity for locally rooted resistance is not singularly a Jewish question or a church question; it has become a question for the shape and viability of humanness in a drastically reorganized world. For Christians and Jews who are situated in and beneficiaries of the expanding world economy, attentiveness to, appreciation for, and support of local resistance—which may take many forms—is an issue of paramount importance.

Because I have framed my discussion in terms of local resistance to universalizing pressures, a framing I think unavoidable in the Old Testament, I must also ask whether such an approach is inevitably sectarian, concerned with funding and authorizing a separatist community. In the instant, I suspect that this approach to ethics is inevitably aimed at the particularity of the community. And certainly the primary concern of the Old Testament is the assertion and maintenance of the distinctive community of Israel. Moreover, I believe that a particularistic ethic of resistance is now urgent in light of the massive power of the Coca-Cola-ization of the world.

Having acknowledged that much, two important qualifications are in order: First, Israel did not live, over time, in a cultural and liturgical vacuum. It was endlessly engaged in interaction with other cultures and regularly appropriated things from the very forces it intended to critique and resist; thus, the materials for this distinctive ethic in the sixth century were very different from what purports to be thirteenth-century resistance. The process of deciding what to appropriate (and how) in the midst of resistance is completely hidden from us. The dual process of resistance and appropriation is unmistakable. Thus, for example, Hosea seems to mount a polemic against "fertility religion," but does so by a Yahwistic appeal to the modes and images of fertility.[16]

Second, while it is not primary, it is evident that Israel's distinctive identity and ethic are an offer, summons, and invitation to the world around it (that is, the imperial world) to share its neighbor ethic. While the texts characteristically focus on immediate concrete crises, it is equally clear that Israel's long-term hope is that the impossible possibility of covenant, rooted in the Creator's practice of steadfast love and justice, can and will be enacted everywhere. Characteristically Israel believes and trusts that an anti-neighbor ethic cannot prevail and that the gods who legitimate such an ethic will be defeated. Israel understands itself at Sinai to be at the edge of YHWH's coming rule, which will indeed reach to the ends of the earth, so that kings and princes will end their futility and join in doxological obedience—the very doxological obedience that is definitional for Israel's life. At its best (but not always), this deep hope is free from Israel's own ideological benefit. That is, the coming rule is a rule of YHWH for the benefit of all, not a rule of preference for Israel.

I conclude with a reference to Jacob Neusner. In his study of Jewish ritual practice, Neusner judges that the stylized gestures and words of ritual are aids in the daily work of being "Jews through the power of our imagination."[17] Indeed, Neusner opines that Jewishness is hazardous and venturesome enough that it requires a daily act of imagination, without which there would not be Jews.

I propose that in Christendom Christians needed no such effort, for identity simply came with the territory, as it always does for dominant faith. The depositioning of Christian faith in the west, however, makes the community of the baptized a community more fully dependent upon daily acts of imagination for the maintenance of identity. The daily acts evoking Christian identity are likely to be ethical as well as liturgical. The beginning point is the recognition that clear identity is not a cultural given, as it might have been in former times of domination, but is now an oddness that requires courageous intentionality.

III.

The Word Shaping a Community of Discipleship

Vision for a New Church and a New Century

Part I: Homework against Scarcity

The beloved James Muilenburg, my teacher and the teacher of us all at Union Theological Seminary, wrote in his chapter on Israel's ethics:

> As the Holy One of Israel, [YHWH] consecrates his people to obedience and service and separateness from the ways of the nations; as King, he rules the world with justice and the peoples with his truth; as Father, he exercises his power and authority, yet with compassion and love; as leader on the way, he guides his people on its way through history; as teacher, he grasps the pupil by the hand and instructs him, and subjects him to his firm but merciful discipline. It is this God to whom Israel is urged to listen, the God who granted the inspiration and motivation to obedience in the glad good news of liberation from slavery and who provided the basis for allegiance and fidelity in the covenant at Sinai.
>
> Amidst all the feverish preoccupation with riches and power and comfort and pleasure; all the bustling commercial activity and the ever-rising prices; the building of fortifications for defense and of fine houses for the privileged; the elaboration of cultic observances with their sumptuous festivals and celebrations, their pilgrimages and rites, their music and choirs, and, withal, the syncretism with the cults of nature and prosperity—amidst all there was one voice that was stifled and repressed. It was the voice of Israel's covenant-making and covenant-keeping God. But was it stilled? Not quite! For there were prophets in the land to sound the cry of protest and outrage, repeating with the urgency born of faith and memory and holy awe, God's categorical and insistent "thou shalt not."[1]

Muilenburg saw the matter of the economy clearly and theologically, as he regularly listened well to the text.

It remained, however, for Norman Gottwald, student of Muilenburg and sometime teacher at Union, to initiate the critical conversation concerning the socioeconomic, political dimensions of what Muilenburg had seen so well and said so eloquently. It was Gottwald who saw clearly that Israel was an experimental social revolution in that ancient world, to see whether social relationships could be organized in human, egalitarian, communitarian ways. He made this case by his controversial appeal to Marxian categories of dialectical materialism, partly to expose and counter the unexamined idealistic theories of Durkheim that largely shaped the discussion. Gottwald has well argued that, propelled by YHWH, Israel is a material experiment in the world whereby neighborly solidarity between haves and have-nots is a form of normalcy. That vision and mandate were laid out clearly at Sinai where Israel, at the behest of YHWH, redescribed the world in all its neighborly potential.

I

But of course Israel did not come innocently to Sinai, nor did Israel begin at Sinai. Excluding for now the problematic of the ancestral memories of Genesis as founding tradition, it is enough to remember the rootage of Israel in Egyptian slavery from which it had been emancipated. It is enough to remember that in contrast to Sinai, in Egypt Pharaoh is the deciding force who defined the world. It is enough to remember that Pharaoh, in the memory of Israel, is famine-driven, always worried about lack of crops and loss of food, always gathering and storing to have enough—good technological procedure for a government that understood "food as a weapon." It is enough to remember that that very Pharaoh, who disrupted the food chain in his clumsy acquisitiveness and in his bottomless anxiety, could never have enough. The slaves who became Israel remembered that they were at work building imperial granaries to abet the royal anxiety. It is of this Pharaoh that the narrative, already in Genesis 47, concluded:

> So Joseph bought all the land of Egypt for Pharaoh. All the Egyptians
> sold their fields, because the famine was severe upon them; and the land
> became Pharaoh's. (v. 20)

And then verse 26 inevitably and soberly adds, without a trace of irony:

> The land of the priests alone did not become pharaoh's.

This is the same pharaoh who later, in the book of Ezekiel, stated his arrogant illusion set deep in anxiety:

> My Nile is my own,
> I made it for myself. (Ezek. 29:3)

The cluster of scarcity, anxiety, technology, and hubris created a land of plenty, bought at the high price of neighborliness. It was a land of plenty completely unbearably for the slaves who made it possible.

And then they were free! There had been cries of pain, daring negotiations, and deep threats. Finally it all happened in the night, when none could see (Exod. 12:29). They did not explain this wondrous rescue; they only sang and danced:

> Sing to the Lord, for he has triumphed gloriously;
> horse and rider he has thrown into the sea. (Exod. 15:21)

The newness was carried, finally, on Israel's lips of doxology, praise for the Holy One who outmaneuvered the famine-driven king of anxiety. Israel departed Egypt joyously, but found itself immediately in the wilderness, out beyond Pharaoh, but also out beyond the imperial food chain where there were no life supports. They complained, even wished again for slavery; no doubt the rate of recidivism was high. For those who stayed with the "departure," however, they came to see and know what could scarcely be imagined. It rained bread! It rained bread from heaven!

> They asked, and he brought quails,
> and gave them food from heaven in abundance.
> He opened the rock, and water gushed out;
> it flowed through the desert like a river. (Ps. 105:40-41)

There was more than enough:

> The Israelites did so, some gathering more, some less. But when they
> measured it with an omer, those who gathered much had nothing over,

and those who gathered little had no shortage; they gathered as much
as each of them needed. (Exod. 16:17-18)

In that odd moment, they learned that when there is escape from Pharaoh's
kingdom of scarcity into YHWH's generous zone of abundance, there is
plenty for all—no famine, no scarcity, no rationing, no acquisitiveness, no
anxiety, enough and more than enough. Never mind that it was wilderness;
it was wilderness taken under the aegis of the creator God who gave plenty.
And all of the contempt from Egypt is lifted in this moment of generous
mercy (see Ps. 123:3-4). The contrast of *scarce, anxious, Egypt,* and *abundant
wilderness* could not be sharper. It is an elemental contrast for Israel as an
experimental social revolution founded on miracle.

II

It is with all of that memory that Israel arrived at Sinai. The problem at
Sinai was how to take this narrative moment of emancipation and well-
being and transform it into a sustainable social practice with institutional
durability. That transformation from narrative to social structure was possible only because YHWH had been pondering the Hittite treaties and
articulated, on the mountain, a manifesto to reorganize social relationships. It is not necessary here to consider all of the ten commandments
that constitute the charter for this social revolution. Two comments suffice.
First, this is the policy formation of the God of generosity and abundance,
fresh from the wilderness, who stand as a sharp, unmistakable contrast to
Pharaoh. So the manifesto begins, as you know:

> I am the Lord your God who brought you out of the land of Egypt,
> out of the house of bondage. (Exod. 20:1)

I am the God who defeated Pharaoh, who eliminated the policies of the
Pharaoh, who overcame the scarcity of Pharaoh, and who nullified the
anxiety of Pharaoh. The choice for Israel at Sinai is the either/or of Pharaoh or the God of manna. Revolutions need stern discipline, and so this
God of Sinai spoke ten times.

Second, the tenth commandment, the final one, has had a curious interpretive history. Some have thought it was, after nine mandates for action,
an introspective, psychological warning against envy. But of course that

has been a highly idealistic reading. When we face the materialism of this God, it is clear that "do not covet" concerns greed, acquisitiveness, confiscation of a neighbor's goods. It is clear that in this tenth command, above all, Israel is not to emulate Pharaoh, for acquisitiveness will defeat and destroy the social experiment to which Israel is summoned. The tenth command against acquisitiveness is so elemental that the writer of Colossians matches it precisely to the first, most foundational command.

> Put to death . . . *coveting* which is *idolatry*. (Col. 3:5)

Cease from violation of the tenth command, for it is a violation of the first command. Indeed, the premise of the entire Sinai experiment is that socioeconomic, political relationships are radically different because of this generous Alternative who presides over the materiality of the world.

It remained for Moses, that most brilliant hermeneutist, to tease out the concrete practices of the new manifesto. Situated precisely between commandment one and commandment ten, as Patrick Miller has noticed, is the command to Sabbath, that holy pause that breaks all vicious cycles of self-preoccupation, destructiveness, and greed.[2] In his ongoing interpretation, Moses lets the Sabbath command provide an alternative to coveting. First in the "year of release" (Deut. 15:1-18), Moses takes the "seven" of the sabbath and makes it an economic mandate for seven years. It is an extraordinary provision that Frank Crüsemann calls the first "social safety net"; it cancels the debts of the poor after seven years; it assures against the formation of a permanent underclass, and it recognizes the inalienable entitlement of the poor to the resources of the community, enough for dignity, security, and well-being.[3] The statute is so familiar and so neglected that we do not notice its stunning, revolutionary reach.

Second, in the "Jubilee," long before our millennial effort at debt cancellation, Moses provides a "seven-times-seven," fiftieth-year social process whereby the reality and claims of communal neighborliness override and curb the destructive disproportion of the market. All of this is premised on the realism of the Exodus:

> For they are my servants whom I brought out of the land of Egypt;
> they shall not be sold as slaves are sold. (Lev. 25:42)

Pharaoh will have no Jubilee, no year of release, no debt cancellation, no sabbath, only a process whereby the privileged work their privilege. But

YHWH has defeated Pharaoh and Israel is YHWH's social experiment to see if the economy can serve the community. The claim is clear and its implications for material practices of the community are clear enough. And so the Torah of Moses develops what is nearly a mantra of social revolution, "widow, orphan, alien," the marginated and vulnerable, now valued, noticed, protected, entitled. Outside of this stringent, costly provision, there is nothing but Pharaoh, nothing but anxiety, scarcity, and eventually fresh waves of bondage.

III

The tilt of the Torah in its sequence of Exodus-wilderness-Sinai is unambiguous. YHWH is indeed a serious, material alternative to Pharaoh. But *then came land.* Indeed that is where the Torah has been headed from the outset. To Abram, "go to the land I will show you" (Gen. 12:1). To Moses, "I have come down . . . to bring you to a good and broad land, a land flowing with milk and honey" (Exod. 3:8). Moses arrives at the Jordan and sees the good land, but does not enter. Thus begins the new history with its huge governance problems—reflected in monarchy—and its immense interpretive requirements reflected in Deuteronomy.

The land quickly requires new agents of oversight, kings; and with kings in Israel, prophets are never far away. Kings are installed to manage the social experiment that is Israel. Moses had already seen in Deut. 17:14-10 that kings are characteristically coveters. They gather, collect, hoard, exhibit—you name it—silver, gold, horses, chariots, wives—it always comes down to money, power, and sex, neighbors' fields and neighbors' wives. Moses offers Torah as an alternative and then shrewdly observes that systemic coveting will land you right back in Egypt, the great land of coveting and enslavement. As an echo to Moses, crusty old Samuel had seen it all coming. Kings are "takers":

> These will be the ways of the king who will reign over you; he will *take*
> your sons and appoint them to his chariots and to be his horsemen,
> and to run before his chariots; and he will appoint for himself com-
> manders of thousands and commanders of fifties, and some to plow his
> ground and reap his harvests, and to make his implements of war and
> the equipment of his chariots. He will *take* one-tenth of your grain and

of your vineyards and give it to his officers and his courtiers. He will
take your male and female slaves, and the best of your cattle and don-
keys, and put them to his work. He will *take* one-tenth of your flocks,
and you shall be his slaves. (1 Sam. 8:11-17)

"Take" six times, programmatic, systemic coveting that will lead to dismay.

What Moses and Samuel, situated in the radicality of Sinai visions of
neighborliness, had anticipated the kings enact. The first royal taker is
David:

So David sent messengers, and he *took* her, and she came to him, and
he lay with her. (2 Sam. 11:4)

It was a quick "take," but one with endless consequences, setting in motion
the deathliness of this governance. David was, for an instant, above
the Torah, outside Sinai, cavorting in the land of Pharaoh where lies
deathliness.

But David's greater son, Solomon, of course outdid David on all counts
of coveting: in the realm of sexual confiscation, three hundred wives and
seven hundred concubines; in the realm of wealth—gold, gold, gold.
So exotic, so extravagant, so indulgent, that when the queen of Sheba
came—no piker of a taker herself—we are told that Solomon took her
breath away (1 Kgs. 10:5). Israel's text gloats a bit over this Solomon who
matched the great ones of the earth. In the same moment, however,
Israel's text knows better. The taking is not condemned for its economic
rapacity; rather the indictment returns from the tenth commandment to
the first. Solomon is an idolater, seduced, in this patriarchal taxonomy, by
his foreign wives:

For when Solomon was old, his wives turned away his heart after other
gods; and his heart was not true to the Lord his God, as was the heart
of his father David. (1 Kgs. 11:4)

But the text knows: idolatry always show up as coveting, for idolatry leads
this wise king outside the zone of Sinai, beyond commandments, beyond
the neighborly mantras that curb Pharaonic coveting, and lead him to deep
and irreversible loss, ten tribes at the outset.

IV

Sinai has a tenuous claim on royal intention. But the God of Sinai, as Muilenburg said, is never without witness. Israel is never permitted to forget. Because as Moses permitted kingship in Deuteronomy 17, so Moses provided prophets in Deuteronomy 18. These Moses-authorized prophets reflected on Israel's inclination to bend too much toward Pharaoh.

Royal Isaiah characterizes the land as the kings had occupied it:

> Their land is filled with silver and gold,
>   and there is no end to their treasures;
> their land is filled with horses,
>   and there is no end to their chariots.
> Their land is filled with idols;
>   they bow down to the work of their hands. (Isa. 2:7-8)

A land of arrogant consumerism about to be turned to grief, because its consumerism cannot be sustained at the cost of the neighbor:

> In that day the lord will take away the finery of the anklets, the head-bands, and the crescents. . . . In that day. (Isa. 3:18)

The acquisitiveness will lead, says this poet, to the shriveling of productivity. His indictment is organized against a kind of agribusiness that is rooted in a Baconian notion of the conquest of nature:

> Ah, you who join house to house,
>   who add field to field,
> until there is room for no one but you,
>   and you are left to live alone
> in the midst of the land. . . .
> Surely many houses shall be desolate,
> large and beautiful houses, without inhabitant.
> For ten acres of vineyard shall yield but one bath,
> and a homer of seed shall yield a mere ephah. (Isa. 5:8-10)

This little poem may be taken as a decisive prophetic marker against an uncurbed, acquisitive market. It's all about buying up land and displacing people. The end result, moreover, is that one needs more and more land because it will, uncared for and unrespected, produce less and less. The land itself will refuse to produce and will withhold its gift of crops, because the land is committed to the Sinai vision. Between verse 8 on acquisitiveness and verse 10 on scarcity stands verse 9:

> The lord of hosts has sworn.

Greedy Israel cannot outflank the intent and restraints of the covenant. Coveting will not work because it defies the Lord of Sinai. Coveting is conduct like that of Pharaoh and he is known in the heavens to be an untrustworthy fraud.

The urban Isaiah is matched by *the peasant Micah*. Micah from the village of Moresheth had watched the greedy urbanites in Jerusalem, the big banks, the land speculators, the large corporate buy-outs. He did not do close economic analysis, but only recited poetry that reflected his peasant passion:

> Woe to those who devise wickedness
> and evil deeds on their beds.
> . . . They covet fields, and seize them;
> houses, and take them away;
> They oppress householder and house, people and their inheritance.
> (Mic. 2:1-2)

He has this image of sleepy men in bathrobes, calling brokers early in the day, coveting fields, seizing them, displacing people, violating the entitlements of Jubilee, gathering, collecting, investing, speculating. The verbs line out until the savage "therefore" of judgment in verses 3-4:

> Now I am devising against this family an evil. . . .
> On that day they shall take up a taunt song against you
> and wail with bitter lamentation,
> and say, "We are utterly ruined. . . ."

There will come a day of reckoning: an irreversible evil sent from YHWH, invading armies, a cry of abandonment in the face of abrupt reversal, and then, finally, a redistribution of land among the peasants. Coveting won't work, because it displaces too many people. The economy will not tolerate such monopoly because the economy, in a Sinai vista, is to serve the community. The community is willed and maintained by the God of covenant who had decisively defeated the powers of acquisitiveness. And now the graspers are on notice.

A century later sounds *pathos-filled Jeremiah*, still engaged with the powers of rapaciousness, only now closer to payout time. The indictment of the covetous is by now familiar:

> They know no limits in deeds of wickedness;
>> they do not judge with justice
> the cause of the orphan, to make it prosper,
>> and they do not defend the rights of the needy. (Jer. 5:28)

The threat is voiced as a question, "Shall I not punish them for these things?" (v. 29). It is a rhetorical question without an answer, and Jerusalem is left to answer. The threat is deep, grounded in the elemental self-deception of the economy that touches every mode of leadership.

> For from the least to the greatest of them
>> everyone is greedy for unjust gain;
> and from prophet to priest,
>> everyone deals falsely.
> They have treated the wound of my people carelessly,
>> saying "Peace, peace,"
>> when there is no peace. (Jer. 6:13-14)

The threat is against those too impressed with commodity, predictably excessive commodity connected to exploitative labor practices (Jer. 22:13-17). It could be different. The community could have the poor and the needy on its horizon. It was different for an instant in the reign of Josiah. But not long enough. Or soon enough. Or not late enough.

The poets—urban Isaiah, peasant Micah, pathos-filled Jeremiah—leave the matter. It is only poetry, and what can poetry matter? W. H. Auden has observed that "poems do not do anything." They do, however, linger and haunt and stand as a testimony, verifying Sinai, subverting uncriticized power, lingering, taken up as canon, lingering and haunting well beyond the city of Jerusalem and the villages of Moresheth and Anathoth.

V

All of that is of course known among us. We may call it "progressive politics" and, Union being Union, I expect we are roughly agreed on this strange tradition entrusted to us. So a step further. The Torah and the prophets together haunted Israel and all its sons and daughters. This Jesus is among those haunted by Sinai and by the poets housed at Sinai. The trajectory we pursue here, the one that links *tradition* and *advocacy for the poor*, surely comes to the narrative of Luke.

In fifteenth-century Florence, Sandro Botticelli painted a portrayal of the baby Jesus held by mother Mary, midst a flood of rich Florentine portrayals. In this one, however, Mary holds a scroll of the Magnificat, and the baby Jesus is fingering the letters of the scroll, fingering the cadences of that song. Mary at that moment is not singing. But she did sing; and while the baby fingered, he inhaled the cadences of mother Mary, all about "the hungry with good things," all about "the rich sent empty away," all about social reversal and social revolution and transformation of the economy for the sake of community. The praise of the poor voiced here has rootage in Hannah's ancient hope. The cadences of social transformation are as old as Israel itself, singing the power and the passion of the God of Israel against every deathly Pharaoh. As Luke tells it, this song rings in Jesus' ears even while he does his teaching. He warns the crowds about "the yeast of the Pharisees" (Luke 12:1-3), and about being called to give an account of faith (12:8-12).

In the midst of that polemical but encouraging instruction, the discourse of Jesus is interrupted by a voice in the crowd, a voice so intent on its own agenda that he is uninterested in Jesus' instruction. The man ignores the invitation to courage just given by Jesus and instead asks, abruptly, out of context, about his inheritance:

> Teacher, tell my brother to divide the family inheritance with me.
> (v. 13)

What a wondrous opening question. The question is as old as Israel itself, for Israel from the beginning has been an intergenerational community worried about the transmission of its material patrimony. The question surfaces already between the shepherds of Lot and Abraham (Gen. 13:5-7), is present in the anxiety of Abraham that Eliezer, his slave, would inherit (Gen. 15:2); indeed, the question haunts the entire tale of Genesis with all our barren mothers. The issue is as urgent as the account of Joshua and his division of the new land of promise, taken by violence from the antecedent population that thought it was their land. The question runs through the acquisitiveness of kings into the loss of exile, the recovery under Ezra, and finally in that telling visionary reallotment of land by Ezekiel in a perfect symmetry.

The tradition we confess is indeed all about inheritance, patrimony, and land—in Palestine surging with promises and too many landless people waiting, in Kosovo where nothing about the land is ever forgotten, in Northern Ireland where religion covers economic affronts, and on and on, until the man's disruptive question is coded in our society as "Welfare Reform" or in Britain as "New Labor," and the inheritance is divided according to the rules and regulations of those who already have most of the patrimony. Give the interrupting man this much, he did seek a judge who would be impartial; he did not want favor, only his proper entitlement. The question he puts to Jesus is exactly the right question for the "progressive" horizon of Union Seminary, and can even allow for entitlements of nonhuman creatures in the allotment of the earth.

We do not know the tone of the man's question, but it must have been urgent, for he interrupts Jesus' discourse in order to get it said. So the plea is at least urgent, likely some indignation at previous treatment by his brother, probably some anxiety, for he was beginning to wonder if there was any place from which to receive right and equitable judgment, and if not with this carrier of the Chalcedonian formula, then where?

Jesus answers the man promptly. Jesus, however, is no fool about which risks he will run. He, like anyone who has witnessed a land dispute in an extended rural family, knows immediately that it is wiser not to render judgment, not to play the role of probate judge, for it is a no-win question. If the question is an entry for the most progressive social ethicists at Union Theological Seminary, then Jesus' answer is enough to delight Union artistic types like Robert Seaver. First, Jesus refuses the role imposed on him:

> "Friend, who set me to be a judge or arbitrator over you?" (v. 14)

Then he warns the man, apparently, spotting in his question a tone of greed and acquisitiveness:

> "Take care! Be on your guard against all kinds of greed;
> for one's life does not consist in the abundance of possessions." (v. 15)

Perhaps the man is so urgent, so angry, so aware of his entitlements that any-one—certainly Jesus—could see that he is going for broke on the question of property and commodity. Such entitlement is, in the horizon of Jesus, at best a penultimate question for the man, and the man has made it ultimate.

And then, "he told him a parable" (v. 16). Jesus conducts a bit of street theater that would not come at the issue of the man's greed directly. Jesus comes storywise, sideways, talking about the crisis of greed enough to be followed, but not directly enough to engage in the family quarrel. He tells a tale of a man who is not present, concrete enough that the listener can rethink his own request, open enough that anybody in the crowd can enter the narrative and recognize herself in the lead role.[4] Economics is turned to art, tradition is turned to drama. Life-or-death commitments are made into a tale where the Voice of the Holy intrudes palpably and audibly: holiness operative in an aggressive economic transaction.

You already know the parable that answers the frantic question of anxiety. "Once there was a rich man." No ducking of social inequity. The rich man—one who in sapiential literature is usually regarded as evil—prepared. His much land produced much revenue; he was blessed. Of course. That calculus of favoritism for the rich had been clearly voiced by Job:

> Why do the wicked live on,
> reach old age, and grow mighty in power?
> Their children are established in their presence,
> and their offspring before their eyes.
> Their houses are safe from fear,
> and no rod of God is upon them.
> Their bull breeds without fail;
> their cow calves and never miscarries.
> They send out their little ones like a flock,
> and their children dance around.
> They sing to the tambourine and the lyre,
> and rejoice to the sound of the pipe.
> They spend their days in prosperity,
> and in peace they go down to Sheol. (Job 21:7-13)

The land of the poor never performs like the land of the rich, no doubt because they lack irrigation pumps, chemical fertilizers, tax write-offs, and advice from agribusiness. But this inordinate prosperity is a premise of the narrative, not a concern.

The story goes wrong when the rich man proposes what to do with his huge capital gains. Right there, in verse 17, he had a choice. He could have chosen differently. But he decides easily and quickly, congruent with his abundance:

Plan part 1:
> I will do this; I will pull down my barns and build larger ones, and there
> I will store all my grain and my goods. (v. 18)

He will store. He will hoard. He will accumulate. He needed bigger barns, partly for storage, partly for conspicuous exhibition of his wealth, his good fortune, his blessing from the God of all crops. His property had given him amnesia, and he no longer remembers the manna warning against storage, where what is stored melts, becomes foul, and breeds worms. It won't keep in storage (Exod. 16:20-21).

Plan part 2:
> And I will say to my soul, "Soul, you have ample goods laid up for many
> years; relax, eat, drink, be merry." (v. 19)

Property leads to congratulations that lead to celebration. He could not remember the manna story; but he conveniently recalled just the right text, albeit perhaps cynical, from Qoheleth:

> Go, eat your bread with enjoyment, and drink your wine with a merry
> heart; for God has long ago approved what you do. (Eccles. 9:7)

Long ago, God approved. By the time this text arrives in the Lucan narrative, the approving God is nothing more than an echo of the self-indulgence of this autonomous self. He calls himself "soul" (*psyche)*, a self-generated, self-authenticated, isolated, subjective self, an "I" with no "Thou" who will call him by name. What a party! He is alone. Nobody else came to the party or was even invited. Perhaps he did not know anybody, because friendship takes effort, and he had none to spare. Likely he did not want to be bothered. Probably he now owned so much land that he had displaced all those who could have been neighbors (see Isa. 5:8-10). Excessive storage makes neighborliness at best unlikely.

So the party begins. He drinks, he eats, maybe he even hums or sings or dances a bit. Conventional wisdom is that family holidays lead to depression, because they never measure up to expectation. Well, if the man in the story had any expectation of joy, his acquisitiveness had blocked it. So alone! So unaddressed, unappreciated, unadmired, unaffirmed, unconnected, the un-selfing of the self by commodity.

But—in the end—not as alone as he had imagined. By verse 20, he is addressed. A voice not stifled, as Muilenburg anticipated! He had eliminated all the neighbors and cut all the phone lines; but one neighbor came, likely had to penetrate the locked gates and the dogs designed to isolate and secure the wealth. There is, however, no finally reliable security system. Late on the night of the party, this unaddressed man is addressed, and now called by his right name. He had called himself *Psyche,* self-invented, autonomous agent answerable to none. His acquisitiveness, however, had caused a massive misperception of his life. Now speaks the God of all truth who names him by his right name: "Fool!" That is, one lacking in judgment and discernment, careless about what is important. Not "self," but "fool." The man in this moment of utterance has been made a self by address, but de-selfed in that very moment by the very voice that could have, under other circumstances, secured his self for him. But self cannot be secured when it makes commodity ultimate.

Perhaps the address by the Holy One who penetrated that night the best security system that money could buy is generic, out of the wisdom tradition, for fools are those who fail to reckon with the shape of life given by God. Or perhaps the Holy One more specifically engages in narrative intertexuality and alludes to 1 Samuel 25. There the woman Abigail turns out to be prudent and wise. But her husband is a fool, such a fool that he is called Nabal, fool. He is foolish in his failure to share with David. David is running a protection racket and Nabal is too intent on his property to see David in larger vista:

> "Who is David? Who is the son of Jesse? There are many servants today who are breaking away from their masters. Shall I take my bread and my water and the meat that I have butchered for my shearers, and give it to men who come from I do not know where?" (1 Sam. 25:10-11)

Nabal is so intent on his property that he refuses to share. And he dies. He loses his life trying to keep his stuff. In like manner, the man in the parable is transformed by Holy Utterance into the fool who will lose his life keeping his stuff:

> "This very night your life is being demanded of you. And the things you have prepared, whose will they be?" (v. 20)

The party ends, abruptly. The conversation is terminated, and so is his life—in the night—by address from his only "Thou," unprotected by his vast wealth. As he dies, you can imagine the LP record running out on his dance music, and the needle turning, turning, turning on the disc, in the quiet until dawn when the maid arrived and knowingly shut it down. The police could not figure it out, no sign of an intruder, so that the death certificate read only, "Killed by his possessions."

Jesus steps out of the parable to address the man with the question and to speak past him to the crowd:

> So it is with those who store up treasures for themselves but are not rich toward God." (v. 21)

The contrast is as clear as Proverbs on "wisdom and foolishness" (Prov. 8:32-36) and as decisive as Deuteronomy on "life and death" (Deut. 30:15-20). The turn in the man's life was not at the party; by then it was too late, and irreversible. The turn was in verse 17, when the man asked a rhetorical question and answered it with "storage." Everything after that was too late. The man with the question went home without his inheritance and even without any encouragement about his entitlement. He was given no advice and no direction, only a haunting.

VI

In this company of "progressive politics," I do not need to say why the haunting is so urgent and our proper subject:

Because commodity produces amnesia,

Because greed tells against neighborliness,

Because the vision of Jubilee has become a grinding calculation among too many money people,

Because shopping among us is no longer for goods, but now is the only entertainment we can think of,

Because the enterprises of sports, entertainment, and politics mostly are about shameless accumulation that vagues the line of violence,

Because daytime greed cannot stop the haunting of the night that defies our control,

Because while the rich are richer, the political process evaporates, and the widow and orphan grow less and less audible (to say nothing of the sojourner),

Because the tale of the Crucified and Risen One is about economics, who though he was rich, yet for our sakes he became poor, so that by his poverty you might become rich (2 Cor. 8:9).

VII

Jesus addresses the man with the question, a man who could have been any one of us. Through the man he addresses the crowd more generally. So the tradition addresses even this company at Union in its generic address; it haunts us with countereconomics, warning against acquisitiveness. The warning and the haunting of course rightly suit our common propensity for progressive politics.

But Jesus is not done in verse 21. Now, after the man and after the crowd, he turns in verse 22 to address the disciples. He wants the disciples to go further and to learn more for themselves from this encounter. He says to them, "Do not be anxious." He knows that anxiety haunts the man who asked the question. He knows, further, that the crowd is like the man, also worried about entitlements. And beyond that, he knows that the same anxiety is present in equal measure among his disciples, anxiety in the church as in the world.

> Do not be anxious about your life . . . your food.
> Do not be anxious about your body . . . your clothing.

What a word to speak to disciples already in on the risks of obedience. What a word to speak at Union where the institution had better worry some about its food and its clothing and its rent and its utility bills, where such anxiety is front and center in the celebration of this new president. The lesson is tough for the crowd. It is even more acute for the disciples. With the crowd, Jesus can do a terse warning about being "rich toward God."

But now, with his disciples, he must factor it out. He must give an account of the alternative to acquisitiveness that is propelled by anxiety rooted in scarcity. Everybody thinks there is not enough, the man, his brother, Jews and Palestinians, Protestants and Catholics, Serbs and Albanians, Muslims and Hindus. Everybody thinks there is not enough, except for this reflection on the providential working of God's creation that refuses the categories of Pharaoh:

> Consider the ravens; they neither sow nor reap, they have neither storehouse nor barn, and yet God feeds them. Of how much more value are you than the birds! And can any of you by worrying add a single hour to your span of life? If then you are not able to do so small a thing as that, why do you worry about the rest? Consider the lilies, how they grow; they neither toil nor spin. (Matt. 6:24-28)

The birds and the flowers are so unlike the man in the parable, and we know about his sorry end, we and the maid the next morning. In this response, Jesus invokes Israel's deepest faith about the generosity of the creator. Israel's largest doxologies are about the God who ensures the food chain, who certifies that there will be more than enough, who protects and guarantees that the world will keep yielding. The ravens count on that abundance and do not hoard. The lilies count on that generosity and never counter scarcity by feverish activity. The birds and flowers, so he says, are not devoured by anxiety.

The disciples are drawn back to rethink and recommit to creation, to the conviction that "this is our father's world," the father who knows you need all these things. The disciples are meant to rethink and reembrace the mothering of this God who births and feeds and nurtures the world that is never designed for autonomy. The birds and the flowers powerfully attest—in the teaching of Jesus—that all the agenda of self-sufficiency and self-security, all the fantasies of the "End of History" and the self-congratulations on a "New World Order" based on the new technologies are never more than penultimate; because ultimately the world lives by gift that can only be matched by trustful gratitude that gives back gladly via the neighbor.

Did you notice the wondrous exegetical marker Jesus has inserted into this affirmation? "Not even Solomon!" Solomon is the master sales rep., the Donald Trump of his time. He believes in free trade and all the rest. He is the master technological enthusiast, the great broker, the Pharaoh of God's chosen people. He is the best and the most and the great pride of Israel, the missile program, the skyscraper, the media event, massive capital gains, nearly unutterable in his acquisitiveness. And he did not get it! Perhaps the man in the parable who died too soon will turn out to be Solomon who was rich toward himself with his exhibitionism; but there is nothing in the tradition about Solomon and the poor, nothing about Solomon and Jubilee, nothing about Solomon and the year of release. His house of extravagant cards, moreover, tumbled in a labor dispute that even his vast military apparatus could not overcome.

The decisive point in Jesus' countereconomics is put in primitive patriarchal form. "Your heavenly father knows." There is generous Agency that gives and gives. At the center of our confession is the affirmation that the faithful generous Giver counters the cold, flat judgment that there is no agency left that will rescue the earth from its deathliness. It is all very well and urgent that Union continue its bold voice in progressive politics and economics. In that it has many important allies.

But my accent finally is, as in Luke, on the "homework." Behind progressive politics and economics there is the theological question, the issue whether the generosity and abundance of God can be confessed as world-defining; because if it cannot, then the ground for anxiety and greed is immense and realistic. I have called this "homework," the hard, less dramatic, nearly unnoticed work of assumptions and premises and basic commitments that take place in more hidden, liturgical ways; and in this the role of Union is greater and more urgent, for it has fewer allies in the project.

The disciples in this exchange are not so much called to instruct the crowd. They are rather to reorder their own life away from deathly foolishness. The temptation to hoard is because there is not enough, not enough guns and missiles, not enough wealth and sex, not enough library money and tenure and curriculum and students and endowments. And now this staggering word of generosity that evokes richness of another kind on our part:

- the kings had not heard well, but the poets insisted;
- Pharaoh could not get it, but Moses knew;
- Gottwald, we say, had it right, even if some do not like his Marxian reading.
- Muilenburg, as always, said it well: "It was the voice of Israel's covenant-making and covenant-keeping God. But was it stilled? Not quite!" The tradition in all these voices attests:

- acquisitiveness in inimical to the human project;
- greed kills;
- anxiety isolates;
- excessive goods produce amnesia.

Jesus adds to this summons his little end-time notation:

> Be dressed for action and have your lamps lit; be like those who are waiting for their master to return from the wedding banquet, so that they may open the door for him as soon as he comes and knocks. Blessed are those slaves whom the master finds alert when he comes. . . . If he comes during the middle of the night, or near dawn, and finds them so, blessed are those slaves. (Luke. 12:35-38)

It occurred to me, surely beyond the intention of Luke, that the man in the parable thought he was the owner and master. It turns out that he is only the slave and steward. His misperception of his own role and office caused him not to be ready. Economics is a long-term project. There are, however, check points and audits. They happen, says the text, when least expected, at night, in circumstances of self-congratulations. Finally, Jesus says:

> "You also must be ready, for the Son of Man is coming at an unexpected hour." (v. 4)

This seminary, long haunted by what Solomon never got, has deep homework to do. The rest of us count heavily upon it.

CHAPTER TEN

Vision for a New Church and a New Century

Part II: Holiness Becomes Generosity

I have suggested that Jesus' summons "Do not be anxious" (Luke 12:22) is an indispensable piece of homework for a sustainable economy of generosity and abundance. Without that homework in faith that commits to a conviction that there is enough, revolutionary or progressive economics has no chance. That judgment about the joining of the *parable to the crowd* (Luke 12:13-21, or more precisely vv. 16-20) and the *instruction to the disciples* (vv. 22-31) set me to thinking about homework. I judge that for ethics in the world and for the shape of humane and generative public policy, homework must be ecclesial. That is, good public policy requires the formation and the nurture of subcommunities of courage and passion that are about the daily business of praise and obedience, that are devoted to the will of God, meditating on it day and night, and that actively await the full and soon coming of God's governance. Such ecclesial homework is a major and central task of Union Theological Seminary, both the tough thinking that is required and the daily, patient practice of nurture in such homework for those who will lead and nurture communities of praise and obedience.

I

I suggest that in largest rubric, intentionality to form subcommunities of praise and obedience is nowhere more clearly or succinctly put than in the mandate:

You shall be holy for I the Lord your God am holy. (Lev. 19:2)

That mandate, rooted, as we say, in the Priestly tradition and writ large in the Torah of Moses, includes three immediate subpoints:

a. Revere father and mother, thus reference to what has become the fifth commandment;

b. Keep sabbath, thus reference to what has become the fourth commandment (v. 3);

c. Reject idols and images, reference to what has become the second commandment (v. 4).

This triad we may take as representative of the core command of Sinai. The critical mandate of the community of Torah, as this tradition voices it, is to be a community matched in its life and practice to the very character of YHWH. The tone of that obedience is command; the substance is holiness, utterly, singularly, peculiarly devoted to and matched with the very character of YHWH. This Torah tradition takes as the central ecclesial task the formation of a holy community, to be weaned from the fears and the hopes of the world, a necessary prerequisite to a radical socioeconomic practice. This discipline, moreover, is surely what has been neglected in the spasms of radical Christian social ethics in recent decades.

But the formation of holiness is not simply instrumental to public policy; it is a characterization that is *intrinsic* to the very being of the church, there being no intended gap between the public engagement of the church and the identity and character of the church as a distinct body in the world. This ecclesial agenda being a holy people of God is worth a rethink among us for quite practical reasons. In the two church traditions I know best, such ecclesial awareness and discipline are largely absent. In the United Church of Christ, there is almost no ecclesial intentionality at all, having evaporated into public policy agenda; in Presbyterianism, the matter has been transposed into judicial management that on the whole lacks the buoyancy or discipline of holiness. As a result, I offer a rather subjective reflection on the emergence of the recovery of ecclesial self-awareness and intentionality in the church body that is roughly the long-term constituency of Union.

II

From the perspective of biblical faith, it was an inexplicable and irreversible moment when YHWH, the God of Israel, entered into a special relationship with Israel by choosing and forming a community that had not been until that moment of God's choosing and forming. Whether that is taken to be in the abrupt divine address to Abraham, in the transformative engagement with Egyptian slaves, or in the solemnity of Sinai, it is confessed that the creator of heaven and earth has entered into the human, historical arena and has allied God's own self with this peculiar people:

> Now therefore, if you obey my voice and keep my covenant, you shall be my treasured possession out of all the peoples. Indeed, the whole earth is mine, but you shall be for me a priestly kingdom and a holy nation. (Exod. 19:5-6)

In quite elemental ways, the reception of this newly identified status as chosen people requires discipline and intentionality, for Israel does not go lightly to this meeting at Sinai:

> Go to the people and consecrate them (that is, make them holy) today and tomorrow. Have them wash their clothes and prepare for the third day. . . . So Moses went down from the mountain to the people. He consecrated the people, and they washed their clothes. And he said to the people, "Prepare for the third day; do not go near a woman" (Exod. 19:10-11, 14-15)

The status of chosen people is variously exposited in the twin trajectories of the Deuteronomic and the Priestly traditions. In the tradition of Deuteronomy, Israel's status as "holy to YHWH" is wondrously put:

> It was not because you were more numerous than any other people that the Lord set his heart on you and chose you—for you were the fewest of all peoples. It was because the Lord loved you and kept the oath that he swore to your ancestors, that the Lord has brought you out with a mighty hand, and redeemed you from the hand of Pharaoh king of Egypt. (Deut. 7:7-8)

Israel's exceptionalism is rooted in God's love, not in the size or virtue of Israel (see 9:4-5). This is of course a costly love, a covenant commitment that expects and insists upon rigorous obedience and attentiveness to YHWH's will for society:

> You are children of the Lord your God. You must not lacerate yourselves or shave your forelocks for the dead. For you are a people holy to

> the Lord your God; it is you the Lord has chosen out of all the peoples
> on earth to be his people, his treasured possession. . . . You shall not
> eat anything that dies of itself; you may give it to aliens residing in our
> towns for them to eat, or you may sell it to a foreigner. For you are a
> people holy to the Lord your God. (14:1-2, 21)

The tradition of Deuteronomy unfolds from holy electedness to a remarkable social ethic with revolutionary attentiveness to widows, orphans, and aliens. The tradition of Deuteronomy is in no doubt that holiness issues in remarkable public policy.

The matter is different in the Priestly tradition, a tradition that is to some extent more enigmatic and likely not accessible to a Christian, especially a Protestant, more particularly a liberal Protestant. We can, however, see enough and appropriate enough to notice the daring insistence of the priests. Holiness—singular devotion to YHWH—requires day-to-day intentionality, disciples that remind of and support the choosing of peculiarity. The primal claim of this tradition is deliberate separateness that is maintained by concrete acts of distinction. The priests reach back to the most elemental distinctions that may strike us as embarrassing:

> You shall not let your animals breed with a different kind; you shall not
> sow your field with two kinds of seed; nor shall you put on a garment
> made of two different materials. (Lev. 19:19; see Deut. 22:9-11)

Holiness, it is affirmed, is not a good idea but a daily practice of enacting a distinct identity that is visible in the world. It entails signs on hands, emblems on foreheads, writing on doorposts in which the family and community boldly announce difference and proceed to act it out. The development of the Priestly tradition indicates that the "other," the non-Israelite, the unchosen other peoples are to be kept out and avoided, because excessive contact will erode identity and compromise vocation.

The practice of holiness as separation, with others as seduction or threat, can be seen in three waves of Torah testimony. As Claus Westermann has seen, the good and lovely orderedness of creation depends on a series of separations, of light and darkness, of waters and waters, of waters and dry land.[1] The separations decreed are so that space is protected and blessed for life and well-being and future. Second, it is now suggested by a number of scholars that the Tabernacle in the tradition of Exodus is intended as a visible, cultic replication of the created order, so that Israel can engage in its liturgic life a model of rightly ordered, safe, blessed life as God intends. YHWH's seven speeches of authorization for the Tabernacle in Exodus 25–31, moreover, correlate to the seven days of creation, culminating in the seventh speech (Exod. 31:12-17) that is inescapably about sabbath as the culmination of creation.[2] Thus no matter how confused and disordered the world may be, Israel, so the text imagines, regularly has access to a series of gradations of holiness that regularize and order the holy zone of life where rests Israel's true home, identity, and vocation.

Third, out of the ordering separateness of creation and tabernacle, the Priestly traditions of Leviticus and Numbers trace out a life for the community that envisions every phase of life free from the seduction and threat of otherness, thus yielding pure, holy separation enacted in sacrifices, priests, and liturgical practices as well as purity in the more mundane daily matters of food and sex.

Now I am aware that this tradition is not normally celebrated in such a progressive place as Union. There is no doubt that the more *civic issues* more widely voiced in Deuteronomy and the *sacerdotal matters* voiced more fully in Leviticus yield very different accents. There is no doubt, moreover, that the traditions of separation, taken by themselves and on their own terms, appear from conventional Christian perspective as excessive and punctilious. Given all of that, the primal insistence is that an ordered life devoted to YHWH is possible, that such ordered life surely has the God of Exodus at its center (see oddly Exod. 29:46), and that ordered life with God yields buoyancy for a different life in the world. The two traditions together yield a mode of community wherein every phase of life is brought under the rule of YHWH, a rule that intends to screen out all the others, for the others are at least a distraction and at worst a deathly seduction. Israel knows, in these traditions, that its peculiar way in the world as the people of God is endlessly at risk.

III

This sense of holiness, especially when pushed logically to the extreme of separation, poses acute problems of alterity: what about the others? The tradition speaks with no single voice on this matter, as honest ecclesial tradition never does. Thus we may notice on the one hand that the maintenance of separation evokes a savage rhetoric of violence, in the ancient text as in the contemporary world. While the Priestly tradition is impervious to the others once they are judged "unclean," the tradition of Deuteronomy is somewhat more open.[3]

In the tradition of D, in the paragraph juxtaposed to the marvelous affirmation on chosenness I have quoted, there is violence toward the unchosen:

> Make no covenant with them and show them no mercy. Do not inter-marry with them. . . . But this is how you must deal with them: break down their altars, smash their pillars, hew down their sacred poles, and burn their idols with fire. (Deut. 7:2-5)

The paragraph on God's choice of Israel is followed by a parallel conclusion:

> You shall blot out their name from under heaven. . . . Do not bring an abhorrent thing into your house, or you will be set apart for destruc-tion like it. You must utterly detest and abhor it, for it is set apart for destruction. (7:24-26)

The rhetoric is overloaded. Sometimes it is destruction of the peoples, sometimes it is their religious symbols.

Either way, the destruction bespeaks immense anxiety. It may be that the rhetoric is to be taken literally as an action to maintain holiness. Most scholars, however, believe that the text as we have it is late and metaphorical, not invoking actual destruction of others, but simply a flood of rhetoric to assert difference in an urgent tome. Either way, holi-ness requires distinctiveness that invites resistance and polemic. It takes no imagination, moreover, to see that this impulse to separation of the truly faithful, by strategies of purgation and excommunication, is alive and well in varying measures of rejection and violence and hate. Holi-ness deals with such elemental claims that it cuts underneath our usual reasonableness.

But one can see, precisely in the text, that Israel knows otherwise as well. We are able to trace an important series of texts that acknowledges in hospitable ways the legitimacy of other peoples who belong on the hori-zon of Israel as they are on the horizon of YHWH, and who constitute no threat to Israel's holiness. Perhaps this acknowledgment of others is in part a pragmatic, experimental one, because Israel always had neighbors and almost always overlords who seemed destined by the same God. But beyond the pragmatic, it is elemental to Israel's faith that the God of its choosing is the creator of heaven and earth and the lord of all peoples. Thus in the very same Sinai utterance of holiness it is also stated, "the whole earth is mine" (Exod. 19:5). In the eloquence of Deut. 10:14-15, moreover, the claim that YHWH "set his heart in love" on Israel is not stated before it is recognized that "heaven and the heaven of heavens belong to the LORD your God, the earth and all that is in it."

Israel's keen sense of exceptionalism is honed in a context of pluralism that accepts the legitimacy of the others and that inchoately and implicitly requires that holiness must be otherwise articulated and practiced. I will cite six clear awarenesses of that pluralism in the midst of which Israel must do its specialness:

1. Most primitively, it is recognized that the covenant with Noah after the flood is YHWH's commitment to "all flesh," to "every living creature," "for all future generations" (Gen. 9:11-12):

> I will remember my covenant that is between me and you and every living creature of all flesh; and the waters shall never again become a flood to destroy all flesh. When the bow is in the clouds, I will see it and remember the everlasting covenant between God and every living creature of all flesh that is on the earth. (vv. 15-16)

This huge divine commitment that is as large as all creation serves Israel well in the exile:

> This is like the days of Noah to me:
> Just as I swore that the waters of Noah
> would never again go over the earth,
> so I have sworn that I will not be angry with you
> and will not rebuke you.
> For the mountains may depart
> and the hills be removed,
> but my steadfast love shall not depart from you,
> and my covenant of peace shall not be removed,
> says the LORD who has compassion on you. (Isa. 54:9-10)

Nonetheless, while claiming the promise for Israel, in its very utterance the poet knows that steadfast love and covenant peace are no monopoly of this little community far from home.

2. It is of course recognized that the initial divine mandate to Abraham is open well beyond the future of Abraham (Gen. 12:1-3). The promise to Abraham and Sarah is of course land, heir, and future; but beyond that it is that "by you all the families of the earth shall be blessed." Israel's existence is in part instrumental for YHWH, a device whereby YHWH's blessings get to the nations; Israel is not an end in this reading but a means toward a larger end.

3. In Deut. 23:1-7 there is a list of uncompromising exclusions from the holy assembly of Israel, no doubt to protect holiness. The list variously precludes forever those with crushed testicles (presumably eunuchs) and bastards as well as Ammonites and Moabites, though allowance is to be made for Edomites and Egyptians. The exclusions do not especially surprise us in context. But two notices testify to Israel's (subsequent?) reconsideration of the matter. In Deut. 2:8-19, it is asserted that Moab and Ammon, excluded in Deuteronomy 23, are recognized as people who are to be respected in their territories, as though they also have received promised lands from YHWH. To be sure, this recognition is less than inclusion in covenantal worship, but it is a huge acknowledgment of the legitimacy of the other. And in Isaiah 56, in a remarkable admission of eunuchs and foreigners into worship, the allowance seems, as Herbert Donner urges, to overcome the exclusions of Deuteronomy 23.[4] One cannot know how to adjudicate these matters except to see that by attentiveness to the other, intense holiness and latitudinal pluralism are kept in the tradition as an unsettled, open, and ongoing question.

4. In one of the most remarkable of texts, Amos speaks against any monopoly Israel may have on YHWH.[5] Amos apparently faces a community mightily convinced of its own peculiar status. Amos does not deny that status (see 3:2) but denies the monopoly. In a full recognition of Israel's founding miracle of the Exodus, Amos has in purview other exoduses done by this God for other peoples:

> Are you not like the Ethiopians to me,
>   O people of Israel? says the LORD.
> Did I not bring Israel up from the land of Egypt,
>   and the Philistines from Caphtor and the Arameans from Kir?
>   (9:7)

The text imagines, with what are perhaps representative examples, at least two other Exoduses done by this Exodus-enacting God who does it everywhere. Indeed the two cases cited were (and continue to be) Israel's most profound enemies, the Palestinians and the Syrians. These "others" share with Israel the founding miracle of Exodus.

5. Whereas Amos 9:7 included the others in theological horizon by citing two other small states commensurate with Israel, the astounding text of Isa. 19:23-25 aims at bigger others. This should not surprise us, for Isaiah is characteristically the most eloquent and most sweeping in vision among the prophets. The poem of Isaiah 19 has begun as an attack on Egypt. By its end, however, it has reversed field as YHWH is wont to reverse field. In the end it is not Israel against the hated empires, but it is Israel alongside the empires, all of whom together may share status with YHWH:

> On the day Israel will be the third with Egypt and Assyria, a blessing in the midst of the earth, whom the Lord of hosts has blessed, saying, "Blessed be Egypt, *my people,* and Assyrians *the work of my hands,* and Israel *my heritage.*" (Isa. 19:24-25)

This must be among the most daring texts in the Old Testament. The poet takes YHWH's pet names for Israel, "My people, the work of my hands, my heritage," and freely distributes them across the Near East. By the end of the poem, YHWH has three chosen peoples. Israel's special status is affirmed, but is now shared with others who have long been nemeses. The poem suggests that YHWH is not yet finished choosing chosen peoples, and may yet choose others. That continuing choosing does not diminish Israel's chosenness, not at all; but at the end of the canon there is this immense vista of chosenness not propelled by Israel's sense of itself, but rooted in Israel's best sense of YHWH, the God of all "others." There are "others"; for YHWH, they are "my others."

6. The fullest articulation of the God of Israel as fully the God of the "the others" is in Second Isaiah. The central gospel message of the poet concerns emancipation and homecoming for exiled Jews. The role of Israel as servant is indeed everywhere enigmatic, as the muddle of scholarship makes clear. It does seem, in any case, that the gospel of news for liberated Jews is at the same time, via Israel, a gospel for the nations beyond Judaism.[6] This rhetoric that seems to point this way echoes and parallels the mandate to Abraham in Gen. 12:3:

> I have given you as a covenant to the people,
>> a light to the nations,
>> to open the eyes that are blind,
> to bring out the prisoners from the dungeon,
>> from the prison those who sit in darkness. (Isa. 42:6-7)

> I will give you as a light to the nations,
>> that my salvation may reach to the end of the earth. (Isa. 49:6)

There are important problems in the text and there are tones of communal triumphalism all around. Nonetheless, the poem seems to acknowledge that YHWH wills the security and well-being of all peoples that inhabit the earth over which YHWH presides, well-being and security that are commensurate with YHWH's gifts to Israel. It is clear that "others" turn out to be "significant others" for YHWH and so are derivatively significant others to Israel, others whom the returning exiles cannot disregard. In some important way, the good future of Israel is twinned to the good future of the nations.

This is not to say that the peculiar holiness of Israel is in any way compromised or abandoned, even by Second Isaiah. It is to say, however, that the tension and unresolveable dialectic belong to the very character of this faith, a dialectic of *peculiarity and plurality,* a dialectic that must be maintained, without regress to either pole if Israel is fully to occupy its special status (see Isa. 66:21-23/24).

In Christian caricature, the fencing out of the other by Judaism is commonplace. And yet it is important to notice that in the current discussion (especially at the impetus of Emmanuel Levinas), the life-giving demands of *alterity* figure large for Judaism. It is Levinas who has seen that it is in the face of the other, the "wholly other," as we Barthians say, that life comes fully.[7] It is a core insight of Judaism that endless preoccupation with "sameness" is indeed a route to idolatry, and therefore faith, among other things, is the full engagement of otherness through whom the God of Israel mediates new life. It is for sure that the deep commitment of *holiness through separation* lingers in the practice of Israel. It is also clear that Israel is on its way to a far different sense of holiness, namely, the unanxious engagement with the other who is indeed threat, but also gift, possibility, and resource.

IV

The issue of *holiness as separation and holiness as unanxious engagement,* with somewhat different nuance, is powerfully present in the life of the early church. Here I will mention four texts and then consider at greater length two texts that tilt the issue:

As Fernando Belo has explicated the Gospel of Mark and especially Mark 7, he has observed that the notion of defilement is powerfully redefined in that Gospel narrative.[8] This presentation of Jesus shows a teaching that is not anxious about the older disciplines of holiness:

> It is what comes out of a person that defiles. For it is from within, from the human heart, that evil intentions come: fornication, wickedness, deceit, licentiousness, envy, slander, pride, folly. All these evil things come from within, and they defile a person. (Mark 7:20-23)

The defilements are not material contaminations, but they are distortions of neighborliness.

In what must be a related text in Matthew 23, Jesus joins issue in the debates of Judaism and asserts in polemical fashion the priorities that belong to his community:

> Woe to you, scribes and Pharisees, hypocrites! For you tithe mint, dill, and cummin, and have neglected the weightier matters of the law: justice and mercy and faith. It is these you ought to have practiced without neglecting the others. You blind guides! You strain out a gnat but swallow a camel! Woe to you, scribes and Pharisees, hypocrites! For you clean the outside of the cup and of the plate, but inside they are full of greed and self-indulgence. (Matt. 23:23-26)

As is commonly recognized, moreover, the polemic is not of Christian against Jew, but reflects a dispute among competing characterizations of holiness; this text puts the Jesus tradition on the side of relational engagement: justice, mercy, faith.

Most dramatically, the trance of Peter (Acts 10) leads to a defining breakthrough in Christian sensibility that eventually leads to a far-reaching decision about the otherness of Gentiles. The trance is an exchange of protest and resolve:

> "Get up, Peter: Kill and eat. . . ."
>
> "By no means, Lord; for I have never eaten anything profane or unclean. . . ."
>
> "What God has made clean, you must not call profane." This happened three times. . . . (Acts 10:13-16)

No doubt it required, as it always does, a trance, a dream, a vision, a gift, in order to break beyond our settled categories. The story of the early church is not the settlement. It is rather the slow, troubled, long-term meditation on the tradition, always probing and moving, and finding itself led to newness where it thought not to go, led there by its Lord who is the pioneer as well as the perfecter. The story in the book of Acts is about openness of the community to those beyond the old categories of holiness, welcoming precisely those who are habitually excluded and disregarded. In such a daring maneuver, over which Paul presides, the church continues that trajectory already strongly at work in antecedent Judaism.

Thus Paul in Romans 12:1, in his great ethical manifesto, can begin with holiness:

> I appeal to you therefore, brothers and sisters, by the mercies of God, to present your bodies as a living sacrifice, holy and acceptable to God, which is your spiritual worship.

Paul employs the rhetoric of sacrifice and so mobilizes all of the sensitivities of the program of Leviticus in its sketch of acceptable, holy offerings—and then leaps to issues of hospitality, generosity, solidarity, and vengeance.

The move from *holiness as separation* to *holiness as relational engagement* is a characteristic one in the early church. It is not simple or uncontested. There is, however, no doubt that the momentum is on the side of recharacterized holiness as one reads both the narrative construal of Acts and the passionate polemics of Paul. There are voices to the contrary that are surely important, not just because they keep connected to older traditions, but because they remind us that pluralistic openness to the other is worth nothing if it entails the loss of God-given peculiarity.

V

Finally I consider in detail two texts about the homework of holiness. (I understand that this rather random lining out of texts is not the way any New Testament scholar would do it, but when one is outside one's discipline, many things are possible.)

The first of two texts I consider is Ephesians 4:17—5:1. This text is surely rooted in the deepest practice of Christian baptism, which means it is focused on the *peculiarity of the community,* on its elect status as God's special people. Remarkably, this deeply rooted *peculiarity* is seen as a pivot from which arises the most radical ethic toward others. Thus *peculiarity* is enacted by *alterity.* Astonishing!

The text begins by contrasting believers with "Gentiles" who live in ignorance, futility, and alienation. They are outsiders to Gospel truth who simply "do not get it." It is remarkable that this writer uses the language of "Gentiles," clearly claiming for the church community all the mandates and entitlements of Jewish tradition, for it is the community in this tradition that knows what is required to end alienation and nullify futility. It is clear that "Gentiles" practice impurity (shades of holiness by separation), but their impurity takes the form of licentiousness and greed, that is, disruptiveness of social relationships. The futility is that they imagine themselves autonomous and not accountable either to holy God or real neighbor.

The community of the baptized is completely contrasted to them. The baptismal community is the one that has dramatically moved from "old self" to "new self," away from lusts to renewed spirit and mind. In cadences echoing Romans 12, what is learned and known "in Christ" is new self. That new learning is taught and available, but the process of transformation to newness is an ongoing one, even as this text is filled with imperatives that urge the process. The body of believers consists in those occupied with the movement *from self to self,* a movement that has been traced in Christ and powered by Christ's spirit.

Most remarkably, the new self to which the believer is summoned is in "the image of God," in true righteousness and holiness. The rhetoric is saturated with the cadences of Israel. The new human self is a reflection of the true character of God, and the true character of God is marked by righteousness and holiness, old terms in Israel that are to be lined out afresh in what follows. Homework in the Gospel consists in, as the old Calvinists said, "improving your baptism."

And now the text becomes quite concrete about the practices of the new self in the new community mandated to a new ethic. Fresh from the terms "righteousness and holiness," we notice that there is nothing here about separation, purity, or denial. Rather the evangelical ethic concerns lived relations in the community, a relationship engagement with others. The new ethic concerns:

- speaking the truth to our neighbors, while the old self might have deceived and dissimulated;
- managing anger in ways that are not destructive;
- honest labor to share among the needy;
- talk that builds up, as a means of grace to those who hear.

And then this remarkable appeal:

> Put away from you all bitterness and wrath and anger and wrangling and slander together with all malice, and be kind to one another, tenderhearted, forgiving one another. . . . (Eph. 4:31-32)

This is the new self in righteousness and holiness, reflective of the image of God.

We are now far from holiness as separation and are into holiness as relationship engagement, the capacity to *be with* and *be for* in ways that heal. This language of "be kind, tender hearted, forgiving" has always struck me as a kind of romanticism that well-meaning, innocent teachers offer little kids in Sunday school as a form of social control. But no, this is adult stuff for men and women in which baptismal identity concerns ceding over self to others in transformative ways, standing on no rights or insistences or entitlements or grudges or resentments or virtues of one's own, for all of that counts for nothing. This ethic, judged outside the community, is indeed the weak doormat that Nietzsche critiqued. Except it is a generative power for newness. Except there is no alternative generative power for newness. This is it.

And then the text offers the clincher in 5:1. We have already seen the phrase "likeness of God." And now in conclusion:

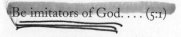

> Be imitators of God. . . . (5:1)

Intentionally act the way God has acted. "Beloved children, live in love." Beloved!—already loved, live as Christ has loved us. The generative clue is the self-giving of God who has kept nothing of self back, but has thrust God's own self into the need of the world. This insight about God in Christ plays upon the deepest notes of divine pathos already voiced in Hosea, Jeremiah, and Second Isaiah. And now the theme comes to fruition in Paul's theology of the cross. This is the divine emptying of the Philippian hymn. This Jesus became obedient to death, to the bottom of risk and self-giving, and now the baptismal community is summoned to such a generative, transformative practice.

My second text is Colossians 3:5-11, a parallel text also rooted in the peculiar vocation of baptism. The rhetoric, after verses 1-4, moves quickly to the ethical mandate and is organized around a negative and a positive.

The *negative:* "Put to death," terminate! The writer is not much into therapeutic nurture but speaks an imperative. Of course, as in Romans 12, the imperative is grounded in the long and deep indicative of the gospel. But finally there is command concerning the kind of relationship engagement that destroys the neighbor:

> Put to death: fornication, impurity, passion, evil desire, and greed.

The list begins with fornication and ends in greed. As always, it's about sex and it's about money. It's about social transactions that are open to abuse and exploitation. It's about making the other into an object to be exploited. As is often noted, moreover, the last item, greed, appeals to the tenth commandment, for the older translation is "covetousness." But the mark of greed is exposited in a parenthesis, "which is idolatry." That is, the tenth commandment is seen as a function of the first commandment; greed is an act of autonomy that denies the singular rule of God over one's needs and desires. Thus the catalogue is set deep in the Decalogue. The second negative inventory in verse 8 becomes more specific:

> Get rid of all such things—anger, wrath, malice, slander, and abusive language. Do not lie.

The practice of "otherness" is not about close rules of contamination. It is about the simple, obvious, daily practices of respect and enhancement that mark the neighbor into well-being.

Verse 9 forms a transition from negative to positive:

> See that you have stripped off the *old self* with its practices and have
> clothed yourselves with the *new self,* which is being renewed in knowl-
> edge according to the image of its creator. . . .

The *positive* does not reiterate in detail but can be deduced from the negative.
The positive appeals again to the "image of the creator." And then this:

> In that renewal there is no Greek and Jew, circumcised and uncircum-
> cised, barbarian, Scythian, slave and free; but Christ is all and in all!
> (v. 11)

Christ is all and in all!

What a breathtaking summing up! The formula of course echoes Paul
from the more familiar Gal. 3:28; it reinforces the Ephesian assertion that
the middle wall of partition is overcome. The most sweeping new circumstance without division has come about by getting rid of anti-neighborly
practices.

Let me say that more succinctly: Engagement in alterity is accomplished through daily, concrete, neighborly practices of self-giving generosity, respect, and affirmation. That of course is what Israel has always
known. Large issues are resolved through concrete, intentional obedience.
The act of baptism, together with its radical ethic, is an awesome act,
because it releases into the world a counter-force for healing, counter to
all the exploitation of alienating sexuality, oppressive economics, and dis-
sembling utterance. Not by magical christological formula but by a daily
counter-ethic the baptismal community matters to the life of the world.[9]

VI

My theme of ecclesial "otherness" concerns the problem of *peculiarity and
pluralism.* The problem of pluralism is deep and large and as of now defies
clear formulation. My more modest agenda is to think about the homework that belongs to the church—and its seminaries—in approaching this
deep problem, a problem in which conservatives characteristically focus
on peculiarity that leads to triumphalism and liberals carelessly embrace
pluralism that leads to evaporation of what is precious among us.

I have tried to trace the deep and defining tension in ancient Israel and the early church about holiness as separated purity and as transformative engagement. In the time remaining, I want to reflect on this problematic and the agility that is required for the issue.

The homework consists in nurturing seminarians who will be responsible in time to come for the tricky process of peculiarity and pluralism. One cannot generalize about seminarians, of course. But I will, on the assumption that everybody who goes to seminary does so out of mixed motives and probably most of us for the wrong reasons. Seminarians, in my purview, have a keen desire to form sects and apply labels and live in camps. And they thereby prepare for the church wars that are to come. Perhaps they are reinforced in this seduction by their strong-willed teachers.

The homework is to become agile, informed hermeneutists, to see that for all of the treasured substance of the tradition, the ongoing work of Moses the hermeneutist is to negotiate, to remember and to forget, to give and to receive, to critique and to trust, about the deepest claims we are able to imagine.

Homework is to be able to *assert* self fully and to *cede* self completely, even if provisionally, to the claim of the neighbor. Roy Schafer has said of good sexuality that it requires the capacity to be a shameless initiator and a glad receiver, and to be able to change roles as needed.[10] In that regard, the process of education is like good sexuality, a capacity to assert and to cede, not simply one or the other.

Homework is to recognize in a critical way one's own huge socioeconomic privilege that is often protected by innocence. I currently correspond with one of my students on a year in India who has in the past resisted categories of social analysis that were threatening to him; and now he writes from India of his glad growth beyond innocence that had, in his own judgment, skewed his discernment. The church has not been a natural habitat for critical reflection on privilege.

Homework is to create an environment of self-knowledge, not excessively "therapeutic," because self-knowledge in the baptismal community is engagement with the self-giving, holy one. Thus beyond all the conventions of seminary, the work is to make it possible for the truth of forgiveness to penetrate the agility, the asserting, the ceding, the innocence, the privilege, the wound, so that the coming leadership of the church is suited and healed for counter-life in the world. Concerning the ordination of Aaron, it is written in Exod. 29:20 that in the ritual blood must

be put on the lobe of the right ear of the priest and on the thumb of the
right hand, and on the toes of the right foot. Indeed, if one thinks of the
wrenching reversal process of forgiveness that makes new self possible,
nurture for leadership concerns exactly healing of ear lobes right down to
the toes. Such education may hope for a toes-up self-awareness of forgiveness rooted in God's strange otherness.

The homework related to peculiarity and pluralism is often taken to
concern Christian engagement with Buddhists and Muslims, and I do not
take that task lightly. But why would any Muslim want to be "in commu-
nion" with Presbyterians who won't countenance Methodists, or Angli-
cans who dismiss Disciples, or conservative Lutherans who battle liberal
Lutherans? My hunch is that our relatedness to other faiths, for all the
hard work to be done, will be relatively a work of joy if the church itself can
be reconstituted according to the mystery of self-giving of which Ephesians and Colossians speak so eloquently.

The truth is that the holiness of separation is very large in the church just
now, so busy are we excommunicating and judging each other impure and
profane. Party spirit, propagated among and by seminarians that remain
unhealed and unforgiven, means that our baptism is rarely enacted in any
full way. Among Presbyterians where I live and work, it appears that the
crowd who supported Colorado's "Amendment B" initiative (which would
have legalized housing and employment discrimination against same-sex
couples) is now in the ascendancy, busily judging impure all those who do
not get it right. In my own church, the United Church of Christ, the shoe
is on the other foot, and multicultural liberals are in the ascendancy and
have no energy or time for any who think otherwise. And I suppose even
in this blessed place with its tradition of progressive Christianity, there is
an unnoticed history of deep exclusiveness as well.

It is instructive to put our church wars alongside the baptismal ethic of
Ephesians and Colossians, and then to ponder the homework that remains
for us to do. In the long run, the very longest run, the key church issues
are not about whose genitalia qualify for ordination or whether everyone
enlists in multiculturalism, but whether a culture of generosity can at all
be fostered midst a world of commodity, a culture that imagines that serious people who live otherwise can be honored and heard, honored in ways
we resist and heard in ways that instruct. The church might indeed be
haunted by the voice that sounded in Peter's trance, "What God has made
clean you must not call profane." The church and its seminaries might

endlessly sort out how the radical mandate of baptism requires that we do our work together differently.

The homework of maintaining leadership and of healing the wars of the church is for the sake of being in the world. Union has been forever in the world, most dramatically in the daring insistences of Reinhold Niebuhr. That place "in the world" now is so much more complex and difficult than in the 1930s, especially while the church is being thinned and deprivileged. It is not difficult to identify some of the crunch points of complexity:

- The lack of will among the powerfully affluent to address concrete injustice;
- The drive of technology for a more comfortable life while assaulting its necessary infrastructures;
- The eruption of old hates in the name of God;
- The new communications capacity that may serve primarily to distance and isolate.

And the church always again is unequal to the task.

That world, so filled with fear, hate, and brutality, so dead-set against neighboring, groans in labor pains, awaiting healing. The church has no gift to give the world when it is so like the world in its fears, its hates, it long-term brutality. The church has gifts to give when it acts out of its own peculiarity, out of its "new self," when it comes to "the other" out of its own being loved and forgiven. Bishop John Shelby Spong has rightly said that the church will die if it does not change.[11] Surely so. But the Second Reformation is not, in my judgment, about demything and remything. It is about the power of transformation carried well enough by old "myths"; the Reformation concerns an ethics of forgiveness for which the world yearns but for which it lacks evidence.

What would it be like if the church in all its manifestations—including its seminaries—understood itself as a "Truth and Reconciliation" Commission? That exercise in South Africa has of course been problematic; but it is impossible to overstate its cruciality. Ponder the terms, *"Truth* and *Reconciliation"*; the terms sound like "full of grace and truth" or "give to us the ministry of reconciliation," in which every meeting, every utterance, every gesture is about truth and about reconciliation.

Truth first, and only then reconciliation. Truth first about wonder and about wound, truth-telling that heals and lets the past be past, for the sake of new embrace. The church of course can be the forum and stage for such utterance; but the church also is the first witness:

> The truth about race and about gender;
> > about money and power,
> > about not caring and not noticing;
> And the reconciliation in quite concrete places.
> But also the truth that makes us free,
> > about the self-giving God,
> > and the self-giving community.
> The truth that losing is gaining,
> > and keeping is losing,
> > that emptying is the only way to fullness.
> The truth that forgiveness is possible and it matters . . .
> > and then reconciliation.

Even the forum, even the acknowledged agenda, is itself a gesture of reconciliation that permits truth-telling, for it can only be told in a place of deep attentiveness.

The real issue in the world and among its religions is whether the vicious cycles of violence and excommunication can be broken and whether there is any ground for an alternative. That possibility and that ground are evident in Israel and in the church: the true holiness of God (and of God's people) is an engagement with the "other" at great risk. The maintenance of peculiarity is crucial, but it is not done any longer by separation, but only by giving away of self in imitation.

President Joseph C. Hough briefly outlined to me the themes of this occasion: *tradition/pluralism/solidarity with the poor.*

The practice of tradition is, of course, a given, for that is what I do. My surprise in my preparation for this occasion is that out of the tradition the other two themes have emerged almost without my notice. I have spoken of scarcity and abundance, of anxiety and well-being in the arena of economics. I have spoken of holiness as serious relational engagement. I have observed that the abundance of God is the sure antidote to both *economic anxiety* that breeds greed and to *ecclesial separateness* that legitimates separatism. At all the pivot points in its life, Israel has learned that from this God there is more than enough for all. When that stunning reality sinks in, there is no call any longer for covetous economics or for dismissive holiness. So consider in conclusion these four random traces:

- "When I broke the five loaves for the five thousand, how many baskets full of broken pieces did you collect?" They said to him, "Twelve." "And the seven for the four thousand, how many baskets full of broken pieces did you collect?" They said to him, "Seven." Then he said to them, "Do you not yet understand?" (Mark 8:19-21)

- In his book *Generosity and the Christian Faith*, George Newlands comments:

Christology, more precisely the kenotic, vulnerable, generous Christ who is the incarnation of the self-giving, creative, responsive love of God, is a basis for public theology, which is also open to dialogue with all humanity, religious or non-religious. As the basis of new creation through the Spirit, a Christology of generosity has cosmological implications for our understanding of theology and the natural sciences as well as the human sciences. A Christology of vulnerable generosity should also be able to contribute to dialogue with Judaism, on the face of it one of the most difficult areas, because it is a statement of identification with radical suffering, with powerlessness and with marginalization. Generosity cannot immediately relieve radical suffering, which may repeat violence suffered in violence inflicted. But it may create the conditions of the possibility of forgiveness, which may lead to reconciliation and so to a weakening in the cycle of violence.[12]

- Martin Luther King has famously said, "The long arc of history is bent toward justice." In parallel we may say on this great day, the long arc of God's holiness is bent toward abundance.

- Finally, a realistic word from Moses on the requirement of a year of release every seven years:

Be careful that you do not entertain a mean thought, thinking, "The seventh year, the year of remission is near," and therefore view your needy neighbor with hostility and give nothing. (Deut. 15:19)

Do not calculate about forgiveness:

Open your hand to the poor and needy neighbor in your land . . . and the Lord will bless you in all that you do. (Deut. 15:11, 18)

Patriotism for Citizens
of the Penultimate Superpower

The "patriotism" that concerns the preacher is not a generic, one-size-fits-all category. Patriotism is state specific, and so the theme of this chapter is the patriotism of the United States of America as concerns U.S. preachers.

I learned about the specificity of patriotism in a poignant way a few years ago when I was in Hungary with a group of seminary students and preached on Sunday morning in a Reformed church in Budapest. During the liturgy, the congregation sang the Hungarian national anthem—I think a regular practice—an anthem that has genuine theological elements and witnesses to the deep history of Hungarian suffering. And then in an act of generous hospitality, the organist played the "Star-Spangled Banner" and we American people dutifully stood—with considerable embarrassment—and sang our anthem. The embarrassment was grounded in the obvious fact that the U.S. national anthem—unlike that of Hungary—is an aggressive war song, bespeaking nothing of suffering or of trustful faith.

The history of patriotism in the U.S. and its contemporary manifestations are rooted in a kind of aggressiveness that forms the issue for the preacher.

I

Indeed, U.S. patriotism is everywhere shaped by a conviction of exceptionalism that began in the Puritan vision of "a city set on a hill." That vision, however, was powerfully transposed into "manifest destiny" and then, in the twentieth century, into "the leader of the free world." It has been transposed again, now into the "last standing superpower," which, under the guise of democratic capitalism, enacts its unchallenged, economic-military will everywhere in the world. In this latter presentation, U.S. patriotism is now tempted to the most astonishing kind of unilateralism that becomes the subject of a pastoral reflection on patriotism.

In such a context, the preacher is obligated to think and speak well about a theological grounding that has been largely transposed into shameless, unrestrained power in quest of empire. The preachable point then is how to love, value, and care for such a nation-state wherein faith supplies some critical distance from the unreflective, largely uncritical passion of popular patriotism. Every preacher knows, of course, how hazardous and difficult it is to maintain enough critical distance to allow space between regnant national ideology and the claims of evangelical faith that resist over-idealizing, and that resist idolatry of a state that has become a practitioner of violence against vulnerable populations, vulnerable cultures, and vulnerable environments.

II

It is likely that the preacher will find standing ground for such a difficult and urgent task in the Old Testament, for the Old Testament offers the largest vista of a public agenda wherein the rule of God is taken seriously with reference to real power in the world. There is, however, at the outset, a problem with our usual appeals to the Old Testament, for we customarily begin with God's concern for ancient Israel and then make a mumbling analogue to God's concern for the U.S.A. Such an analogue, even if mumbled, does not work because Israel, according to its own articulation, is always a small, exposed, vulnerable state; by contrast, patriotism in the U.S. entertains no thought of smallness, exposure, or vulnerability. Thus, the customary interpretive move from *Israel* in the Old Testament to the U.S. is a seductive mistake. For that reason, I suggest that the preacher must seek elsewhere in the text for an analogue that makes critical distance possible.

When we look elsewhere in the Old Testament for texts that ground our thinking about patriotism and public policy beyond the scope of small, exposed, vulnerable Israel, we may focus on the other nations—small states and great empires—and their direct relationship to YHWH. To be sure, Israel is enmeshed in the work of other states, but characteristically prophetic rhetoric speaks about YHWH's direct engagement with other states without regard to Israel.[1] These texts, particularly the oracles against the nations, seem to me the most fruitful way to think biblically about patriotism, because these oracles eschew any notion of exceptionalism and because they think theologically about states other than Israel. Clearly, in the Old Testament all states are understood theologically because YHWH governs all states. That, it seems to me, is at the heart of patriotism in a superpower that imagines itself immune to such realities, as indeed every superpower has been tempted to imagine.

III

I propose as a defining category in biblical faith for the preacher concerning patriotism the direct action of God for the several states of the ancient Near East and particularly the great empires of Egypt, Assyria, Babylon, and Persia. Each of these powers in turn imagined itself to be an ultimate power that was free to use its power in unrestrained ways, an imaginative posture that characteristically led to oppression and brutality. Textual evidence of this interaction of God with the nations is especially evident in the so-called oracles against the nations (as in Amos 1–2, Isaiah 13–23, Jeremiah 46–51, Ezekiel 25–32), but it is not limited to them.

We may identify three dimensions to the God–state relationship that is evidenced with a variety of nuances but with a recurring primary plot. First, YHWH can recruit and mobilize the nations to enact God's will, since in principle all nations are subjects of YHWH and are destined, soon or late, to conform to YHWH's will. Thus, the nations—even the great nations—are understood as vehicles and instruments for God's will in the world, a will that is said to be YHWH's own will, even if mediated through the rhetorical venue of Israel as a small, dependent state that has a great vested interest in YHWH's dealing with the great states.

The evidence for states as *vehicles and instruments for God's will* include the following:

1. In the eighth and seventh centuries B.C.E., *Assyria*, especially under the leadership of Senacherib, is reckoned to be YHWH's instrument of judgment against Israel, and of course Assyria did move aggressively against Israel and Judah:

> Ah, Assyria, the rod of my anger—
>   the club in their hands is my fury!

Against a godless nation I send him,
   and against the people of my wrath I command him,
to take spoil and seize plunder,
   and to tread them down like the mire of the streets. (Isa. 10:5-6)

2. In like manner, in the late seventh century the traditions of Jeremiah imagine that *Babylon*, under Nebuchadnezzar, is YHWH's tool of judgment against Jerusalem:

> I am going to send for all the tribes of the north, says the LORD, even for King Nebuchadrezzar of Babylon, my servant, and I will bring them against this land and its inhabitants, and against all these nations around; I will utterly destroy them, and make them an object of horror and of hissing, and an everlasting disgrace.

> It is I who by my great power and my outstretched arm have made the earth, with the people and animals that are on the earth, and I give it to whomever I please. Now I have given all these lands into the hand of King Nebuchadnezzar of Babylon, my servant, and I have given him even the wild animals of the field to serve him.

> And say to them, Thus says the LORD of hosts, the God of Israel: I am going to send and take my servant King Nebuchadrezzar of Babylon, and he will set his throne above these stones that I have buried, and he will spread his royal canopy over them. He shall come and ravage the land of Egypt, giving
> those who are destined for pestilence, to pestilence, . . .
> and those who are destined for the sword, to the sword.
> (Jer. 25:9; 27:5-6; 43:10-11)

It is evident in the crisis of 587 B.C.E., at the time of the destruction of Jerusalem, that YHWH does not characteristically act "directly" in public affairs, but rather acts through proximate human agents. Of these texts, 27:5-6 is of particular interest because the dispatch of Nebuchadnezzar is preceded by a self-announcement of YHWH, "It is I." The juxtaposition of the self-praise by YHWH in verse 5 and the summons of Nebuchadnezzar in verse 6 is ordered to assert the ultimacy of YHWH in public affairs and the penultimate role of Nebuchadnezzar at the behest of YHWH. A key part of the presentation of an unfettered superpower is the theological assertion that nation-states, even those with imperial pretenses, are decisively an inescapably penultimate in the expenditure of power in the world.

3. In the sixth century, the Isaiah tradition anticipates the nullification of Babylonian power by the rise of *Persia*, a turn of power accomplished under Cyrus, the initial Persian leader. In one of the most spectacular of all statements in the Old Testament concerning public power, YHWH declares:

> Thus says the Lord to his anointed, to Cyrus,
>   whose right hand I have grasped
> to subdue nations before him
>   and strip kings of their robes,
> to open doors before him—
>   and the gates shall not be closed. (Isa. 45:1)

The term "Cyrus" as "his anointed" is stunning enough, more so when it is recognized that in the Septuagint the phrase is rendered *mou christou*; Cyrus is designated to accomplish in human scope the intent of the divine king.

In each of these cases, prophetic rhetoric effectively links imperial conduct to divine intention, in each case establishing the subordinate, subservient position of state power. In this way, prophetic discourse keeps alive the tricky interface between realpolitik and divine purpose in public history.

IV

Human power, however, is endlessly seduced into the quest for more victories, more power, more territory, more wealth, more commerce—*more* because in a penultimate position there is never enough. Such imperial states are endlessly restless to override the divine intent of penultimacy for the human state. Every such state in the Old Testament is portrayed as lusting for ultimacy, a kind of autonomy that need not acknowledge the elemental restraint of divine purpose. We have just seen that each of these states is said to be mandated by YHWH in prophetic horizon; however, every such state oversteps its mandate in an aggressive attempt to be unrestrained and without accountability to divine purpose and therefore *stands under divine judgment.*

1. After the mandate to *Assyria* in Isa. 10:5-6, the poem proceeds immediately to report on the Assyrian refusal to accept such a limited mandate
from YHWH:

> But this is not what he intends,
> nor does he have this in mind;
> but it is in his heart to destroy,
> and to cut off nations not a few.
> For he says:
> "Are not my commanders all kings?
> Is not Calno like Carchemish?
> Is not Hamath like Arpad?
> Is not Samaria like Damascus?
> As my hand has reached to the kingdoms of the idols
> whose images were greater than those of Jerusalem and Samaria,
> shall I not do to Jerusalem and her idols
> what I have done to Samaria and her images?" (Isa. 10:7-11, 13-15)

Such arrogance that boasts of autonomy and that practices usurpatious
policies of plundering and overthrowing inescapably evokes YHWH's
judgment. That judgment leads to the destruction and demise of the state
that flaunted its awesome power:

> Shall the ax vaunt itself over the one who wields it,
> or the saw magnify itself against the one who handles it?
> As if a rod should raise the one who lifts it up,
> or as if a staff should lift the one who is not wood!
> Therefore the Sovereign, the LORD of hosts,
> will send wasting sickness among his stout warriors,
> and under his glory a burning will be kindled,
> like the burning of fire.
> The light of Israel will become a fire,
> and his Holy One a flame;
> and it will burn and devour
> his thorns and briers in one day.
> The glory of his forest and his fruitful land
> the LORD will destroy, both soul and body,
> and it will be as when an invalid wastes away.
> The remnant of the trees of his forest will be so few
> that a child can write them down. (Isa. 10:15-19)

In this way, prophetic imagination chronicles the demise of the Assyrian empire, a demise that culminated in the sacking of Nineveh, its capital city. The great superpower, in its refusal to accept penultimate status in YHWH's world, came to a prompt and abrupt termination.

2. It is the same story with *Babylon,* only this empire gets more airtime in the Bible. According to the tradition of Jeremiah, Babylon under Nebuchadnezzar was mandated to act for YHWH against Judah. But of course Babylon overstepped its mandate and enacted uncommon brutality. After the tradition of Jeremiah, the tradition of Isaiah must circle back to deliver the hard word to Babylon. It is true that YHWH, in anger, had authorized Babylon to act against Jerusalem:

> I was angry with my people,
> I profaned my heritage;
> I gave them into your hand. (Isa. 47:6)

But of course Nebuchadnezzar could not stop there:

> You showed them no mercy;
> on the aged you made your yoke
>   exceedingly heavy.
> You said, "I shall be mistress forever."
>   so that you did not lay these things to heart
>   or remember their end. (Isa. 47:6b-7)

The text goes on to voice Babylon's illusion of ultimacy:

> Now therefore hear this, you lover of pleasures,
>   who sit securely,
> who say in your heart,
>   "I am, and there is no one besides me;
> I shall not sit as a widow
>   or know the loss of children" . . .
> You felt secure in your wickedness;
>   you said, "No one sees me."
> Your wisdom and your knowledge
>   led you astray,
> and you said in your heart,
>   "I am, and there is no one besides me." (Isa. 47:8, 10)

The Babylonian assumption of ultimacy—no more penultimate status under YHWH!—had been played out in brutality. The empire is indicted for a lack of mercy toward Israel. I am sure that Nebuchadnezzar responded to such prophetic indictment in indignation: "You never said anything about mercy! You are indicting me for the violation of a limit about which I have known nothing."

I am sure that YHWH's sovereign retort to such imperial indignation would go something like this: "I never mentioned mercy because I assumed you, like all the others, know that mercy is the bottom line for me. I assumed that you, in your hegemonic power, did not need to be told of something so elemental. Mercy is always the last word and you have violated it." The indictment for lack of mercy, according to prophetic discourse, properly defines the ultimacy of YHWH and the penultimacy of every hegemonic state. Mercy as restraint upon imperial arrogance and imperial autonomy is a non-negotiable given in YHWH's creation. Any state that imagines that it can use its power in unrestrained ways against any other state or any vulnerable population—no matter how weak—misunderstands its place in a world under divine rule.

3. I notice only in passing that the Old Testament contains no explicit terminal judgment against the empire of *Persia*. The reason for that, we are led to believe, is that Persian policy was not so unspeakably ruthless toward Israel. (It may be, moreover, that the makers of the scripture in the Persian period were themselves so inured to Persian power that divine judgment against Persia was not a wise utterance, indeed was not even thinkable.)

V

The powers are instruments of divine purpose. The powers are under judgment for violating divine purpose. Now third, and briefly, I note that there are a few texts that imagine *the reestablishment of states* that have been judged by God, a reestablishment wherein such state power accepts its penultimate position and cedes ultimacy to YHWH and to YHWH's will.

1. The narrative of Daniel 4, albeit late, traces in an imaginative way the fall and rise of *Babylon*. At the outset, Nebuchadnezzar has a harsh nightmare, and the Jew Daniel interprets the dream: Nebuchadnezzar stands under judgment and will be reduced to an animal eating grass—

until you have learned that the Most High has sovereignty over the kingdom of mortals, and gives it to whom he will. (Dan. 4:25)

This formulation, closely parallel to Jeremiah 27:5, indicates that Nebuchadnezzar is under judgment because he has imagined autonomy and did not discern his true state of penultimacy. In due course, the dream comes to fruition. That state of humiliation for the leader of the hegemonic state, we are told, will last "until you have learned."

Only after the dismantling of imperial power and shame and humiliation does the narrative turn. It turns only when Nebuchadnezzar "lifted my eyes to heaven," that is, when Nebuchadnezzar acknowledged God and ceded final authority to the God of heaven. We are told that "my reason returned to me," a clear acknowledgment that the exercise of unrestrained imperial power had driven the Babylonians insane (see Dan. 4:34). Only when ultimacy is credited to YHWH does Nebuchadnezzar get over his craziness. In the event, Nebuchadnezzar is rehabilitated in imperial power; his power, however, is in the context of doxology that acknowledges that even imperial power is subject to the God who governs all states:

> Now I, Nebuchadnezzar, praise and extol and honor the King of heaven,
>   for all his works are truth,
>   and his ways are justice;
>   and he is able to bring low
>   those who walk in pride. (Dan. 4:37)

2. I have not yet mentioned *Egypt,* who, at the beginning, in Exodus 1–15, is brought resistantly under the rule of YHWH. In the prophetic oracle of Isaiah 19, the Egyptian empire is brought to its demise, most radically, the Nile River is dried up (Isa. 19:5; see Ezek. 29:3). Most remarkably, after the undoing of the Egyptian empire according to 19:1-4, 5-10, and 11-15, the account of each vis-à-vis YHWH turns decisively. We are not told why, but we may speculate that Egypt eventually comes to terms with the rule of YHWH. It is now declared,

> The Lord will make himself known to the Egyptians; and the Egyptians will know the Lord on that day, and will worship with sacrifice and burnt offering, and they will make vows to the Lord and perform them. The Lord will strike Egypt, striking and healing; they will

return to the LORD, and he will listen to their supplications and heal them. (Isa. 19:21-22)

Egypt, even recalcitrant Egypt, which practice brutalizing policies, will "return to YHWH," accede to YHWH's intention, and so be rehabilitated as a viable state in the world. The oracle culminates in 19:24-25 with the astonishing expectation that Egypt will become—along with fearful Assyria and precious Israel—a treasured people of God. Thus both Babylon and Egypt, upon acknowledgment of YHWH, can resume the practice of state power in a viable and effective way.

VI

The following are reflections that have come to me about preaching patriotism, as I have pondered these remarkable texts in the bold, theological conviction that they articulate:

1. Superpowers—in the ancient world and until our own time—characteristically imagine themselves to be autonomous and unrestrained because there is no visible power to challenge them. There is a sense of being ultimate, especially if the power is unmatched or unchallenged by another commensurate power. (I wrote this on the day a U.S. State Department functionary declared, "All that counts for us is Britain. The rest of Europe is irrelevant in our making of policy.") That sense of autonomy, in turn, produces an arrogant sense of entitlement that, in unrestrained ways, justifies the use of economic, political power in exploitative and eventually barbaric ways. That, of course, is the characteristic charge made against the powers in these texts we have considered.

2. Preachers equipped with the sorts of texts I have cited here have opportunity to declare the penultimacy of such seemingly autonomous power. It is the relentless insistence of prophetic imagination that states that seem to lack a check on power in fact are under restraint and would wisely proceed on that basis. The claim of the text that the preacher utters concerns the reality of God, who finally and decisively governs the public processes, whose ultimacy and sovereignty resituates every national and imperial power as penultimate and finally subservient to a purpose and will beyond itself.

These prophetic oracles make the claim in a straightforward way that at first reading seems to be a simplistic supernaturalism. Closer reading indicates that at most the holy God authorizes, stirs up, counter powers almost ex nihilo who will check the superpower (see Jer. 50:9). That declaration concerns the righteous will of the holy God, who will not be mocked. If the same claim is put in less direct form, it may be asserted that there is an inscrutable quirkiness to the historical processes upon which penultimate worldly power must not presume. Such inscrutable quirkiness is voiced, for example, in Proverbs 21, a remarkable claim made without explanation:

> No wisdom, no understanding, no counsel,
>   can avail against the LORD.
> The horse is made ready for the day of battle,
>   but the victory belongs to the LORD. (vv. 30-31)

Either way—as righteous will or as inscrutable quirkiness—the ultimacy of divine sovereignty resists barbaric power and sides with the weak and the vulnerable. Thus the holy God is an Equalizer between strong and weak, rich and poor, a premise of the petition of Psalm 10:12-13:

> Rise up, O LORD; O God, lift up your hand;
>   do not forget the oppressed.
> Why do the wicked renounce God,
>   and say in their hearts, "You will not call us to account"?

The arrogant autonomy of the superpowers characteristically operates on the mistaken conviction that, "You will not call us to account." The preacher, witness to the inscrutable holiness of God, vouches otherwise. There is an accounting!

3. The rhetoric of supranational sovereignty concerning the One who stirs up is indeed odd and awkward. I imagine that there is hardly a congregation in mainstream U.S. Christianity where such texts can be credibly uttered. The reason for that difficulty, of course, is that for a very long time theological-ethical rhetoric in our society has withdrawn to private or family spheres and has ceded the public domain to secular assumptions and therefore secular discourse.

Thus, if a preacher is to work *theologically* at patriotism, it seems essential that the preacher, along with the congregation, must dare to recover the rhetoric of prophetic imagination concerning God's governance in the public sphere. When the preacher concedes discourse to secular assumptions, it is likely that a serious theological critique of popular patriotism is already rendered impossible. Thus, I suspect that from these texts the preacher must proceed to give testimony about quirky ultimacy that inescapably repositions the penultimate, for it belongs to preaching to make such witness. Preachers may find comfort in the awareness that in that ancient world, such articulations were then also received as dubious and embarrassing.

4. I take, then, the preacher's task on preaching patriotism to be the recovery of the discourse of a particular rhetoric rooted in these texts that is counter to the accepted rhetoric of patriotic ultimacy. The recovery of such rhetoric is indeed very difficult work. It is clear, however, that critical thought and critical action in the public domain will not go beyond the edges of rhetoric; for that reason, keeping God's sovereignty connected to political reflection is an urgent assignment for the preacher.

In support of such an enterprise of recovery of particular rhetoric, I cite the astonishing book by Peter Brown, *Poverty and Leadership in the Later Roman Empire*).[2] Brown studies the way in which Christian bishops in the third and fourth centuries introduced an entirely new rhetoric of wealth and poverty—a rhetoric rooted in the complaint Psalms of the Old Testament—and thereby decisively altered the public horizon of the ancient world concerning poverty:

> I would suggest that an almost subliminal reception of the Hebrew Bible, through the chanting of the Psalms and through the solemn injunctions of the bishop in connection with the *episcopalis audientia,* came to offer a meaning to the word *pauper* very different from the "pauperized" image of the merely "economic" poor. The pauper was a person with a claim upon the great. As with the poor of Israel, those who used the court of the bishop and attended his church also expected to call upon him, in time of need, for justice and protection.[3]

The infiltration of an ancient Near Eastern model of justice may explain a certain "upward slippage" of the notion of the "poor" in Christian texts of this time.[4]

> The language of "poverty" and the image of the poor as the bearers of claims on the great, which had been so present in ancient Israel, came

to seep out of the churches. It added a novel tincture to the language of public relations. It became a language that was increasingly found to be apposite to describe the quality of the relation of the emperor to his subjects, and of the weak to the powerful.[5]

Mutatis mutandis, I suggest that when preachers attend to the peculiar discourse of prophetic imagination, such a construal of public life may well "seep out of the church" into public discourse; the consequence of such a seep might well be that the capacity of a superpower might be reimagined and reconstrued.

5. The preacher has the task of articulating holy ultimacy that recharacterizes the penultimacy of every worldly hegemony. It is important to recognize that the articulation of restraints upon unbridled, entitled power can well be done in secular categories without reference to God's sovereignty. Thus Paul Kennedy, for example, can compellingly make the case that "great powers" "fall" when matters of territory, resources, and population become out of balance due to overextended militarism.[6] Surely such an argument in substance is paralleled to the polemic against arrogant state autonomy offered by the prophets in their Yahwistic imagination.

While the preacher thus has important allies in secular conversation, it is important that the preacher keep at the task of *theological* critique that parallels the wise critique offered by secular political science. The reason that the preacher's peculiar work is important is that the preacher finally is not engaged in analysis (important as that task is) as it is practiced by secular allies. The preacher moves beyond analysis to alternative, and finally has the evangelical task of empowering the faithful to alternative forms of citizenship, alternatives that are informed by loyalty and love for country. The impetus for such alternative never arises simply from analysis, but must come from an affirmation that belongs peculiarly to prophetic discourse, namely, the glad acknowledgment of the rule of God. Thus, the preaching of patriotism has a distinctly doxological flavor:

> "The kingdom of the world has become the kingdom of our Lord
> and of his Messiah,
> and he will reign forever and ever." (Rev. 11:15)

Such an anticipation articulated in gospel parlance is congruent with Israel's old liturgical claim that lies behind prophetic imagination:

Say among the nations, "The Lord is king!
    The world is firmly established; it shall never be moved.
    He will judge the peoples with equity." (Ps. 96:10)

Abbreviations

AB	Anchor Bible
BJS	Brown Judaic Studies
BTB	*Biblical Theology Bulletin*
CBQ	*Catholic Biblical Quarterly*
ConBOT	Coniectanea biblica: Old Testament Series
HUCA	*Hebrew Union College Annual*
JBL	*Journal of Biblical Literature*
JSOT	*Journal for the Study of the Old Testament*
JSOTSup	Journal for the Study of the Old Testament Supplement Series
NRSV	New Revised Standard Version
OBT	Overtures to Biblical Theology
OTL	Old Testament Library
RelSRev	*Religious Studies Review*
SWBA	The Social World of Biblical Antiquity
SBLDS	Society of Biblical Literature Dissertation Series
SBT	Studies in Biblical Theology
SVTP	Studia in Veteris Testamenti pseudepigraphica
ThTo	*Theology Today*
VTSup	Vetus Testamentum Supplements
WMANT	Wissenschaftliche Monographien zum Alten und Neuen Testament
ZAW	*Zeitschrift für die alttestamentliche Wissenschaft*
ZTK	*Zeitschrift für Theologie und Kirche*

Notes

1. A Text That Redescribes

1. George A. Lindbeck, *The Nature of Doctrine: Religion and Theology in a Postliberal Age* (Philadelphia: Westminster, 1984).

2. Gerhard von Rad, "The Problem of the Hexateuch," in *The Problem of the Hexateuch and Other Essays* (London: SCM, 1966).

3. Julian of Norwich, *Revelations of Divine Love of Juliana of Norwich*, trans. M. L. Del Mastro (New York: Doubleday, 1977), 123-25.

4. Norman K. Gottwald, *The Tribes of Yahweh: A Sociology of the Religion of Liberated Israel, 1250-1050 B. C.* (Maryknoll: Orbis Books, 1979).

5. Patrick D. Miller, *Deuteronomy.* Interpretation Commentary series (Louisville: John Knox, 1990).

2. Proclamatory Confrontations

1. See Philip R. Davies, *The Canonization of the Hebrew Scriptures*, Library of Ancient Israel (Louisville: Westminster John Knox, 1998); and John L. Berquist, *Judaism in Persia's Shadow: A Social and Historical Approach* (Minneapolis: Fortress Press, 1995).

2. See Walter Brueggemann, "On Scroll-Making in Ancient Jerusalem," *DTD* 33 (Spring 2003): 5 11.

3. See James Muilenburg, "Baruch the Scribe," in *Proclamation and Presence*, ed. John I. Durham and J. Roy Porter (London: SCM, 1970), 215–38; and, more critically, Andrew J. Dearman, "My Servants the Scribes: Composition and Context in Jeremiah 36," *JBL* 109 (1990): 403–21.

4. For good reason, James A. Sanders calls for the church "to produce more 'wisemen' [read "scribes"] and fewer 'prophets'" (*Torah and Canon* [Philadelphia: Fortress Press, 1972], 100).

5. George A. Lindbeck, *The Nature of Doctrine: Religion and Theology in a Postliberal Age* (Philadelphia: Westminster, 1984), 31–32 and passim.

6. Sumner Welles, *Naboth's Vineyard: The Dominican Republic 1844–1924* (New York: ARNO, 1972).

7. See Walter Brueggemann, "Praise and the Psalms: A Politics of Glad 'Abandonment,'" *The Psalms and the Life of Faith*, ed. Patrick D. Miller (Minneapolis: Fortress Press, 1995), 112–32.

8. See Walter Brueggemann, "The Preacher, the Text, and the People," *ThTo* 47 (1990): 237–47.

9. William T. Cavanaugh, *Torture and Eucharist: Theology, Politics, and the Body of Christ* (Oxford: Blackwell, 1998), 278.

10. Ibid., 279.

11. Ibid.

3. A Fresh Performance amid a Failed Script

1. C. H. Dodd, *The Apostolic Preaching and Its Developments* (New York: Willet, Clark & Company, 1937), chap. 1.

2. It is a primary contribution of Gerhard von Rad to have shown the way in which the Pentateuch developed as an ongoing dynamic process of reinterpretation (*Old Testament Theology*, vol. 1, trans. D. M. G. Stalker [San Francisco: Harper & Row, 1962]).

3. It is the great merit of Terence E. Fretheim to have suggested a fresh way in which to understand the relationship between the Exodus narrative and creation faith ("The Plagues as Ecological Signs of Historical Disaster," *JBL* 110 (1991): 385–96). See also Walter Brueggemann, "Theme Revisited: Bread Again!" in *Reading from Right to Left: Essays on the Hebrew Bible in Honour of David J. A. Clines*, ed., J. Cheryl Exum and H. G. M. Williamson, JSOTSup 373 (New York: T. & T. Clark, 2003): 76–89, which proposes a closer linkage between creation and faith and the sojourn tradition.

4. On Israel's "narrative world," see Amos N. Wilder, "Story and Story-World," *Interpretation* 37 (1983): 353–64.

5. Robert Alter, *Canon and Creativity: Modern Writing and the Authority of Scripture* (New Haven: Yale University Press, 2000), 15. Here, in speaking of the Samuel narrative, Alter writes:

> The Hebrew imagination, as early as its founding biblical phase, laid the grounds for what could be called a culture of exegesis. Prose narrative was its first instrument for expressing the reality of the

nation's historical experience, but unlike the lucid, leisurely narrative of Homer's sunlit world, it is a kind of abrupt story that turns on dark places, that is riddled with unsettling enigmas—in the instance of the text that stands behind Faulkner's novel [*Absalom, Absalom!*], incestuous rape, fratricide, insurrection, a bloody struggle for succession, and the spectacle of a once-powerful man on the throne who seems to have lost the capacity to wield power. The primary narrative is, as we have noted, composite, a redactor's orchestration of tensions among divergent or even clashing views of the represented figures and events. . . . One readily understands how such a narrative would generate three thousand years of exegesis, with no end in sight." (15–16)

6. On tradition history as process and as method, see Douglas A. Knight, *The Traditions of Israel: The Development of the Traditio-Historical Research of the Old Testament, with Special Consideration of Scandinavian Contributions,* SBLDS 9 (Missoula: Society of Biblical Literature, 1973).

7. On this text, see Walter Brueggemann, *Theology of the Old Testament: Testimony, Dispute, Advocacy, with CD-ROM* (Minneapolis: Fortress Press, 2005), 215–24.

8. See Gerhard von Rad, *The Problem of the Hexateuch and Other Essays* (New York: McGraw-Hill, 1966), 26–33; and Martin Noth, "The 'Re-Presentation' of the Old Testament in Proclamation," in *Essays on Old Testament Hermeneutics,* ed. Claus Westermann, trans. James Luther Mays (Richmond: John Knox, 1963), 76–88.

9. On the problematic of "strict constructionism," see Samuel J. Levine, "Unenumerated Constitutional Rights and Unenumerated Biblical Obligations: A Preliminary Study in Comparative Hermeneutics," *Constitutional Commentary* 15, no. 3 (1998): 511–27.

10. On interpretative issues related to land, see Walter Brueggemann, *The Land: Place as Gift, Promise, and Challenge in Biblical Faith,* 2nd ed., OBT (Minneapolis: Fortress Press, 2002), and Norman C. Habel, *The Land Is Mine: Six Biblical Land Ideologies,* OBT (Minneapolis: Fortress Press, 1995).

11. See Claus Westermann, *Basic Forms of Prophetic Speech* (Philadelphia: Westminster, 1967).

12. Brevard S. Childs, *Introduction to the Old Testament as Scripture* (Philadelphia: Fortress Press, 1979), 311–72; Ronald E. Clements, "Patterns in the Prophetic Canon," *Canon and Authority: Essays in Old Testament*

Religion and Theology, ed. George W. Coats and Burke O. Long (Philadelphia: Fortress Press, 1977), 42–55.

13. Frank Crüsemann nicely says, "Sinai is, however, a utopian place. It is temporarily and physically outside state authority. . . . The very real survival of Israel . . . depends on a fictional place in an invented past" (*The Torah: Theology and Social History of the Old Testament Law* [Edinburgh: T. & T. Clark, 1996], 57).

14. See Walter Brueggemann, "Always in the Shadow of the Empire," in *The Church as Counterculture*, ed. Michael L. Budde and Robert W. Brimlow (Albany: SUNY Press, 2000), 39–58.

15. In a longer version of this chapter I suggest that the world rendered unfamiliar by the prophets is shown in the wisdom traditions to be the world of daily *familiarity*, only now reconfigured by God's holiness that places the familiar in jeopardy and yet permits buoyancy.

4. Faith at the *Nullpunkt*

1. See the summary of Donald E. Gowan, *Eschatology in the Old Testament* (Philadelphia: Fortress Press, 1986).

2. See Rolf Rendtorff, "Die theologische Stellung des Schöpfungsglaubes bei Deuterojesaja," *ZTK* 51 (1954): 3–13; and, more generally, Walter Brueggemann, *Theology of the Old Testament: Testimony, Dispute, Advocacy, with CD-ROM* (Minneapolis: Fortress Press, 2005), 413–17.

3. Unlike the ancestral narratives, the Exodus tradition is deeply permeated with violence whereby YHWH acts and secures the future of Israel. This defining violence in Israel's faith is critically explored by Regina M. Schwartz, *The Curse of Cain: The Violent Legacy of Monotheism* (Chicago: University of Chicago Press, 1997).

4. On the relationship between the two traditions, see R. W. L. Moberly, *The Old Testament of the Old Testament: Patriarchal Narratives and Mosaic Yahwism*, OBT (Minneapolis: Fortress Press, 1992).

5. On the cruciality of this moment of "if," see Martin Buber, *Moses: The Revelation and the Covenant* (Atlantic Highlands, N.J.: Humanities Press International, 1988), esp. 101–9; and James Muilenburg, *The Way of Israel: Biblical Faith and Ethics* (New York: Harper, 1961), esp. 54–62.

6. See the definitive study of Torah by Frank Crüsemann, *The Torah: Theology and Social History of Old Testament Law* (Edinburgh: T. & T. Clark, 1996).

7. On the relation of promise and command, see Jon D. Levenson, *Sinai and Zion: An Entry into the Jewish Bible* (New York: Winston, 1985); and, from a Christian perspective, John Bright, *Covenant and Promise: The Prophetic Understanding of the Future in Pre-Exilic Israel* (Philadelphia: Westminster, 1976).

8. See Peter R. Ackroyd, *Exile and Restoration: A Study of Hebrew Thought of the Sixth Century B.C.*, OTL (Philadelphia: Westminster, 1968); and Ralph W. Klein, *Israel in Exile: A Theological Interpretation*, OBT (Philadelphia: Fortress Press, 1979).

9. Walther Zimmerli, "Plans for Rebuilding after the Catastrophe of 587," in *I Am Yahweh* (Atlanta: John Knox, 1982), 111, 115, 133.

10. Amos Wilder, "A Hard Death," *Poetry* 107 (1965–66): 168–69, quoted by John D. Crossan, *A Fragile Craft: The Work of Amos Niven Wilder* (Atlanta: Scholars, 1981), 66.

11. This resolve is forcefully expressed in the formula, "I will be your God and you shall be my people," a formula especially crucial in the exile when most of the uses cluster.

12. In using the term, "Israel-less," I intend to allude directly to the Christian formulation of Jürgen Moltmann, *The Crucified God: The Cross of Christ as the Foundation and Criticism of Christian Theology* (New York: Harper & Row, 1974), 243: "The grief of the Father here is just as important as the death of the Son. The Fatherlessness of the Son is matched by the Sonlessness of the Father."

13. Gerhard von Rad, *Old Testament Theology*, vol. 2: *The Theology of Israel's Prophetic Traditions* (London: Oliver and Boyd, 1965), 263–77; see also Walter Brueggemann, *Hopeful Imagination: Prophetic Voices in Exile* (Philadelphia: Fortress Press, 1986).

14. On the formula, see John Martin Bracke, "The Coherence and Theology of Jeremiah 30 31" (Ph.D. diss., Union Theological Seminary, Richmond, Va., 1983), 148–55; and more generally, Thomas M. Raitt, *A Theology of Exile: Judgment/Deliverance in Jeremiah and Ezekiel* (Philadelphia: Fortress Press, 1977).

15. See Walter Brueggemann, "The 'Uncared For' Now Cared For (Jeremiah 30:12-17): A Methodological Consideration," in *Old Testament Theology: Essays on Structure, Theme, and Text* (Minneapolis: Fortress Press, 1992), 296–307; Hans Walter Wolff, "What Is New in the New Covenant? A Contribution to the Jewish-Christian Dialogue according to Jer. 31:31-34," in *Confrontations with Prophets: Discovering the Old Testament's New*

and Contemporary Significance (Philadelphia: Fortress Press, 1983), 49–62; and more recently, Norbert Lohfink, *The Covenant Never Revoked: Biblical Reflection on Christian-Jewish Dialogue* (New York: Paulist, 1991).

16. William McKane, *Jeremiah 1–25,* vol. 1, International Critical Commentary (Edinburgh: T. & T. Clark, 1986), 1–83, has contributed the felicitous notion of a "rolling corpus."

17. On "home" beyond exile, see Frederick Buechner, *The Longing for Home: Recollections and Reflections* (San Francisco: HarperSanFrancisco, 1996), and Walter Brueggemann, *Cadences of Home: Preaching among Exiles* (Louisville: Westminster John Knox, 1997).

18. See Brueggemann, *Hopeful Imagination,* 69–87.

19. A close parallel concerning YHWH's shame before the gods is voiced in Num. 14:13-19.

20. See Jon D. Levenson, *Theology of the Program of Restoration of Ezekiel 40–48,* Harvard Semitic Monograph 10 (Missoula, Mont.: Scholars, 1976); and especially Kalenda Rose Stevenson, *Vision of Transformation: The Territorial Rhetoric of Ezekiel 40–48,* SBLDS 154 (Atlanta: Scholars, 1966).

21. See Walter Brueggemann, *Biblical Perspective on Evangelism: Living in a Three-Storied Universe* (Nashville: Abingdon, 1993), 14–47.

22. Sigmund Mowinckel famously proposed that the formula refers to a specific liturgical enactment whereby YHWH is made to be sovereign. See a critical assessment of the hypothesis by Ben C. Ollenburger, *Zion, the City of the Great King: A Theological Symbol of the Jerusalem Cult,* JSOTSup 41 (Sheffield: JSOT, 1987), 24–33.

23. See Jacob Neusner, *Understanding Seeking Faith: Essays on the Case of Judaism,* vol. 1: *Debates on Method, Reports of Results* (Atlanta: Scholars, 1986), 137–41.

24. See Walter Brueggemann, "The Loss and Recovery of Creation in Old Testament Theology," *ThTo* 53 (July 1996): 177–90.

25. See two works by Bernhard W. Anderson: *Creation Versus Chaos: The Reinterpretation of Mythical Symbolism in the Bible* (Philadelphia: Fortress Press, 1987); and *From Creation to New Creation: Old Testament Perspectives,* OBT (Minneapolis: Fortress Press, 1994).

26. An important exception to this interpretive consensus is Walther Eichrodt, "In the Beginning," in *Israel's Prophetic Heritage: Essays in Honor of James Muilenburg,* ed. Bernhard W. Anderson and Walter Harrelson (New York: Harper, 1962), 1–10.

27. Isaiah 54:10 is an important reference for our argument because there the poetry likens exile to the flood waters of chaos.

28. Oscar Cullmann, *Immortality of the Soul or Resurrection of the Dead? The Witness of the New Testament* (London: Epworth, 1958).

29. Mitchell Dahood, *Psalms,* AB 17A (Garden City, N.Y.: Doubleday, 1970), 3:101–50; Nicholas J. Tromp, *Primitive Conceptions of Death and the Nether World in the Old Testament* (Rome: Pontifical Biblical Institute, 1969).

30. Dahood, *Psalms.* 3: xli–lii. In a very different idiom and without reference to Dahood, James Barr, *The Garden of Eden and the Hope of Immortality* (Minneapolis: Fortress Press, 1993), has sought to refute the dominant categories of Oscar Cullmann, arguing that positive consideration be given to the theme of immortality. Barr's argument is not fully clear to me, because he asserts that "our story does not speak of 'life after death,'" nor about the "immortality of the soul," and "I am not opting for immortality" (19, 41). Barr's argument attends especially to Genesis 2–3 and the same Psalms and is concerned with the durability of the "soul" (*nephesh*) in a direct challenge to Oscar Cullmann.

31. See Fredrik Lindstrom, *Suffering and Sin: Interpretations of Illness in the Individual Complaint Psalms,* ConBOT 37 (Stockholm: Almqvist and Wiksell International, 1944).

32. Claus Westermann, *The Praise of God in the Psalms* (Richmond, Va.: John Knox, 1965). See the fuller exposition by Patrick D. Miller, *They Cried to the Lord: The Form and Theology of Biblical Prayer* (Minneapolis: Fortress Press, 1994), 55–177, and passim.

33. On this vocabulary, see Walter Brueggemann, "Crisis-Evoked, Crisis-Resolving Speech," *BTB* 24 (1994): 95–105.

34. Hans Heinrich Schmid, "Rechtfertigung als Schöpfungsgeschehen: Notizen zur alttestamentlichen Vorgeschichte eines neutestamentlichen Themas," in *Rechtfertigung: Festschrift für Ernst Käsemann zum 70. Geburtstag,* ed. Johannes Friedrich et al. (Göttingen: Vandenhoeck & Ruprecht, 1976), 403–14.

35. Hans Joachim Begrich, "Das priesterliche Heilsorakel," *ZAW* 66 (1934): 81–92. The theme is fully exposited in the work of Miller, *They Cried to the Lord.*

36. See the discussion of Edgar W. Conrad, *Fear Not Warrior: A Study of 'al tira' Pericopes in the Hebrew Scriptures,* BJS 75 (Chico, Calif.: Scholars, 1985).

5. The City in Biblical Perspective: Failed and Possible

Note: An earlier form of this chapter was presented in May 1998 to a group of pastors reflecting on urban ministry.

1. The issues concerning the early history of Israel are exceedingly vexed and unclear. This essay is an exercise in theological exposition that operates with the "constructed" version of history that became canonical and normative for Israel. While not unaware of the historical questions, my exposition concerns Israel's normative self-understanding, which may in turn contribute to our self-understanding as a community attendant to that normative act of imagination.

2. The classic presentations of the hypothesis are by George E. Mendenhall, "The Hebrew Conquest of Palestine," *The Biblical Archaeologist Reader,* vol. 3, ed. Edward F. Campbell Jr. and David Noel Freedman (Garden City, N.Y.: Anchor, 1970), 100–120; and Norman K. Gottwald, *The Tribes of Yahweh: A Sociology of the Religion of Liberal Israel, 1250–1050 B.C.E.* (Maryknoll, N.Y.: Orbis, 1979).

3. See Frank S. Frick, *The Formation of the State of Ancient Israel,* SWBA 4 (Sheffield: Almond, 1985); and David Noel Freedman and David Frank Graf, *Palestine in Transition: The Emergence of Ancient Israel,* SWBA 2 (Sheffield: Almond, 1983).

4. See the definitive study by James W. Flanagan, *David's Social Drama: A Hologram of Israel's Early Iron Age,* SWBA 7 (Sheffield: Almond, 1988).

5. See George W. Ramsey, who cites the two quite old but influential articles by H. H. Rowley ("Zadok," *Anchor Bible Dictionary,* 6 vols., ed. David Noel Freedman et al. [New York: Doubleday, 1992], 6:1034–36).

6. This notion goes back to the old hypothesis of Albrecht Alt, *Essays on Old Testament History and Religion* (Oxford: Blackwell, 1966), 171–259.

7. The sociological background of Micah in his village context has been articulated by Hans Walter Wolff, "Micah the Moreshite—The Prophet and His Background," in *Israelite Wisdom: Theological and Literary Essays in Honor of Samuel Terrien,* ed. John G. Gammie et al. (Missoula: Scholars, 1978), 77–84. See also Itumeleng J. Mosala, "A Materialist Reading of Micah," in *The Bible and Liberation: Political and Social Hermeneutics,* ed. Norman K. Gottwald and Richard A. Horsley, rev. ed. (Maryknoll, N.Y.: Orbis, 1993), 264–91.

8. The connection is important between the *remembered* elder Micah and the *present* elders who protest on the basis of him. The elders, remembered

and present, offer a memory and a social vision that stand outside the horizon of the urban consciousness of the power players in Jerusalem.

9. Tod Linafelt, *Surviving Lamentations: Catastrophe, Lament, and Protest in the Afterlife of a Biblical Book* (Chicago: University of Chicago Press, 2000).

10. While the three prophets Jeremiah, Ezekiel, and Second Isaiah can be distinguished from each other in important ways, it is equally important for our purposes to see them as a coherent offer of a future to Israel, an act of hope that refused to accept present circumstance as definitive. For the power of that shared testimony, see Gerhard von Rad, *Old Testament Theology*, vol. 2: *The Theology of Israel's Prophetic Traditions* (London: Oliver and Boyd, 1965). See also Walter Brueggemann, *Hopeful Imagination: Prophetic Voices in Exile* (Philadelphia: Fortress Press, 1986).

11. For the work of the church, it is important to embrace the task of imagination against the given. Engagement in that process eventually arrives at the awareness that what has been taken as given turns out to be an act of imagination long practiced and honored. For the work of imagination against givenness, see Wesley Kort, *Take, Read: Scripture, Textuality, and Cultural Practice* (University Park, Pa.: Pennsylvania State University Press, 1996), and his focus upon John Calvin's *sicut* ("as if") as the principle for the freedom and authority of scripture. Less directly see also Garrett Green, "'The Bible as . . .': Fictional Narrative and Scriptural Truth," in *Scriptural Authority and Narrative Interpretation*, ed. Garrett Green (Philadelphia: Fortress Press, 1987), 79–86; and Garrett Green, *Imagining God: Theology and the Religious Imagination* (San Francisco: Harper & Row, 1989). The emancipated imagination of the church is crucial for revisioning the city. At present, of course, the church is characteristically enthralled by the dominant imagination of the city that appears as a given.

6. Evangelism and Discipleship: The God Who *Calls*, The God Who *Sends*

1. The phrasing is from the "Statement of Faith" of the United Church of Christ, http://www.ucc.org/faith/faith.htm.

2. Hans Walter Wolff, "The Kerygma of the Yahwist," *Interpretation* 20 (1966): 131–58; Patrick D. Miller, "Syntax and Theology in Genesis 12:3a," in *Israelite Religion and Biblical Theology: Collected Papers*, JSOTSupp 267 (Sheffield: Sheffield Academic Press, 2000), 492–96.

3. For a New Testament counterpoint, see C. S. Song, "The Politics of the Resurrection," in *Proclaiming the Acceptable Year,* ed. by Justo L. Gonzales (Valley Forge, Pa.: Judson, 1982), 25–39.

4. See Walter Wink, *Naming the Powers: The Language of Power in the New Testament* (Minneapolis: Fortress Press, 1984).

5. Wendell Berry, *Jayber Crow: A Novel* (Washington: Counterpoint, 2000), 181.

6. Ibid., 182.

7. Jacob Neusner, *The Enchantments of Judaism: Rites of Transformation from Birth through Death* (New York: Basic, 1987), 212–16, and passim.

7. Options for Creatureliness: Consumer or Citizen

1. In U.S. scholarship, the most influential statements were by G. Ernest Wright, *God Who Acts: Biblical Theology as Recital,* SBT 8 (London: SCM, 1952); and *The Old Testament Against Its Environment,* SBT 2 (London: SCM, 1950).

2. Gerhard von Rad, "The Theological Problem of the Old Testament Doctrine of Creation," in *The Problem of the Hexateuch and Other Essays* (New York: McGraw-Hill, 1966), 131–43. The article was first published in German in 1936.

3. See my summary of the matter: Walter Brueggemann, "The Loss and Recovery of Creation in Old Testament Theology," *ThTo* 53 (1996): 1,977–90. The matter has been fully explicated by Rolf P. Knierim, *The Task of Old Testament Theology: Method and Cases* (Grand Rapids: Eerdmans, 1995), esp. 57–138. See also William P. Brown and S. Dean McBride, Jr., eds., *God Who Creates: Essays in Honor of W. Sibley Towner* (Grand Rapids: Eerdmans, 2000). From a theological perspective, see especially Joseph Sittler, *Evocations of Grace: Writings on Ecology, Theology, and Ethics* (Grand Rapids: Eerdmans, 2000).

4. On the qualification of "attested by Israel," see Walter Brueggemann, *Theology of the Old Testament: Testimony, Dispute, Advocacy, with CD-ROM* (Minneapolis: Fortress Press, 2005), 117–44.

5. There is, of course, a rich and extensive literature on providence. Among the helpful works for me are from a historical perspective, Horton Davies, *The Vigilant God: Providence in the Thought of Augustine, Aquinas, Calvin, and Barth* (New York: Peter Lang, 1992), and from a

pastoral perspective, Frank E. Tupper, *A Scandalous Providence: The Jesus Story of the Compassion of God* (Macon, Ga.: Mercer University Press, 1995).

6. See my discussion, which is informed by Barth: Walter Brueggemann, *Genesis*, Interpretation (Atlanta. John Knox, 1982), 191–92.

7. See the splendid discussion by Rolf Knierim, "Food, Land, and Justice," in *The Task of Old Testament Theology*, 225–43.

8. This sentence is intended to note that the Hebrew term *'aretz* translates as both "land" and "earth"; it is not always clear which is intended. In any case, the plush land promised in Deuteronomy is surely the vision of "earth" in creation made specific.

9. It is clear that "food," in the several ways I have referenced, is at the same time quite concretely nourishment for life and at the same time a metaphor for all that makes life joyous and well. One need not choose between the two intentions in any concrete usage.

10. Mike Royko, "Viet Verdict: Mostly Guilty," in *One More Time: The Best of Mike Royko* (Chicago: University of Chicago Press, 1999), 71–73.

11. Ibid., 71.

12. Ibid., 72.

13. On YHWH's relation to Israel as an epitome of YHWH's relation to creation, see Walter Brueggemann, *Theology of the Old Testament: Testimony, Dispute, Advocacy, with CD-ROM* (Minneapolis: Fortress, 2005), 413–49.

14. For a review of the scholarly conversation, see Ernest W. Nicholson, *God and His People: Covenant and Theology in the Old Testament* (Oxford: Oxford University Press, 1986).

15. See the argument summarized by Charles S. McCoy and J. Wayne Baker, *Fountainhead of Federalism: Heinrich Bullinger and the Covenantal Tradition* (Louisville: Westminster John Knox, 1991).

16. Robert N. Bellah, *The Broken Covenant: American Civil Religion in Time of Trial* (New York: Seabury, 1975).

17. Robert N. Bellah, ed., *The Good Society* (New York: Knopf, 1991).

18. I am greatly indebted to Terence E. Fretheim for helping me to see the Exodus narrative in relation to issues of creation ("The Plagues as Ecological Signs of Historical Disaster," *JBL* 110 (1991): 385–96). See also his commentary, *Exodus*, Interpretation (Louisville: Westminster John Knox. 1991).

19. See Walter Brueggemann, "Pharaoh as Vassal: A Study of a Political Metaphor," *CBQ* 57 (1995): 27–51.

20. See Patrick D. Miller Jr., "The Human Sabbath: A Study in Deutero-nomic Theology," *The Princeton Seminary Bulletin* 6 (1985): 81–97.

21. I particularly make reference to Gen. 41:14-36. Pharaoh's entire strategy for famine, as in Gen. 47, is based in the nightmare that he reports to Joseph. I submit that much of the anxiety about scarcity is rooted in nightmares of anxiety and not in facts on the ground.

22. Patrick D. Miller, "Deuteronomy and Psalms: Evoking a Biblical Conversation," *JBL* 118 (1999): 3–18, has explored the way in which the "cry from below" also becomes a dominant practice in the Psalms, so that the cry is not an occasional item but belongs to the most elemental assumptions and practice of faith. Israel's faith cannot do without the "voice from below."

23. The savage language and the brutal activity of YHWH as judge and as deliverer constitute an ongoing interpretive problem. On the issue, see Regina Schwartz, *The Curse of Cain: The Violent Legacy of Monotheism* (Chicago: University of Chicago Press, 1997); and Renita J. Weems, *Battered Love: Marriage, Sex, and Violence in the Hebrew Prophets*, OBT Minneapolis: Fortress Press, 1995).

24. The data and its significance for the faith of Israel has been shrewdly summarized by Mignon R. Jacobs, "Toward an Old Testament Theology of Concern for the Underprivileged," in *Reading the Hebrew Bible for a New Millennium: Form, Concept, and Theological Perspective*, ed. Wonil Kim et al. (Harrisburg: Trinity Press International, 2000), 205–29.

25. See Marvin L. Chaney, "You Shall Not Covet Your Neighbor's House," *Pacific Theological Review* 15 (Winter 1982): 3–13; James Luther Mays, *Micah*, OTL (Philadelphia: Westminster, 1976), 65–66.

26. Elsa Tamez, *When the Horizons Close: Rereading Ecclesiastes* (Maryknoll, N.Y.: Orbis, 2000), 116–18.

8. Ecumenism as the Shared Practice of a Peculiar Identity

1. It is this awareness that has produced thinking, especially evoked by Lesslie Newbigin, that "the west" is a mission field for the church. See *Between Gospel and Culture: The Emerging Mission in North America*, ed. George R. Hunsberger and Craig van Gelder (Grand Rapids: Eerdmans, 1996).

2. I am of course aware that internally there were certainly hegemonic groups that prevailed. By focusing on the impact of the international empires, I do not overlook internal domination. I assume that patterns of domination are roughly the same, whether by external or internal agents.

3. On this motif in Israelite perspective, see Donald E. Gowan, *When Man Becomes God: Humanism and Hybris in the Old Testament,* Pittsburgh Theological Monograph Series 6 (Pittsburgh: Pickwick, 1975).

4. Norman K. Gottwald has offered an analysis of the realities of class in the formation of the monarchy ("A Hypothesis about Social Class in Monarchic Israel in the Light of Contemporary Studies of Social Class and Social Stratification," *The Hebrew Bible in Its Social World and in Ours* [Atlanta: Scholars, 1993], 139–64).

5. Theodore H. von Laue, *The World Revolution of Westernization: The Twentieth Century in Global Perspective* (New York: Oxford University Press, 1987); Charles Reich, *Opposing the System* (New York: Random House, 1996).

6. See R. Frankena, "The Vassal-Treaties of Esarhaddon and the Dating of Dt," *Oud-Testamentlische Studien* 14 (1965): 122–54; Dennis J. McCarthy, *Treaty and Covenant: A Study in Form in the Ancient Oriental Documents and in the Old Testament,* Analecta Biblica 21A (Rome: Biblical Institute, 1978); and Moshe Weinfeld, *Deuteronomy and the Deuteronomic School* (Oxford: Clarendon, 1972).

7. John van Seters, *Abraham in History and Tradition* (New Haven: Yale University Press, 1975).

8. See Walter Brueggemann, "A Poem of Summons (Is. 55:1-3)? A Narrative of Resistance (Dan. 1:1-21)," *Schopfung und Befreiung,* ed. Rainer Albertz et al. (Stuttgart: Calwer, 1989), 126–36.

9. Jeffries M. Hamilton, *Social Justice and Deuteronomy: The Case of Deuteronomy 15* (Atlanta: Scholars, 1992); Moshe Weinfeld, *Social Justice in Ancient Israel and in the Ancient Near East* (Minneapolis: Fortress Press, 1995).

10. David Daube has suggested links between the year of release and the exodus narrative (*The Exodus Pattern in the Bible* [Westport: Greenwood, 1979]).

11. Norman K. Gottwald has most recently adopted the term "communitarian" to characterize the vision of revolutionary Israel ("Pro-legomenon: How My Mind Has Changed or Remained the Same," *The Hebrew Bible*

in Its Social World and in Ours, xxv). Gottwald has employed this word after his earlier term "egalitarian" was roundly criticized.

12. See Walter Brueggemann, "Reflections on Biblical Understandings of Property," *A Social Reading of the Old Testament: Prophetic Approaches to Israel's Communal Life* (Minneapolis: Fortress Press, 1994), 276–84.

13. On the use of the term "triage" in such a way, see Richard L. Rubenstein, *After Auschwitz: History, Theology, and Contemporary Judaism,* 2nd ed. (Baltimore: Johns Hopkins University Press, 1992). Zygmunt Bauman has shown how the Holocaust was a most modernist approach to the problem of surplus people (*Modernity and the Holocaust* [Ithaca, N.Y.: Cornell University Press, 1992]).

14. See Robert G. Hall, "Circumcision," *Anchor Bible Dictionary,* 6 vols., ed. David Noel Freedman et al. (New York: Doubleday, 1992), 1:1028–29.

15. "A Prayer for the Continuity of American Jewish Life," *New York Times,* 6 September 1996.

16. See Walter Harrelson, *From Fertility Cult to Worship: A Reassessment for the Modern Church of the Worship of Ancient Israel* (Garden City, N.Y.: Doubleday, 1969).

17. Jacob Neusner, *The Enchantments of Judaism: Rites of Transformation from Birth through Death* (New York: Basic, 1987), 211–16, and passim.

9. Vision for a New Church and a New Century: Part I: Homework against Scarcity

Note: This chapter was originally an address presented at Union Theological Seminary on April 7, 2000, as part of the inauguration of Joseph C. Hough as president of the seminary.

1. James Muilenburg, *The Way of Israel: Biblical Faith and Ethics* (New York: Harper, 1961), 65, 81.

2. Patrick D. Miller, "The Human Sabbath: A Study in Deuteronomic Theology," *Princeton Theological Seminary Bulletin* 6 (1985): 81–97.

3. Frank Crüsemann, *The Torah: Theology and Social History of Old Testament Law* (Edinburgh: T. & T. Clark, 1996), 224–34.

4. Thomas F. Green shrewdly suggests that public speech is constituted by public utterance in which the listener can accept what is said as

a candidate for his/her own speech (*Voices: The Educational Formation of Conscience* [Notre Dame, Ind.: University of Notre Dame Press, 1999], 148–67).

10. Vision for a New Church and a New Century: Part II: Holiness Becomes Generosity

Note: This chapter was originally an address presented at Union Theological Seminary on April 7, 2000, as part of the inauguration of Joseph C. Hough as president of the seminary.

1. Claus Westermann, *Creation* (Philadelphia: Fortress Press, 1971).

2. See Peter J. Kearney, "The P Redaction of Exodus 25–40," *ZAW* 89 (1977): 375–87; and Joseph Blenkinsopp, *Prophecy and Canon: A Contribution to the Study of Jewish Origins* (Notre Dame, Ind.: University of Notre Dame Press, 1977), 54–69.

3. This difference is what caused Wellhausen to judge that D was earlier and P was later when the issues were no longer contested.

4. Herbert Donner, "Jesaja lvi 1-7: Ein Abrogationsfall innerhalb des Kanons—Implikationen und Konsequenzen," SVTP 36 (1985): 81–95.

5. See Walter Brueggemann, "'Exodus' in the Plural (Amos 9:7)," *Many Voices, One God: Being Faithful in a Pluralistic World*, ed. Walter Brueggemann and George W. Stroup (Louisville: Westminster John Knox, 1998), 15–34.

6. It may well be that this is a particularly Christian reading of the matter, for Harry Orlinsky, my teacher here at Union Theological Seminary, filed an important protest against any universalist reading.

7. See especially Emmanuel Levinas, *Totality and Infinity: An Essay on Exteriority* (Pittsburgh: Duquesne University Press, 1969).

8. Fernando Belo: *A Materialist Reading of the Gospel of Mark* (Maryknoll, N.Y.: Orbis, 1981).

9. See Rodney Stark, *The Rise of Christianity: A Sociologist Reconsiders Christianity* (Princeton: Princeton University Press, 1996).

10. Roy Schafer, *Retelling a Life: Narration and the Dialogue in Psychoanalysis* (New York: Basic, 1992), 94–95.

11. John Shelby Spong, *Why Christianity Must Change or Die: A Bishop Speaks to Believers in Exile, a New Reformation of the Church's Faith and Practice* (San Francisco: Harper & Row, 1998).

12. George S. Newlands, *Generosity and the Christian Future* (London: SPCK, 1997), 266.

11. Patriotism for Citizens of the Penultimate Superpower

1. See Walter Brueggemann, *Theology of the Old Testament: Testimony, Dispute, Advocacy, with CD-ROM* (Minneapolis: Fortress Press, 2005), 492–527.

2. Peter Brown, *Poverty and Leadership in the Later Roman Empire,* The Menahem Stern Jerusalem Lectures (London: University Press of New England, 2001).

3. Ibid., 70.

4. Ibid., 71.

5. Ibid., 73.

6. Paul M. Kennedy, *The Rise and Fall of the Great Powers: Economic Change and Military Conflict from 1500 to 2000* (New York: Random House, 1987).

Index of Names

Index of Biblical References